Citizens

OF THE

Eastern Shore

OF

Maryland

1659-1750

Volume I

Compiled by

F. Edward Wright

HERITAGE BOOKS
2007

CONTENTS

Introduction i
Taxables:
    Tax List of Chester Hundred, Kent County - 1721 1
    Tax List of Somerset County - 1723 2
    Tax List of Talbot County - 1733 17

Marks of Cattle:
    Cattle Marks of Kent County, 1659-1676, 1694-1726, 1732-1734 .. 31
    Cattle Marks of Somerset County, 1666-1705 34
    Cattle Marks of Talbot County, 1741-1748 42

Overseers of Roads:
    Overseers of Roads, Dorchester County (complaints), 1690 43
    Overseers of Roads, Talbot County (appointments), 1702 - 1713 . 44

Petitions:
    Kent County support of Lord Baltimore, 1689 48
    Talbot County support of Lord Baltimore, 1689 48
    Cecil County support of Lord Baltimore, 1689 48
    Somersett County to King and Queen, 1689 48
    Christ Church Parish, Kent Island, (after 1713) 49
    Indian Tribes, Somerset County, 1721 49
    Upper Chesapeake Bay, farmers and traders, after Mar 3, 1737 .. 49
    Somerset County, to export surplus grain, 1738 50
    Talbot County, to erect new parish, 1738 50
    St. Peter's Parish, Talbot Co, to erect parish, ca. 1740 51
    St. Luke's Parish, Queen Anne's Co, Chapel of Ease, ca. 1741 ...51
    Coventry Parish, Somerset and Worcester Counties, 1748 51
    Coventry Parish, Somerset County, (after 1745) 52
    Friends (Quakers) of Cecil County, 1696 53
    For Ferry over An... River, Somerset County, 1722 53
    Licenses, Presby. Church, Roads, in Kent County, 1739-42 54
    Supporting John Anderson, Dorchester County, 1734 54

Excerpts from Levy Court Records:
    Levy Book of Kent County - 1722 55
    Levy Book of Talbot County - 1724 59
    Levy Book of Somerset County - 1724 60
    Levy Book of Queen Anne's County - 1728 - 1729 62

Colonial Militia Returns:
    Militia of Cecil County - 1740 68
    Militia Officers of Dorchester County 72
    Militia of Queen Anne's County - 1732, 1748, 1749 73
    Militia of Somerset County - 1732, 1749 77
    Militia of Talbot County - 1748 81
    Militia of Worcester County - 1748 83

From Church Proceedings and Sessionals:
    Pew holders of Manokin Presby. Church, Somerset Co., ca. 1747 .. 85
    Pew holders of St. Luke's Chapel at Wye, Queen Anne's Co., 1723 .85
    Gift and subscriptions, St. Stephens Parish, Cecil Co., 1703 ... 85

Index of slaves 86
General Index of personal names 89

INTRODUCTION

The main purpose of this compilation is to aid in locating an ancestor in respect to time and place. The following lists help to locate over 7,000 persons whose presence was noted on various official records. Sometimes much more is revealed on these persons and their family relationships. Tax lists show father and sons who lived in the same household. Recordings of cattle marks sometimes included gifts to relatives, named therein.

In order to save the reader the time of searching an entire page, one name after the other, I have re-arranged many of the lists alphabetically. When I felt that the order of the names as originally recorded might imply groupings of relatives, friends or neighbors, I retained the original order.

When a name appears more than once in these lists it may not mean the existence of more than one person with such a name. For instance the Levy lists contain the names of the same person more than once when more than one payment was made during the year.

I attempted to gather lists of names with equal weight to each county of the Eastern Shore. But Dorchester County continues to elude our efforts. Aside from the loss of so many of its early court records and church records, the colonial militia rolls are also meager, for the most part only revealing the names of the officers.

Tax lists - The tax act of 1712 states that all male persons and all female slaves of the age of 16 or above shall be accounted taxable except clergymen and such poor people as receive alms from the county and all such slaves as adjudged to be past labour. Although excluded as a non-taxable, the name of a white woman may appear on these lists, in which case we would assume her to be the owner. The term "At," (sometimes written as "Att") indicates the name of the owner (who is living elsewhere). Frequently the number of slaves is stated, followed by the total number of taxables. This numbers should be noted as a check on the data; however, sometimes the figures are unexplainable.

In addition to the tax lists given in this work there are others covering Somerset County. Tax lists for Somerset County are available at the State Archives for the years, 1723-1725, 1727, 1730, 1731, 1733-1740, 1743-1754, 1756, 1757 and 1759.

Cattle Marks were recorded for not only cattle but also fowl, pigs and other animals. The record actually notes the shape and location of notches or other markings on the animal. I did not include all marks of cattle that are available for this period. Somerset land records include cattle marks up to 1723, whereas this book concludes with those of 1705. The recording of cattle marks for Kent County also continue beyond the period covered by this work. I feel a significant number are included here. Others may be published at a later date.

Overseers of roads - These men were appointed to ensure that the roads were properly maintained, with the help of his neighbors. As the text reveals, many persons were found wanting in fulfilling these responsibilites and consequently summoned to court to explain. Sometimes these persons were fined; on occasion the overseer was fined.

Petitions - I have included any type of petition in which I could group five or more names. The user should note all the names in juxtaposition since they may imply a family or neighborhood connection.

Levy books give us a glimpse at a diverse cross section of the upper, middle and lower classes, the officials, persons receiving payments, those fined for infractions and the charity cases. One of the longest lists to be found is the one showing bounty payments for killing crows, squirrels, and wolves. The list of payments in 1729 for Queen Anne's County contains approximately 400 names, many of whom did not own real property and were unlikely to appear in other public records.

The existence of the militia reflects, primarily, the fear of Indian attacks, and to some extent, although ill founded, Catholics and slaves. Although the threat of Indians was far greater in the back country of Western Maryland, the governor required all counties to contribute. These rolls are held by the State Archives, many of which have not been labeled as to county, although familiarity with the names will readily suggest the county of residence, as I have annotated.

The records of convicts have not been included in this project. I am unclear as to what extent these persons remained in the county in which are recorded their previous trials and sentences in England. The existence in Maryland county court records of trials in England along with information on the ship and time of servitude in America, suggests that these persons were turned over to the custody of citizens or officials in the same Maryland county in which the sentence is recorded. However I note, as have others, that very few of these names surface in later records of that county. These records offer a potentially rich source of genealogy, but merit more background research than I was able to do at this time. These will probably be included in future volumes.

Only a page of this work is devoted to Parish Proceedings and Sessional Records (Presbyterian). For those who limit their use of church records to the registers, I recommend the proceedings (or minutes, sessionals, etc.) of churches as an additional genealogical source, albeit oft times much more time consuming. Some of the Eastern Shore church proceedings and minutes have been transcribed and made available at the Maryland Historical Society.

There is a great wealth of genealogy in the court records and church proceedings, beyond that covered here. I feel certain that they will be exploited further for their genealogical value and eventually published.

F. Edward Wright

Tax List of Chester Hundred, Kent County - 1721
From the Scharff Collection (State Archives)

"A list of the White men Taxables, negro men, women and children in Chester
Hundred in Kent County Taken and Returned to the Sheriff by me Edwd Worrell
(constable)"

Coll. Edwd Scott, John Tilden, Edwd
　Scott Junr, George Black/4
John Fanning, Wm. Peters, David
　Bailey, John Osburn/3
James Smith, James Calder, John
　Mills, John Ranger/4
Thomas Piner, Jonathan Fisher/2
James Piner/1
Simon Willmer, David Davis, Andrew
　Brown, James Smith/4
John Moll, James Cruickshanks, David
　Moll/3
At the widow Gillagues, John Lyman/1
Sam'll Burrell/1
Francis Lewis/1
John Beech, Thomas Larcum/2
John Austin/1
Philip Davis, Charles Newman/2
Arthur Barker, David Dewlin/2
Thomas Williams, David Jones/2
Roger Murphy, Thomas Ambras/2
Robert Hane(?)/1
Wm. Dicus/1
John Fiddis/1
John Hambleton/1
James Davis/1
Aurthur Foreman, Francis Foreman,
　Wm. Stanley/3
James Dill/1
Mich'l Hacket, Charles Jones/2
Phillip Carroll/1
Rich'd Davis, John Nusan, John
　Williams/3
James Tornley/1
Nath'l Rickets, John Deparner/2
Nehemiah Powel, Phillip Frahil/2
Robert Foreman/1
At the widow Foreman's - Wm. Foreman,
　Denis(?) Carroll, Wm.(?) W...,
　John Worton/2
Joseph Wright/1
James Fanning/1
James Watson/1
At Andrew Spaulins, Thomas Chadock/1
James Kaw (Kane?)/1
John Young, Kinven Wroth, Wm. Bivan/3
Edwd. Worrell/1
Rice Jones, Thomas Jones/2

Sam'll Thomas, Gilbert Macknesh(?),
　John Tillard, Jacob Goodin/4
Daniel Duliente, Wm. Sheperd/2
Sam'll Fillips/1
James Glascock/1

Negroes men/women/children
At Coll. Edwd Scott 6/3/6
At John Fannings 1/1/1
At James Smith 2/4/6
At Thomas Piner 1/0/0
At James Piner 0/1/0
At Simon Willmer 1/1/4
At John Moll 1/0/1 (negro girl)
At Widow Gillages 0/1/2
At Francis Lewis 1/0/0
At Robert Willmer 2/0/0
At Arthur Barker 1/1/0
At Jos. Durden 2/0/1
At Micha. Hackett 2/0/2
At Richd. Davis 0/0/1 (negro boy)
At Rebeckah Piner 0/1/0
At John Young 0/0/1 (negro boy)
At Edwd. Worrell 2/0/0
At Sam'l Thomas 0/2/4
At Daniel Dullient 1/0/0

1

(Number of slaves/total number of taxables)

Tithables Belonging to Pocomoke
Hundred - 1723
Mr. Joseph Gray/negroes 4/5
Mr. Francis Allen, Richard Ashley
negroes 2
Even Laws negro 1
Fenix Hall
Peter Wattson
Jno Bivens negro 1
Benja. Houston, Joseph Davis negro
1/3
Sam'll Tayler, Solomon Taylor/2
James(?) Turner, Sam'll Turner Junr,
Jno Turner, Henly Turner/4
Chas. Nicolas, Jno. Nicolas, Sam'll
Nicolas/3
Jam. Nicolas 1
Mr. Wm Whittington, negros 5/5
Esther Skirvin, negros 8/?
Daniel Doron, Jno. Clark/?
Jam. Tayler/?
Joseph Houston, negro 1/2
Jno White of Nasseango/1
Thos. Bytler/1
Nath'll Davis, Lazarus Davis/2
Mr. Southey Whittington, negros 4/5
Elisabeth Johnson.../8
(2 or more entries obliterated)
Rob... Peale(?) negros 2/4
Else Roberts, Wm Wroth/1
Thos. Bivens(?)/1
Hugh Porter(?), Wm ... /2
Jno ..., Jonathan .../2
Patience Wilkisson(?), Isaac
Wilkisson(?), Joshua
Wilkisson(?), Angelo
Wilkisson(?)/3
Jno White of Hasswaddy/1
Jno Scott, negros 4/4
(3 or 4 entries obliterated)
Wm Donohow/1
Edward Dickeson, Cornelius Dickeson,
Edmund Dickeson, negros 2/5
Jno Townsend, senr, Wrixham Townsend,
Littleton Townsend, negro 1/4
Chas. Townsend, Chas. Townsend, Jno.
Townsend/3
Jno Townsend Junr/1
Dan'll Townsend, negro 1/2

Elizab'th Townsend, Jams. Townsend,
negro 1/2
Sam'll Mayo/1
Jno Coulbourn/1
David Shockley/1
Jno Fleming, Jno Lane, negroes 2,
Henry Philip/5
Francis Otwell, Chas. Otwell
(entry unreadable)
Jno Smith, Jno Smith Junr/2
Bivens Morris/1
Jno Denston/1
Wm Denston/1
Patarick Dealy/1
Joseph Ward/1
Rand'll Smullens, Thos Vallens/2
Ambrose Rigen, Ambrose Rigen, Wm
Boneam/3
Arthur Warwick/1
Robt Harris, negros 2/3
Teague Riggin, negro 1/2
Caleb Harris/1
Edw'd Harper/1
Jams. Harris/1
Richard Knight, Joseph Rigen, Jno.
Brillehane, Sam'll Miller/4
Jno Harris, Thos Truet/?
Hugh Colleg..
Isaac Costen, negro 2/?
Peter Benton, negros 6/?
Stephen Costen/1
Jno Harper, Rich'd Harper/2
George Tull, Wm Tull, Noble Tull/3
Rich'd Tull, Wm. Caine/2
Wm Handy, negros 2/3
Grifen Thomas, Jno. Deane/2
Robt Mitchell, Wm Bosh(?), negros 3,
James Tenly/5(?)
Geo. Lane/1
Dan'll Cawdry, Moses Virgin, Josp'h
Morgan/?
Widd'w Alexander(?), Jno Porter, Jam:
Noble
Edw'd Clash(?), Andrew Pound/2
Aron Jordine/1
Thos: Dukes/1
Ellenor Stevens, Wm Stevens, Sam'll
Stevens/2
Gedieon Tillman/1
Jno Broughton, Philip Parker/2
(3 entries obliterated)

Samuel(?) Purkins(?), Jno. Purkins,
Thos. Purkins/2
Jno Burk/1
Thos. Newbold, Jno Newbold, Francis
Newbold/5
Thos. Brown/1
(entry unreadable)/2
James Cathell/1
Moses Fenton, negro 1/2
Edw'd Peacock/1
Jno Powell/1
.. ...ston, ...ton/2
(3 entries obliterated)
Madam Mary Hampton, Alex'r ..ickey,
Edw'd Goggin, negros 8/10
Robt Truem..(?), Robt Boyer/2
Sam'll Tomerlin/1
Archabald White, Thos. Pryer/?
Jno White Pocomoke, negro 1/?
Allen McDanel/?
Mr. Robt Nearen(?), Robt Nearen, Jam.
Nearen, negros 2/?
Alexr McCready, Francis Carey/2
Thos Evans, Nath'll Evans/2
Mrs. Mary Milburn, negros 2/2
(unreadable entry)
Thos Bellin, negro 1/2
Wm Holland, negro 1/2
Jno White at the point, Thos Ellis,
negro 1/3
Jno Ellis, Jacob Philips/2
Wm Cox, negros 3/?
Som.set(?) Dickeson, Jno White, negro
1/?
Peter Dickeson, Peter Dickeson,
Abram: Dickeson, Teague Dickeson,
negro 1/5
Sam'll Rigen, negro 1/2
Teague Mathews/1
Elizabeth Rigen, Th: Rigen, negro 2/3
Jno Rigen, .../3
(entry obliterated)
...Jun/1
... Jno Mathews, Sam'll Mathews,
negro 1/4
Geo Godard, Longland Godard, Tho:
Godard/3
Isaac Boston, Geo: Marshall, negro
1/3
Tho: Adams, Tho: Adams, Philip Adams,
Wm. Giles, negro 1/5

Jacob Adams, Francis Porter, negro
3/6
(4 entries obliterated)
Hope Taylor/1
Edw'd Beachamp, Mercy Beachamp,
Manuel Mallatto, negro 1/4
Tho: Jolly/1
Robt. Mills/1
Sam'll Dorman/1
Robt Melven/1
John Webb/1
James Philbett/1
Sarah Carey, Jno. Carey/5
Robt. Cook/1
John Pereson(?)
John Dennis/1
Wm Lane, Abraham Lane/2
David Goggin/1
Edward Jones/1
Jno. Gillet(?), Jno. Gillet/2
Sam'll Gillet
Geo: Beans
Isaac Piper/1
Sam'll Mills/1
Jennet Mills, negros 2/2
Wm Brazer/1
John Mills, Wm. Mills/2
Silas Chapman/1
Edward Chapman/1
Abram Lamberson/1
Jams. Henderson/1
Chas: Ramsey/1
Barnet Ramsey, Chas: McHenderick(?),
negro 1/3
Jno Merrill/1
Wm Deaker/1
Philip Quinton, negro 1/2
Joseph Schoolfield, negroes ../?
Jacob ..., Mark ... Peter Morris(?)
Thos. Bea..., Joshua Me..., Jams.
Ange...
Ralph Smith, negro 2/3
Thos. Layfeild, negros 2/3
Jams. Dickeson/1
Sarah Lamberston, Jno .../?
.... , Ja. Houston, Josp'h Houston,
negros 2/5
Jams. Henderson, & son of Jno
Henderson/1
Jno Henderson Junr/1
Francis Henderson/1
John Williams/1

John Pa...
John S..., Thos. Lea...
Isaac W...
John H..., Benja. ... negro...
Chars. Henderson/1
Robt Blades, Jno Blades/2
Jno Pitts, negros 2, Francis Brooks/4
Sam'll Marchment, Sam'll Marchment
Wm. Marchment/3
...ton/1
...ws/2
... Tayler/21
... Porter/1
... Brittingham, John Brittingham/1
Non residents ...... Rob: Gibs/1
(names of Henry Philips and others
    (unreadable), scratched through)

A list of the Taxables persons of
Munney Hundred Taken June 18th 1723
Levin Denwood, Ffranis Graden, negros
    Hercules, Brissa, Joe, Samson,
    Ceasar, Munday, Peter, Robin,
    Jacob, Henny, Pallina, Merando,
    Penelopy, Holiday/16
Betty Gale, George Gale, Denis Foley,
    negros Jemy, Ceaser, Bess, Pheby,
    Rose/7
Thomas Dashiell, Charles Dashiell,
    negros Will, Ffrank, Jack, Peter,
    Bess, Jean/8
John Jones, Robert Jones, William
    Jones, David Evans, Thomas Loyd,
    negros Bristo, London, Jean,
    Diner/9
John Laws, Charles Polk, negros
    Dirna, Prince & Ceasar/5
Thomas Laws, William Waller, Arthur
    Cuningham, Murreas negro/4
Thomas Roe, James Wilkison/3
Will'm Stoughton, Thomas Howard,
    negros Bussey, Jupiter, Attey,
    Catoe, Fendo, Sue & Sabina/9
Philip Covington, William Wheatly,
    negros, Sambo, Joe, Theadore &
    Betty/6
William Lobins/1
William Jones, John Hust/2
George Downes, negros Tobie &
    Bendoe/3
Robert Laws, Bess negro/2

George Martin/?
Att Muny for Eph. Willson, William
    Thomson, negros Jeffrey, Tobie and
    Judah/4
John Waller, Major Waller, George
    Waller, Jenny negro/4
Lewis Jones, James Jaggers, negros
    Pompy & Hanna/4
Charles Williams, William Pollett,
    James Betsworth/3
James Brucksher/1
Nicholas Roe/1

Added at end of column after the
    entries had been totaled:
Levin Gale, Mark Noble, William
    Brien, Jno Dunkin, William
    Person/5

Rachell Crouch, Thomas Cary Junr,
    Robert Maycome, Lemon & Hanna,
    negros/43
Joy Hobbs Senr, Joy Hobbs,
    Marsilleous Hobbs/3
Thomas Hobbs/1
Noble Hobbs/1
James Jones, Negros Sambo, Tobie,
    and Moll/4
William Story, John Jones, Negros
    Whitehaven and Doll/4
Thomas Dixson, James Maitland, Hago
    negro/3
Abraham Wilson, negros Cook, Tobie,
    Nottingham Matthers and Sara/6
Henry Dorman, Henry Dorman Junr/2
John Roberts, William Roberts, Bess
    negro/3
Ffrancis White/1
Thomas Willson/1
John Miller/1
William Paul/1
John Hill/1
Wilks Churme/1
Thomas Wright/1
George Stringer, David Thomas/2
James Crazy/1
James Polk, David Polk, negros Samboe
    and Roger/4
Benjamin Saser, Thomas Saser/2
William Saser, John Maycome/2
Joseph Polk/1
Edward Roberts/1

4

Richard Wallace Senr, Thomas Wallace,
  Mathew Wallace/3
Richard Wallace/1
Thomas Jaggers Senr, Thomas Jaggers,
  Mendum Jaggers/3
Benjamin Horner/1
Joseph Roe/1
John Windsor/1
Lazarus Windsor/1
Randell Feden/1
John White/1

-----signed John White, Constable

A List of the taxables of Anomesex
  Hundred Taken Ju...1723

Samuel Horsey, Samuel Horsey Junr/2
William Wilson, Joseph Ames/2
Randoll Mitchell/2
John Oton, negro Dick/2
Thomas Madox, Alexander Madox, Thomas
  Madox/3
John Conor/1
Philip Conor/1
Thomas Word (Ward), James Word,
  Stephen Word/3
John Starling/1
Hopkin Word, negro Jerry, negro
  Silis/3
Peter Frazer/1
Michael Oor/1
William Conor/1
Thomas Poter, Thomas Poter Junr;
  Henery Poter/3 (Potter)
Samuel Word, She..y(?), negro/2
Henry Miles, Henry Waters(?),
  Frites(?), negro/3
Jonathan Cotingim, Thomas Linsey/2
David Adams/1
Edmon Beachom/1
William Beachom/1
Elisabeth Scott, John Shard, negro
  Will/2
Samuel Long, Walter Tayler/2
John White, William White/2
John Taylor, Coulbourne Tayler/2
Robart Wers/1
John Taylor Junr/1
Edwart Woodley(?)/1
Henry Smith/1

John Benston, William Benston,
  William Hall, William Taylor/4
Josep Lahn 1
Ann Coulbourn, negro Abram/1
Francis Lord, Randall Lord/2
Will Lisher (Lister?)/1
Jeffery Long, William Long, John
  Layton, Cato, negro/4
John Dancaster/1
Stephen Handy, negro Suslu..ker(?),
  negro Jan../3
Michael Holland Junr, negro Dick,
  negro Moll/3
Solomon Coulbourne, negro Jack, negro
  Dide/3
Cornelos Word, Cornelos Word Junr/2
  (Ward)
Thomas Sumurs, Jonathen Sumurs/2
John D..te/1
Stephen Horsey, William Revull(?),
  negro Coy(?), negro Horsy/4
Thomas Prior/1
Sarah Davis wido, John Davis, Thomas
  Davis, negro Sambo, negro Harsy,
  Negro cox(?), negro Jany/6
Thomas Stockwell, John Waler/2
James West/1
Samuell Wheler/1
John Mathes/1
Marget Somurs wido, Isac Somurs(?),
  Thomas Sumurs/2
William Catting, William Boston/2
Edward Hull, Daniel Hull/2
Elizabeth Waters wido, William
  Waters, Richard Waters, Edwart
  Waters, negro Elik, negro
  Lyreo(?), negro Hager, negro .../7
Elexander Argo one (?) the (?)
  Handy/1
Jeramiah Heris/1
John Gordin/1
John Taylor, Thomas Taylor Junr/2
John Taylor Junr 1/
Artor Parks/2
Samson Croket/1
John Parks/1
William Mister/1
John Eavens/1
John Horner(?)/1
Jerge Hopkings/1
Thomas Timens/1
Richard Hall/1

Charls. Hall/1
John Cotman, William Waters, negro
  Mingo, negro Dick/4
Thomas Dixon, negro Harry, negro
  Fong(?)/3
Aron Orn(?)/1
Capt William Planer, negros: Peter,
  Sambo, Watt, Tom, Georg, Tites,
  Jone, Gase, Hana, Bes, Hector/12
James Burnet, John Hall/2
John Wilins(?)/1
Samuell Handy, negro Sherper(?),
  negro Nan/3
Benz Walston, Joy Walston, negro
  Dick/3
Sarah Tull wido, Samuel Tull, Thomas
  Tull, negro Jemimo(?), negro
  Peter/4
Solomon Tull/1
Thomas Wilens, negro Dick, negro
  Harey/3
Isaɛc Wiliams/Benjeman/2
Wiliam Dixon, negro Bes/2
Ffrancis More/1
Daniel Clary, Ablosom Ford/2
John Sumers(?), Jonathan Williams,
  Lopes negro/3
Henry Caton/2
Robert Dise/1
Edwart Stockwell, Charls.
  Canhar..(?)/2
John Medcalf, Richard Corken(?), John
  Wilson/3
James Trehearn/1
James Ward/1
John Colhowne, John Colhoune Junr/2
Joseph Lankford, William Lankford,
  John Bosmon/3
Daniel Long, Solomon Long/8
Sarah Roach wido, Samuel Roach,
  William Gulet
John Trehearn, Janey negro/2
John Jenson, James Smith/2
Joseph Porter, William Roberson/2
Antony Bell, Thomas Bell, John Bell,
  Anton Bell, negro Robin, negro
  Cate/6
John Gunby, Kurk Gunby, negro Moll,
  Negro Cate, negro Jack/?
John Kilom, George Dikes/2(?)
William Scott/1
Martha Halos(?)/1

Richerd Orgin, Joseph Orgin, William
  Orgin/3
Mary Bolitho(?), negro Jim(?), negro
  Morsar(?)/2
Michael Holland, negro Will/2
William Coulbourne, negro ..(?)
Isaac Horsey, Isaac Borsmon
John Riging, negro Darkus/4
Nathaniel Horsey, John Mott, Cate
  negro, negro Ned/4
Michael Roach, Thomas Persons, Edward
  Hearn/3
Charls. Cotingim, negro Robin/2
Robart Scott, Isac Scott, negro Bes/3
Randolph Long, Samuel Mashell/2
Mary Ciyser (Cixer?), Samuel Ciyser
  (Cixer?)/1
George Lane/1
Elizabeth ...
James Davis/1
wido Blaney(?)
Abraham Trice(?)/1
John Rigen/1
Samuel Miles(?), Narthaniel
  Williams(?)/2
Michael Holland Junr, Constable

A List of .... Wicomico Hundred 1723
Mr. James King/1
Robt Hasting/1
George Hanes, Jno Haines/2
Tho: Lindall/1
Wm Hairne/1
Tho: Hairne/1
Jno Titum/1
Jno Johnson/1
Jno Caldwell, Joseph Warren, Andrew
  Rathber, negro Tom, negro Will,
  negro Tom Junr, negro Ishmall,
  negro Coffee/8
Margrett Caldwell, Patr: Caldwell,
  Tho: Caldwell/?
Tho: Covington, negro Tom/?
Jno Cayton/?
Thos: Vincent Senr/1
Thos: Vincent Junr, Jam: Vincent/2
Edw'd Shorte, Dan'll MagLaghlin/2
Rich'd Collins/1
Jno. Heatick, Edw'd Marglamary/2
Wm Heatch/1

Edwd Cawderry/1
Jno. Cawderry, Isac Cawderry/2
Jno Riccords Sen, Philip Riccords,
   Sam: Ricords/3
Bryan: Snee, Jno: Mulphey/2
Andrew Sphear/1
Cornel: Lynch(?)/?
Jos: Pemberton, negro Edinbergh/2
Wm Elgitt/1
Sarah Johnson, Purnell Johnson, Geo:
   Maglamary/2
Adam Heatch(?), negro Toby, negro
   Hanah/3
Fran: Landcake, Geo: Landcake, Wm
   Wainwright, negro Toby, negro
   Bess/3
Tho: Humphreys, negro Cuffy, negro
   Enomony, negro Taby/4
Tho: Humphrys Sen, Wm King, negro
   Dick/?
(entries obliterated)
Wm Johnson, Geo: Hutchins/2
Rich'd Nicols Jr, Jam: Nicols/2
Rich'd Nicols Senr, Abel Samuells/2
Geo: Hutchins, Henry Hutchins/2
Tho: Bartlett/1
Jno. Anderson/1
Jos: Vennables, Ben: Vennables, negro
   Mingo, negro Coffe/4
Jno Goslin, Rich'd Goslin/2
James Hardy Sen, Jam: Hardy Junr, Jno
   Hardy, Patr. Shiels/4
... Handy/?
Jno Handy, negro Santy, negro Murry,
   negro Jane/4
Jam: Macmurry, Jno Macmurry, negro
   Ball, negro Rose/4
Sar: Dashiell, Harb: Dashiell, negro
   Cesar, negro Major, negro Grace,
   negro Bess, negro Jane/6
Rob: Dashiell, negro Tite/2
Geo: Scott, Day: Scott, Thos: Pettis,
   negro Sam, negro Hector, negro
   Pomp/6
Ben: Wailes, Pat'r. Bun, ..tt: Swan,
   negro Sib, negro Bess/5
.. Cawderry/1
... Tilletts/1
Mary Rownds, negro Gibbs(?)/1
Geo: Collier, negro Sib/2

Rachell Evans, Wm George, negro
   Robin, negro Mercer, negro Dol,
   negro Sib/5
Robt. Prentice/1
Jno Evans Junr, Geo: Dashiell, negro
   Toby, negro Tom, negro Robin,
   negro Abbo/6
Tho: Willin, Jno Reynolds, negro
   Sarah/3
Jno Evans Senr, Nic: Evans, negro
   Abbo/3
Rich'd Crockett, Rob: Crockett, Jno.
   Crockett, Peter Miller, Jno.
   Foster, negro Coop, negro Monk,
   negro Wapping, negro Tom, negro
   Grace/10
Edw: Fowler, negro Mol/2
Tob: Burk/1
Naomi Shils, Tho: Shiels/1
Tim: Adkinson/2
Wm Nelson, Jno Nelson/2
Jno Shiels, Pet'r D. Brasier/2
Wm Wright/1
Jno Everton, Peter Furbus/2
Ben: Hickman/1
Rich'd Harris, negro, Jago/2
Wm Harris, Wm Harris Junr/2
Tho: Dashiell Junr, Wm Lockwood/2
Tho: Rensher, negro Peter, negro
   Pompey/3
Charles Ballard, Cha: Ballard, negro
   Jack, negro Meareak, negro Mary,
   negro Molle/6
Hen: Johnson/1
Merrick Ellis, Jno Banister, Jam:
   Webster, negro Mary, negro Bobo,
   negro Hannah, Jo: Carr
Tho: Holebrook, Tho: Boswell/2
Geo: Dashiell, James Smith, Step:
   Stanton, Jno: Howard, negro Gift,
   negro Nann, negro Polidore/7
Betty Gale, David Jno:son, Jno:
   Wilcoxs, Cha: Lowe, negro
   Messenger, negro Dublin, negro
   Simus, negro Scipio, negro Binda,
   negro Nanny/9
Levin Gale to be charged for negro
   Hope, negro Pleasant, negro Nabb/3
Tho: Walker, negro Tom, negro Jack/3
Tom: Benston, negro Saunders/2
Wm Robinson/1
Mary Heysom, negro Phillis/1

7

Benj. Cottman, Ben: Cottman Junr, Wm
   Cottman, Jos: Cottman, Geo: Terry,
   negro Bubo, negro Sarah/7
Jno: Leatherbury, Jon: Stanton, negro
   Pompey, negro Sampson, negro
   Sambo, negro Bridgett, negro
   Rose(?)/7
Wm Sullivan/1
Mary: Mangor/ Jno. Mangor/1
Wm Denson/1
Geo: Goddard/?
Jno. Goddard, Philip Harris/2
Pet'r: Sherman/1
Wm Alexander, Sam: Alexander/2
Moses Alexander, Jno Murray/2
Robt: Knox/1
Tho: Bruerton, Wm Chapnite(?), Isaac
   Hyway/3
Jos: Stanfurd/1
Tho: Pullett/1
Geo: Willson/1
Jam: Chaddwick, Peter Moode/2
Alex'r Vance/1
Wm Adley/1
Jonat: Raymond, Jon: Raymond Junr/2
Jno Cope/1
Alex'r Adams, Jno Tompson, Rich'd
   Puckam, Rob: Smith, Edward Fla..,
   negro Qua...
Wm Bruerton/?
Wm Hayman/?
Jno: Cristopher Junr/1
Jno Cristopher Sen, Eph:m
   Cristopher/2
Step: Baily/1
Geo: Baily/1
Jno Mears/1
Peter Magee/1
Isaac Noble, negro Tom/2
Owen Odaw/1
Jno Booth/1
Peter Sherman, Jon Sherman/2
Edw: Sherman, Tho: Sherman/2
Edw: Sherman Junr/1
Abigal: Stevens, negro Jack, negro
   Bess/2
Joh: Bounds, negro Bess
Edw: ..., negro Beleck(?)/3
Rich'd Philips, Step: Hall, negro
   Grace/3
Jacob Crouch, Abrah: Puckum/2
Wm Vennables/1

Jno Vennables/1
Sam: Jackson, Wm Evans, negro
   Bridgett/3
Tho: Taylor/1
Rose Moore, Peter Gordon/2
Jarvis Jenkins/6(?)
Pat'r. McDull/1
Jno: Mackdowell/1
Tho: Anderson, Jos: Jackson/2
Jno Parsons/1
Andrew Lakey/1
(several entries obliterated)
Jno: Kibble/1
Wm Kibble
Peter Parsons/2
Rich'd Stevens, Robert Miller, negro
   Pompey/3
Jno: Magloghlin/1
Cris: Dowdell/1
Mary Girrard, Rich: Hodggen,negro
   Will/2
Tho: Collier, negro Grace/2
Frenk(?) Boardman, Wm Boardman/2
Tho: Bashaw, Gerrard Bashaw, Jam:
   Bunn, Rich'd: Pope/4
Alex'r Carlile, negro ??, negro Dino
(obliterated entry)
Jno: Layton/1
Jno: Brady(?)/1
Edw'd Hillman/1
Ann: Crouch, Jno: Crouch, Isaac
   Crouch/2
Sarah Howgin(?), Alex'r
   Tullington(?)/1
Cha: Hill/1
Jno Disharoon, Mic: Disharoon, Wm
   Stevens, Tho: Stevens, negro
   Coffee/5
Jno: Stevens/1
Jno Roach, Wm Roach, Jno Roach Junr,
   Cha: Roach, negro Joseph, negro
   Kitt, negro Patience/7
Jno Maggee, Geo: Maggee/2
Robt Adkins/1
... Dickson/1
And: Bashaw/1
Hen: Toadvine, Nicol: Toadvine, negro
   Goliah/3
....., negro Toby/2
Isaac Toadvine/1
Wm Cary, Wm Cary, Junr/2
Edward Nichols/1

Jam: Mauhawn(?)/1
Arth'r Hayman, Wm Hayman/2
Mos: Dusky, Jam: Dusky, Rich'd:
  Dusky/3
Jno: Shockley, Alex'r Sermon, Sam:
  Davis/3
Lewis Disharoon, Jno: Disharoon/2
Pat'r Kersey/1
Nath: Dunaho/1
Jno: Davies, Dan: Davies, Jno: Davies
  Junr, Jos: Paby, Jno Ruark/6
Alex'r Lukey (Leckey?)/1
David Barnhill/1
... Hill /1
... rdue/1
James Smith, Jam: Smith Junr/2
Tho: Hugg, Robt. Polk/2
Jeremiah Wright/1
Timothy Kennedy/1
Nicolas Ready/1
Jno. Goulden, Dennis Duskey/2
Tho: Cox Junr/1
Tho: Cox: Senr/1
Ebenezar Handy, Ralph Winterton,
  negro Tom, negro Monfurd, negro
  Hannah/5
Jno: Ricords Junr, Geo: Owens, Jno:
  Paris/3

Manokin Hundred Taxables
...(Aprroximately half this sheet is
  worn away)
... C...well
...Will'm Clark, .. Ned, Coffee,
  Jack, Nancy, Mary, Jane, negros/9
Joseph Hust, Joseph Hust/2
Thos(?) Brown, ... Harry, negros/4
(several entries obliterated)
... Maddox, Geo: Low... negros:
  Coffee, Dick, ..., Moll.../7
Capt. John Tunstall(?), thirteen
  negros...
Mrs. Esther Denwood widw, Jack,
  Jacob, Toney, negros/6
John Denwood, Will., Harry, Sue,
  negros/4
David Brown, Thos Brown, Cudgo negro
Rich'd Magraw, Henry No... Domingo...
Capt R..., Alex'r ..., Wm ... Rich'd
  Ma..., Matt'w Jon..., Fortune,

Jessey(?), Min, Mack... , Pompey,
  Vio..., Moll, .../?
(entry obliterated)
W..., ..., ..Tom, ..., Jack,
  Phillis, .../8
Thos. Gilles(?), Will'm... John
  Ha..., Robt' Do..., Dominique, ...
  Pegg, Pegr.../?
Owen Conne.../
(Ge)orge Benstone, James Cane/2
James Strawbridge, David, Tom,
  Coffee, Hagar, negros/5
Rich'd Whittey Senr, Rich. Whittey
  Junr/2
... Gray, ... Gray... son/3
(middle portion of column
  obliterated)
... ...orney
... Frances
Will'm Collins/1
Will'm Bowland/1
And'w Moo.dey, Will'm Jarvis(?)/2
John Mores(?), ... Riggby/1
Jarvis Ballard, Robt Shein, Amy
  negro/?
John Fergerson/?
Daniel Burgin
Geo. Bosman Junr, Sambo, negro
Willm Bosman Junr
Will'm Bosman Senr, James Staples,
  Philip Sp...
Doso, negro
John Young, Jam. ... Jonath...
Wm. ..., Abra ..., Jams. ...
John Scot, James D..., ... negro/?
John Chamberlaine(?)
Robt. Smith
...wood Rencher, ... Fisher ...,
  ..., ..., Bess negro
George Hiebus, Geo Hiebus, Into,
  Sambo....
John ..., Wm M..., Jam. M...
Will'm Jones, Joy negro...
Widow Til(1man), Coffee negro
Aaron Tillman/1
Patrick Matthews/1
Moses Tillman, Ewd Hielley(?)/3
Stephen Deare (Doare?), Stephen
  Deare (Doare?)
John Philips
Clear Thompson, Wm. Thompson, John
  Murry, Jack, negro/4

Benjamin King, Sam'll Miles, Will'm
    King, Tho: Paterson, Dick & Ben,
    negro/6
Col Roger Woolford's act (large
    portion missing)
Willm. Ak...
Edmond Cullen/1
John Elzey, John H..., Sambo.../5
James Lin..., Moses, Bess, .../3
George Horner/1
Rich'd Waters, Edmund .../2
Jam. Lawes, Cha. Dulap/2
Willm. Flemming/1
    (large portion missing
John Fountain/1
Mercy Fountain, Sam'll Fountain, John
    Smith, Hercules, negro/4
Nich'o Fountain/1
... Fountain/1
Jam's Willes
Burnaby Willes
Joseph Henderson/1
William Miles
Alex'r Maddux/1
Wm Fountain/1
Daniel Maddux, Jacob negro
Thos. Maddux, Frans. Crowder, Sue
    negro
Benja. Fosque, Thos. Fosque
Charles Revell(?), Price, ...
Randall ..., Toby, ...
Joseph Tillman
John Horsey Senr , Will'm Horsey(?),
    Peter ...on...
(several entries missing)
John ...an, Willm. Mcdorman(?), Morey
    negro
Abell Wright, Randal Wright
Thos Mitchell, Thos Mitchell, John
    Hill, Mingo, ...
Willm. Eskridge, Tom, Moll
Wm Prosser/?
Joseph Butler
Daniel Munrooke/?
John Brown/1
Will'm Brown/1
John Evenes/1
Abraham Heath/1
Will'm Eliphant/1
Wm Noble/1

Capt John King, Henry Fisher, John
    Goldsmith, Harry, Ciss, Patience,
    Toney, Rose, negros/8
Alex'r Hall Senr, Alex'r Hall Junr,
    Bryan Gilliagan, negro Peter/4
... King, negro ... /2
Richard(?) Chambers(?) Senr,
    Richard(?) Chambers(?) Junr
(entries missing)
Anthoney West
Benj'a Sharp, Nath'll Plumb
Jacob Heath
Thos. Banister, Lilence, negro
Revil Horsey, Patience negro
Rich'd Saunders(?)
Alex'r Hall(?)
Robt ... Ann..., Will'm...
Sarah ..., Henry... James...
Joshua Shaw
Will'm Evenes, Edw..d (Edmond?)
    Malavell(?)

A True List of Taxeables of Nanticoke
    Hundred by James Bound Constable
    taken in June 1723

Ebenezer Cottman, Patrick Donnison,
    Patrick Donnison, John Bowwhannan,
    negro Roger/4
George Greer, Mark Greer/2
Henry Lackey/1
John Carter, Phillop Carter/2
John Carter Junior/1
James Nicholson, Rich'd Nicholson,
    Robert Twolly(?)/3
James Weatherlee, Jacob Bound, negro
    Tom, negro Pegg/4
William Weatherlee, negro Tobby/2
Franis Prices/1
Solomon Hitch, negro Bess/2
John Acworth, negro Sarry/2
James Larrimore, John Gurrly, William
    Gray/3
John Chesman/1
Richard Acworth, Senr, Richard
    Acworth, Thomas Acworth, John
    Smith, negro Will/5
Charles Acworth/1
John Gillis/1
Henry Carter/1
John Willson/1

Thomas Gravener/1
Gabrell Cooper Sr, Gabrel Cooper,
　Samuell Cooper, James Cooper,
　Isaac Cooper/5
Thomas Relph, John Relph/2
Robert Downes/1
Thomas Parrimore/1
Peter Calloway, Peter Calloway
　Junior/2
William Calloway/1
William Relph/1
Phillop King/1
Thomas Wood/1
Cornelis Watkinson/1
Edward Whetly, Thomas Smith, William
　Russell/3
George Scot/1
Edward Killum, John Darby, William
　Tully/3
William Young, James Gossling, Thomas
　Gossling/3
John Huffington, Thomas Huffington,
　William Tayler, James Tully,
　Jonathan Huffington, Rowland
　Maklond/6
Charles Young, Nathannl Lawly
　(Lanely?)/2
John Price/1
Peter Freene/1
William Twifoot/1
Edward Nowells/1
John Allfee/1
Richard Huffington/1
Rich'd Ellingworth, Robt.
　Ellingoworth/2
James English, Thomas English,
　William English/3
Thomas Marvell/1
Zeakell Green/1
Samuel Mellson/1
John Phillops/1
Thomas Lester/1
Richard Gefferyson/1
John Stuard/1
John Sharp/1
John Lingly/1
Andrew Speer/1
Henry Speare, Samuell Garvis/2
Thomas Waller/1
Nathanel Waller/1
William Harvy/1
John Caldwell, one negro/2

John Calloway/1
John Marey/1
John Read/1
John More/1
Thomas Gorden/1
James Jones, William Jones/2
James Jones Junior
Soloman Turpin/1
Edward Wooden, John Wooden/2
Mathew Hossey/1
John Tatman/1
John Winsor/1
Henry Winser/1
James Bogger/1
Henry Friggs, Robert Friggs/2
William Robertson/1
Charles Newton, Johen Newton/2
Chales Huggins/1
Edmon Huggins, John(?) Huggins,
　Nehamiah Huggins/3
Thomas Price/1
Richard Killum/1
Peter Samwells Senior/1
Thomas Johnson/1
William Phillips/1
Ralph Tindall, Charles Tindall,
　Sam'll Tindall/3
Jacob Ingram/1
Isaac Ingram, Fredrick Joseph/2
Henry Williams, Charles Williams/2
John Lankstone/1
Abraham Ingram, Robert Ingram/2
John Fleetwood/1
Samuel Owens, Robert Owens/2
John Gray/1
Joshua Eddgs(?), To Joseph Wailes/1
John Neale to John Eavens Junior/1

1723. A List of all the Taxable
Persons in Mattaponie Hundred taken
by the Constable of the said Hundred,
as followeth

Mr. John Purnell senr, John Purnell
　Junr, John Tinley and .. slaves
　...ner/9
Wm. Turner(?) & Thomas Oxford/2
Thomas(?) Odue/1
Jacob Waggaman & one slave/2
Michael Tar/1
James Cherrex/1

John Pope, William Stevens and one
 slave/3
Tobias Pepper/1
John Allen/1
Joseph Allen/1
Edward Bennett/1
William Pepper & Wm Becksborne/2
William Kenetson/1
Thomas Lilliston/1
William Cord & two slaves/3
Parker(?) Selby/1
Penry Brownbill & Wm Ainsworth/2
Christopher Parradice/1
Robert Watson Senr, Robt Watson Junr
 and one slave/3
Samuell Hosier/1
Thomas Newton/1
John Sturgis Junr/1
Roland Hogg & John Hogg/2
Comfort Ayres & Tho Glenden/1
William Ayedolett/1
Samuell Tar/1
John Dreaden/1
Abraham Hill/1
Ambrose Wilit & Nixon Coner/2
J... & William Stuckley/2
Charles Vesey & William Vesey/2
John Sturgis Sen, Wm.(?) Sturgis,
 Jonathan Sturgis, Joshua Sturgis,
 his sons/4
James Hall, Nehemiah Holland and two
 slaves/4
Richard Conner/1
Johnson Hill Sen, Johnson Hill Junr,
 Hutten Hill & Robert Hill/4
Edward Million/1
Wm Daniell/1
Umphery Chapman/1
John Chapman/1
Steven Walton/1
David Price/1
Bishop Henderson/1
Manuell Harman/1
Abraham Mason & Luke Watson/2
Joseph Fitteman/1
Mathew Scarbrough, John Scarbrough
 Mathew Wise, Thomas Wise and one
 slave/5
Thomas Milborne/1
Phillip Selby, Mathew Selby, Charles
 Davis and three slaves/6
John Walker and two slaves/3

Mary Pope payes for George Pope and
 two slaves/3
Fisher Walton, Samuell Hudson and one
 slave/3
William Richardson Senr William
 Richardson Junr and one slave/3
Thomas Robins, Boden Robins and three
 slaves/5
Peter Johnson, John Johnson and
 Robert Johnson/3
John Watson/1
Peter Claywell & Tho Claywell/2
Peter Watson/1
Nathaniell Hopkins Senr, Matthew
 Hopkins, Nathaniel Hopkins Junr,
 Samuel Hopkins, John Ferrell/5
Wm.(?) Southey/1
Joseph Taylor/1
Hugh Wilson, Robt Ogelby & John
 Holston/3
William Wilson & Wm Duer/2
Robt Scott & William Scott/2
William Bratten/1
John Dillaha/1
Benjamin Ayedolett/1
Richard Sturgis/1
Nathaniell Brownbill & John Taylor/2
John Onions/1
Sam'll Hopkins Senr, Sa. Hopkins
 Junr, Wm Hopkins, Josiah Hopkins
 and John Walker/5
Christopher Glass/1

Signed by --- Christ Glass

A List of Tyethable Persons In
 Baltimore Hundred taken by Edmond
 ----, Constable

Wm Stevenson, 3 negroes/4
Jno. Miller/1
Littleton Bowin/1
Joseph Wait/1
Wm Cobb/1
John Linch Senr & Sons, Alexander and
 Abraham(?)/3
Nathanael Racklif/1
Wm Reed/1
Wm Winders/1
Wm Smith/1
Richard Webb/1

John Tull/1
Race Clark/1
John Lathbery/1
Richard Hudson Junr/1
Gabriel Powell/1
Joseph Kenny/1
John Cobb/1
John Linch Junr/1
David Hudson/?
Jonas Smith/?
John Wats, Peg & ne...
Thomas(?) Cofen(?)/?
Thomas Bowdin/?
Thos Quillen
Isac Rappoon(?)/?
Hugh Tingell senr, Son Jno. Tingell/2
Hugh Tingell Junr/1
Mary Woodcraft, son Rich'd and 1
    negro/2
John Ellison/1
Peter Robinson/1
John Robinson/1
Mary Robinson, 1 negro/1
Michael Robinson/1
John Woodcraft/1
John Rickets & 1 negro/2
John Smith, 3 negroes/4
James Perry/1
Wm Powder Wm. Waley/2
Wm Evens/1
Thos Dasey/1
John Marsey/1
... Godwin/?
Henry Brueing/?
Edward Clark, Robt. West/?
Joncs Rickets, Sons John & William/3
John o Norton, Robt. Tyre, & 2
    negros/4
Daniel Wharton and Hinman & Frances/3
Tho. Robinson & John Wharton/2
Sarah Moriss, Sons John & Charles/2
Leonard Johnson & Jonathan Dixon/2
Sturgis Dixon/1
John Dixon/1
George West/1
John Wellbone/1
Thos. West/1
Thomas Harney/1
George Howard, Sons, John, Joseph &
    Samuell, Samuel Davis, 2 negroes/7
Thos. Roberts/1
John Barnit/1

... Polit/1
Samuel Derexson & Joseph Derexson/2
John Painter(?) & 1 negro/2
William Sammons/1
Bowman(?) Townsend/1
Wm. Burton, son William & 2 negros/4
Joseph Lewis/1
William Groom/1
Wm Pepper, Arnold Pepper & Benj'a
    Blizard/3
Gabriel West/1
Paul Waples/1
Ebenezer Jonnes/1
Abraham Endless/1
John Blizard/1
Wm Freeman/1
Lazerus Kenny/1
David Hazard, Cord Hazard & 1 negro/3
Wm Turvile, son Wm & 1 negro/3
Wm Robinson/1
Mary Godwin, Sons, Michael & Cezar/2
Thos. Mumford, Son ..., 2 negros/4
... Mumford/1
Franklyn Fassit & 1 negro/2
John Turvile/1
Wm .../?
Ken..t ..../?
Robert Gault/?
Francis Hamlin & Wm Marsey/2
John Hamlin/
John Fassit/
Joseph Gray & Jno. Deal/2
Edward Moor/1
Rich'd Murrow, Sons Rich'd & James/3
Mary Collings, Son Ebenezar/1
John Collings, Wm Collings/2
George Taylor/1
John Pattey & Sam'l Powell/2
John Hennesey/1
Rich'd Hudson Senr, & 2 negros/
Richard Lodgwood/
Walter Taylor/1
Henry Alexander/
Thomas Wallace & John Wallace & John
    Stinson & 1 negro/
John Camill/1
Archbald Deal/1 negro/2
John Johnson/1
James Hog & 1 negro/2
Alex'r Marsey/1
Wm Kennit Senr/1
Alex'r McGrigory/1

Peeter Collier/1
Wm Fassit, Son Wm, Jno McWilliams, 7
    negroes/10
Wm Walton, Sons, John & Wm, Jno
    Morrison, & 6 negros/10
John Mumford/1
Thos. Ferill/1
Widow Bowin, 1 negro/1
John Gilleland & Nicholus Coffey/2
Nathanal Crapper, Son Sollomon &
    Francis Coffey/3
Rich'd Holland, 3 negros/4
Stratton Burton, David Allford/2
Rich'd Manklin, ...
Charls.(?) Racklif & ... negros/6
Nath'l(?) W..., Wm Marriss/
Isaac Atherly/1
John Purnil, Allan Dunbar, John
    Hammon, 3 negros/6
Isaac Marshal & Henry Scott/2
John Wheeler/1
Wm Davison/1
Daniel Davis/1
Widow Fawl, Son John/1
Isiah Bredil, Son Wm Gray, George
    Chansellor & 1 negro/4
... Holloway/1
... ...ison & Erasmus Harrison/2
Widow Evens, son John/
Joseph (or Josiah?) Britingham/
... Johnson, 1 negro
... O Flanagon/
Edmond Crapper, Joseph Miller, Henry
    Bradley, 4 negros/7
Total 243
Non-Residents - Abraham Highway
Examined the within List and found to
    be 243 Taxables Jo'n McClester,
    Sheriff

A List of the Tiathables of
Bogueternorton Hundred Taken by
George Truitt, Constable - 1723

Thomas Selby Snr/1
Thomas Selby Jr, Charles Holstone/2
William Porter/1
John Bishop Senr
Wm Bishop
Benjamin Bishop

Elisabeth Pope Widd, Joseph Porter,
    McClintuck Porter, negro Donke/3
Thomas Outon, Richard Blizard/2
Mathew Patrick/1
Roger Patrick/1
John Victor/
Alexander Stewart, James Henderson/2
John Cammull(?)/1
John Pepper, Christopher Pepper/2
Thomas Slinger
Wm Brittingham/1
Charles Richardson, Robert
    Richardson, Charles Richardson/3
Adam Terence Senr, Christopher
    Mullan/2
Wm Davis, Cooper/1
Elis Hutson, Widd, Wm Hutson, negro
    Tom/2
John Bishop Junr(?)/1
John Webb(?)/1
John Hutson Jnr/1
Benjamin Tull/1
Cornelius Ennis/
John Swan(?)
Robert Hutson, Negro Tobey, negro
    Betty/3
Denis Hutson, negro Ceaser/2
Abraham Smith, Wm Wilson/2
Charles Clark/1
John Dreadon, Robert Dreadon/2
Robert Hall/1
Samuell Broten Junr/1
Henery Bishop
Afria Doze Johnson, George Johnson,
    John Johnson, negro Guy, negro
    Lesley(?)/5
Wm McClamery, negro Boson/2
Samuel Deverix, John Deverix, negro
    Bess/3
Charles Godfrey, Joseph Godfrey,
    negro Joan/3
Mark Scott, Thomas Scott Jnr(?)/2
John Timmons/1
James Woods/1
Daniell Denison/1
Robert Martin, Owen O Cassady, negro
    Toney, negro Ceaser, negro
    Mall(Matt?)/6
Price Collins, negro Jefery, negro
    Yocko/
Edward Davis, Nehemiah Cropper/

Ephraim Heather, negro Fisher, negro
  Bess/
Parker Selby son of Daniel/1
Wm Bowin Snr, John Bowin, David
  Bowin, negro James, negro Dick/
Benjamin Truitt, Joseph Truitt/2
Edward Hammond son of John/1
Elisabeth McClemey, widd, negro
  Phillis/1
James Tomson/1
Edward Bownd, negro Ben, negro Geney/
John Murray, Cornelius Tayler, Wm
  Williamson, negro ..., negro
  Augna(?)/
Andrew Smith, John Smith, Wm Smith/
Joseph Johnes (Jones?), Richard
  Simpson/
Thomas Midsley/1
Wm Richards/1
John Ironshire/1
Warrin Hadder/1
John Bradford, Nathaniel Bradford/2
John Greer/1
Robert Hodge/1
Lodowick Fleman/1
Elisabeth ..., Widd, Robert Stinson/1
Nicholas Warrin/1
Robt Warren/1
Wm Beatheard(?), Robert Jarman/2
Peter Beckett/
Walter Tayler/
John Abbott/1
Robert Hill, Thomas Railey, Wm
  Morris, negro Will, negro Bess/5
... Timmons/1
... Timmons, James Timmons/2
Joseph Timmons/1
Samuell Timmons/1
Thomas Timmons/1
Wm Timmons/1
Jobe Truitt Jnr/1
Jobe Truitt Snr, Mordica Truitt/2
Mrs. Mary Hampton, Benjamin Godgin,
  ..., negro James Pompey, negro
  Patience, negro Genney/5
John Bassitt/
...e Jarman/1
John(?) Hammond son of Edward/1
...d, .../2
Antony Hadder/1
John Jarman/1
... Morris, Joseph Morris/2

John Cavenough/1
Mr. (?) Tho: Fletcher, Wm Smith, John
  Bishop, Henery
  Coulman(?)(Cotman?)/3
Roger Hook, Wm Hook/2
Henery Jarman, Wm Truitt/2
John Burbage Senr, John Burbage
  Junr/2
Edward Burbage/
Henery Mock(?)/1
... Truitt, Carpenter, ... Truitt,
  negro Sarah/3
Thomas Pointer son of Thomas, Thomas
  Bishop/2
Elias Pointer/1
Thomas Pointer son of Wm/1
Jeremiah Townsand Snr, Brickhouse
  Townsand, negro Touse/3
Jeremiah Townsand Jnr/1
George Truitt son of John/1
Samuell Broton Snr, Wm Stevenson,
  John Truitt/3
Daniell Handcok, Wm Handcok/2
John Patrick Junr, John Patrick, John
  Baker/3
Thomas Collins/1
John Holland/1
Ebenezar Crapper/1
Wm Griffin/1
Charles Collins, negro James/2
Wm Simson, negro Peter/2
Isaac Brittingham/1
John Williams/1
John Truitt son of John/1
John Denis Snr, Wm Denis, Wieb
  (Webb?) Prier, negro Joe, negro
  Cate/5
Doneck Denis Jnr/1
Samuell Davis, negro Will/2
Thomas Grover(?)/1
Timothy Brumley (Drumley?)/1
Ebynezar Franklin/1
Col John Franklin, negro Herkulus/2
Wm Hall, negro Coffey/2
Thos Patton, Robert Patton/2
Edmand Hough/1
James Stevenson/1
James Steale/1
James Mumford, George Mumford/2
Philip Truitt/1
Mathew Raine/1
John M'Caley Snr, John McCaley Jnr/2

Eliner Truitt widd, negro Ben, negro
   Mall/2
Tho: Nathaniel Williams, Presgrave
   Williams/2
Quanton Broton, Peter Lindall/2
Katharine Purnall widd, negro Jack,
   negro Coffey, negro Moriah, negro
   Titus/4
Thomas Purnall, Robert Warrin,
   Deverix Drigas, negro Dorithy,
   negro Sambo, negro Dina, negro
   Will
Mathew Purnall, negro Will/2
John Parker Senr, George Parker, John
   Parker Junr, negro Jack, negro
   Tom, negro Daniell, negro Nan/7
Richard Pennell, John Pennell, Tho:
   Pennell, Charles Pennell/4
Wm Davis, Robert Davis, Wm Davis/3
Robert Davis, Wm Davis/2
Samuell Truitt, John Porter/2
James Truitt, George Truitt/2
Stanton Atkins/1
Andrew Collins/1
Jonathan Williams/1
Jobe Jarman/1
Emanuel Bridgewaters/1
Wm O Shohannas/1
Wm Selbey(?), negro Mingo, negro
   Sambo, negro Tobey, negro Hannah
   Snr, negro Hanah Jnr/6
Adam Spence Junr, Charles Henderson,
   negro George, negro Sambo, negro
   Hector, negro Mall/6
Wm Robison, negro John/2
Benjamin Burton, John Parker/2
Wm Fausitt son of John/1
James Rownd, negro Tom, negro Peter,
   negro Hannah/4
Richard Newman/1
Richard Beatheard/1
John Hutson Snr/1
Robert Ponton/1
Wm Whittington, negro Harvey, negro
   Simon, negro Sam, negro Mall,
   negro Bettey, negro Sarah/7
Wm Ennis/1
James Broton/1
Wm Pointer, Nathaniell Pointer/2
Edward Pointer/
John Purnall Junr/

Indian Pipgrin(?)
George Truit Son of George/1

A List of Taxables in Talbot County 1733

Island Hundred
Edward Lloyd, Ditto Security for
  Thos. Higgins and William Henesay,
  Christopher Hughes, Negroes:
  Toney, Mary, Dick, Will, Sampson,
  Ulysses, Hector, Polydore, Harry,
  Sabina/14
Thomas Hopkins, Arthur Oneal,
  Negroes: Harry & Betty/4
William Sampson, John Welton and
  Robert Ling/3
Thomas Pirkins, William Martin,
  Thomas Sinclair and Phillis a
  Negro/4
David Clemens, John Fleming and
  Thomas Fisher/3
Hannah Springer, Thos. Scott/1
Francis Storey, Joseph Storey and
  Richard Storey/3
William Benny, Samuel Fisher/2
Charles Walker, William Hugg/2
Hugh Morgan, Thomas Walker/2
Mary Morgan, Robert Morgan, William
  Smith, Rowland Saman/3
John Naylor, Joseph Naylor/2
Thomas Foster/1
Thomas Lenox, Negro Peg/2
John Parr, Thomas Higgins, William
  Lenegar, John Craduck, Negro Nan/5
Samuel Cockayne, Isaac Faulkner,
  Negro Dinah/3
Thomas Roberts/1
Alexander Willson/1
Phil. Banning, Eneas Mcdonald/2
Archibald Valentine/1
Marmaduke Storcy/1
Margaret Roberts a Mulatto/1
John Benny, Henry Best/2
James Benny/1
James Morgan/1
Nicholas Brown/1
John Hage, Edward Pratt(?)/2
William Johnson/1
William Edmondson, Thomas Scot.
  Negroes, Mingo, Dido & Moll/5
Thomas Springer, Negro Jack/2
Robert Beswicks, Richard Strawhan,
  Negroes: Caesar, Simon/4
William Warner, John Warner/2
Daniel Baker, William Baker/2
Henry McNish, William Jones/2
John Sweat, Vaule Sweat/2

William Pratt/1
The Widow Noble, Robert Noble, Andrew
  Best, Negroes: Danby & Joan/4
Joseph Hollins, William White/2
Gilbert Barrow, ditto secry for
  William Dyer, Edward Herd(?)/3
John Blackwell, Dido a Negro/2
The Widow Shield, Archibald Douglis,
  Alice a Negro/2
William Ryon, William Ryon junr/2
Thomas Beasly, William Gad/2
Ambrose Kinnimmont, Edward Brown,
  Negroes Toby, Peter, Simon, Pegg/6
At John Dolvin's, John Dolvin junr/1
Thomas Keets, William Sanseton/2
Richard Bennett Esqr. At Jacks
  Quarter John Dolvin, Negroes,
  Jack, Cloe, Jack/4
George Beswicks Negroes: Tony and
  Peter/3
Richard Beswicks, James Thomas,
  negores: Joseph, Jack/4
William Cole, Jarrat Heath, John
  Cole, Negroes: Pompey & Sarah/5
Steven Baker/1
John Miller, John Puskell/2
Michael Allison/1
John Jaggerman/1
John Parker/1
John Pitts/1
Thomas Adams/1
Jacob Williams/1
William Harper/1
David Prichard/1
James Saunders, ditto secry for Wm.
  Glover/2
At the Widow Finneys, William Finney,
  Humphry Bowe, negroes: Tom,
  Jenny/4
Ferdinando Callahane, James Callahan,
  William Stewart/3
Roger Clayland, Harris Clayland, John
  Hesketh(?)/3
At Tamerlane Davis his quarter,
  Thomas Turner, Negroes: Tom,
  Harry, Occoba(?), Ege/5
At Mr. Hemsleys quar., James Virgin,
  Negroes Pompey, Will, Peter,
  Judith, Sarah/6
Anthony Williams, Auldin Williams,
  Charles Kingston, Negro Dick/4

17

At the Widow Hewy's, Anthony Williams
Guy, Negro Doll/2
Esqr. Bennett quarter Henry McQuead,
Negroes: Jack, Nan, Sarah/4
Francis Pickering, Negro Pompey/2
John Corkerill/1
James Williams Guy/1
John Porter/1
John Allen/1
Bryan Cavanaught/1
Richard Hughs senr, ditto for Edward
Corse(?), Richard Hughs, Richard
Hughs Junr/4
Andrew Henesey, Thomas Wantland/2
Francis Wrightson, John Gordon,
Negroes: Moll, Jenny/4
At Coll. Wards quarter, James
Wantland, Negroes Will, Will,
Caesar, Matthew, Peter, Sarah/7
William Elbert, Ditto junr, Thomas
Jones, Thomas Owens, Abraham
Severy, Negroes Mingo, Robin,
Abraham, Toney, Diana, Hagar,
Abington/12
William Clayton, Evan Evans, John
Cedar, Vincent Jones, William
Clayland, John Ross, Negroes:
Mingo, Tony, Pompey, Bristo, Jack,
Ned, Sarah, Dido, Rose, Ben, Sam,
Daphney, Mingo, Rose, Lydia, Joe,
Rose, Dick/24
Philip Emerson, Michael Penkind,
Littleton Ward, Negroes: Jack,
Andrew, Dick, Scipio, Andrew,
Simon, Phillis, Cate/11
At Esqr Bennetts quar. at Wye town,
Thomas Rowland, James Miller,
Richard Kickley, Negroes: Jack,
Tom, Mansaul, Caesar, Peter, Esop,
Maffro, Sarah, Betty, Rose, Lydia,
Sam/15
Richard Skinner, Robert Summers,
Andrew Gresham, Negro: Sue/4
Aaron Higgs, ditto Security for
Joseph Parker, Samuel Simpson,
John Sevill/4
Samuel Kinnamont/1
William Pickering/1
John Willson, Joseph Kinninmont,
Negroes: Durham & Bess/4
John Nutter, Nathaniel Nutter/2

Joseph Porter, Nathaniel Saintee,
John Blake, Negroes: Tom, Sue.
Laurence Cork, George Davis/7
Alexander Ray/1
Robert Bishop/1
Richard Gresham, Daniel Tarr/2
George Gresham/1
William Dehorty, Morgan Dehorty/2
At Woolmans belonging to Mr. Saml.
Chew: Charles Brown, Thomas
Garratt, Negroes: Scipio, Sampson,
Abigail, Hannah/6
Perry Benson, William Russell, Thomas
Russell, William Whaley, Nicholas
Deverix, Negroes: Caesar &
Phillis/7
William Edwards/1
John Willson/1
Michael Meginny/1
Richard Bruff, John Roberts/2
John Higgins/1
John Christian/1
William Whaley/1
The Widow Whaley, John Whaley/1
Thomas Ward, Ephraim Start/2
Andrew Kinninment/1
John Kinninment, William White/2
Woolman Gibson, Francis Stokes, John
Ranstead, Negroes: Tom, Mingo,
Daphny, Bess, Moll/8
John Davison, James Davison/2
Richard Gibson, Charles Cannon/2
William Tarr/1
Robert Hall, William Oxingham, Thomas
Simmons, George Smith, Negro:
Jacob/5
Coll. Jacob Gibson, Bartholomew
Gibson, Francis Hazeltine,
Negroes: Tom, Moll, Sam./6
George Garey, Edward Shropshell,
Daniel Peaks, William Jones/4
John Rennalds, William Mansfield/2
The Widow Cooper, William Cooper,
John Cooper/2
Lewis Jones, Francis Jones/2
John Ray, Thomas Christian/2
James Horney, Andrew Kinninmont,
Richard Dickinson, Negroes:
Hannah, Moll/5
Thomas Bruff, Thomas Butler, Joseph
Rashfield, Charles Floyd/4
John Osment/1

At Bab's quarter belonging to Richard
Bennett, Esqr. Negroes: Bab, Sam,
James, Sue, Moll/5
At Millers quarter belonging to ditto
- Henry Downes, Negroes: Charles,
Tom, Walle, Pompey, Phillis, Rose,
Phillis/8
Henry Downes his Negro woman/1
Thomas Russam, Peter Russam/2
Richard Marlip/1
James Higgins, Thomas Harris/2
John Tarr junr/1
Edward Fottrell, Robert Lloyd, James
Lloyd, Edmond Kelly, Leonard
Sales, Christopher Lewis, Robert
Constantine, Samuel Douglass,
Negroes: Sam, Kitt, Esau, Denbigh,
Maria, Dorcas, Sarah/15
William Robinson/1
James Hollyday, Edward Garatt, John
Rooks, Thomas Tarr, Thomas Johns,
William Davis, Negroes: Bob,
Leander, Ulysses, Will, Alice,
Nancy, Affey, Nell, Wally, Mingo,
Fortune, Peacock, Sue, Sarah,
Moll, Joan/22
Solomon Warner, Edward Griffin/2
John Davis, John Macfall, Daniel
Tunen, John James, Negro: Dido/5
William Jones, his son Pool Jones/1
James Steward/1
James Baker/1
John Henry/1

Thirdhaven Hundred
Thomas Bozman, Joseph Brown, Negroes:
Isaac, Caesar and Mingo/5
Jonathan Taylor, John Newman,
Negroes: Frank, Robin, Mingo,
Jamey, Whitehaven, Ned, Betty,
Beck, Mall, Mereah, Lyla,
Judith/14
Major John Sherwood, Negroes: Ned,
George, Sam, Nan, Doll, Sarah/7
Gabriel Sales, Daniel Osey, Thomas
Sullevant, Negroes: Crowtop,
Nell/5
John Vaughn/1
John Padison, Thomas Roberts/2
William Doberly, Jacob Mansfield/2

Edward Oldham, Negroes: Nick, Jack,
Judith, Toping/5
William Coombs, John Dewland/2
Thomas Alexander, Rigby Foster/2
John Cotter, Thomas Lander/2
William Clark/1
Vincent Lowe/1
Thomas Barnes/1
Henry Dean/1
Robert Lowry/1
John Lurty, James Mace, Negro:
Phillis/3
William Skinner, Negro: Rose/2
Thomas Simson, William Herring/2
Thomas Pamphilion/1
Edward Kelly/1
Solomon Songo/1
John Gibson/1
Samuel Chamberlain, George Townsley,
William Spencer, Thomas Cook,
Jeremiah Belhook, Negroes:
Charles, Toney, Flora, Cheshire,
Rose, Nan, Leverpool, Lilly, Jack,
Pompey, Sue, Sarah, Phill, Oxford,
Shot Wick. Richard Chance/21
Thomas Guning, Richard Broocks,
Edward Cronean, Thomas Didis/4
Joseph Cowley, Neah Cornish, Solomon
Cornish/3
Jacob Cole/1
Alexander Domahoy/1
Jacob Brumwell, James Ogle/2
Andrew Rennalds, William Jones/2
Charles Markland, Darby Dunnovan/2
John Prichard, Charles Lowno, Joseph
Graham, Robert Willson, Thomas
Jolley, Negro: Mereah/6
Mrs. Mary Oldham, Thomas Pitchfork,
Charles Mooning, James Chessey,
Negro: Betty/4
William Colehale/1
Benjamin Stuard/1
John Coward, Negroes: Robin, Sarah &
Peter/3
Robert Wadell, William James/2
Mrs. Wilkinson, James Barness,
Nicholas Lundey, John Dawsey,
Negroes: Mall and Jenny/5
David Robinson, John Robinson, Peter
Stevens, John Slater, Thomas
Allen/5
James Murphoy/1

A List of Taxables in Talbot County 1733

Henry Hart/1
Nicholas Lowe, Ralph Coggs,
  Christpher Brown, Edward Brumey,
  Negroes: George, Sarah, Betty,
  Hannah, Lydia, Deborah, Adam,
  Betty, Sarah, Cobb/14
Daniel Thomson/1
Mr. Nichs. Goldsborough, James
  Murphey, Joseph Synors, Owen
  Tagan, Joseph Jones, Samuel Price,
  Negroes: Ben, Flora, Scipio,
  Dinah, Mall, Jemmey/12
Thomas Ford/1
Thomas Bradshaw/1
Saml. Prichard/1
James Cobourn, William James/2
George Robins, Stanley Robins,
  William Herring, Thomas Martin,
  Samuel Broocks, William King,
  Anthony Brick, Joseph Crouch, John
  Tyder, Negroes: Jack, Lydia,
  Caesar, Tom, Coffey, Phillis,
  Betty, Diana, Chester, Harry,
  Pompey, Elither, Joe/22
Samuel Jenkins/1
William Thomas jun., Joseph Lehay,
  William Lehay/3
Mrs. Loockerman, John Cahell,
  Negroes: Jack, Jemey, Phillis,
  Sarah, Tom, Bettey/7
John Edmondson, William Alexander,
  Ben Guy, Negroes: Robin, Spindelo,
  Steven, Will, Black Nan, Sebery,
  Harry, old Sarah, little Sarah,
  Tom, Doll, John, Robert Studd/16
William Bush/1
John Jones/1
Richard Bush/1
Farril Gallaher, Abednego Bodfield,
  Shadrach Bodfield/3
Francis Armstrong, Francis Armstrong,
  Robert Hopkins, George Wicks,
  Negroes: Spindelo, Blowes/6
Dennis Hopkins, William Hopkins,
  Samuel Hopkins, Joseph Hopkins,
  George Latham, Negro: Jenny/6
John Guy Williams, John Frith/2
Dominick Kirven, Richard Harman/2
George Shannahane, Negro: Judith/2
Michael Fletcher, John Alliss, Andrew
  Spence, Negroes: Tom, Jemey,
  Coffey, Robin/7

John Chance/1
John Barlett/1
William Bush, senr, Joseph Bush,
  George Bush, Solomon Bush/4
Michael Howard, William Reden/2
William Goldsborough/1
Edmond Ffish, Edmond Ffish junr,
  Negroes: Sampson, Will, Adam,
  Jenny, Daphney/7
Joshua Grasham, Alexander Rassey,
  Negro: Esther/3
James Ferrell, John Lered/2
John Ferrell/1
Thomas Bush/1
Henry Woods/1
James Robson/1
Thomas Price/1
Park Webb/1
Philip Jenkins, James Webb/2
John Webb, Richard Webb, Philip
  Porter, Ralph Elston, Edward
  Cathe/5
John Price, John Price, Thomas
  Ewbanks/3
Richard Dove/1
Charles Blackwell/1
Hugh Mcderment, David Shehawn, John
  Whaling/3
James Walker/1
Patrick Flood/1
Black Jack/1
James Buckley/1
William Buckley/1
Richard Porter, Thomas Porter, Garrat
  Rouch, James Cane, John Hutchens,
  Thomas Studson, Negro: Jack/7
William Cullinder/1
The Widow Hutters, Thomas Hutters/1
Philip Fray/1
James Milner, Robert Gill, Negro:
  Beck/3
Patrick Spence, James Coleman/2
Arthur Conner, John Hallcey, William
  Giles/3
Francis Megrah, William Corn/2
Daniel Conner senr, Daniel Conner,
  Solomon Burn, John Conner/4
Henry Parrott, Isaiah Parrott,
  William Parrott, John Davison/4
At the Widow Bayly's Negro Walley/1
Edward Lee/1
Nathaniel Fox/1

Henry Bayly, John Wallice/2
John Merrick/1
Samuel Winier/1
Thomas Skillington/1
Kenelm Skillington, Kenelm
  Skillington, Elijah Skillington,
  Negro: Huck/4
Edward Berry, Daniel Berry/2
Edward Man Sherwood, John Clark,
  Michael Thomas/3
William Nannin, James Stuart/2
Roger Rogers/1
James Hickey/1
The Widow Prichard, Peter Prichard/1
John Studham/1
James Willscott/1
Jeffery Cox, John Cox, Joseph Cox,
  Nathaniel Cox/4
Patrick Mullikin, John Prichard, John
  Hutton/3
Daniel Coffey/1
Edward Leg/1
John Norriss/1
Samuel Mullikin, Samuel Hutchins/2
Douglass Chance/1
Richard Morgan/1
James Webster, Andrew Brown/2
The Widow Acres, Meredith Puck/1
Francis Formiller/1
Elizabeth Stevens, Elisha Stevens,
  Negroes: Will, Sarah/3
Doctor Wm. Sharp, Isaac Sharp,
  William Sanders, William Marderey,
  Negroes: Hornens, Vago, Jack,
  Joney/8
Solomon Sharp/1
Philip Martin/1
Henry Bowdle, John Casey, Daniel
  Shehawn, Negro: Phillis/4
Joseph Parrott, John Potter, John
  Burgess/3
Adam Brown, Negro: Dick/2
Joseph Sillson, Sarah Sillson/2
Thomas Farehurst/1
Peter Winstedley/1
Loftus Bowdle, Thomas Bowdle,Richard
  Gorsuch, John Snowling, Negroes:
  Mall and Doll/6
Joseph Eason, Francis Eason/2
Thomas Browing/1
David Mills, William Mills, Edward
  Prichard/3

William Foreman/1
William Edmondson, Negroes: Charles,
  Jack, Hannah/3
William Saunders senr/1
John Saunders/1
Thomas Martin senr, Thomas Martin,
  William Martin, Will, Bess, Megg/6
James Bradford/1
Charles Gorsuch/1
James Sheapard, William Harrison,
  Thomas Kenderdine/3
Andrew Yeaman/1
Alexander Boyce/1
Joseph Cox/1
William Adams/1
Solomon Robinson, John Robinson,
  Garrot Fitzgerald, Negro Phillis/4
Thomas Rathell, Henry Hill/2
Israel Cox, Peter Williams/2
John Dawley, Thomas Dawley/2
John Harden, Negro: Bristoll/2
George West/1
Lothan West, Henry West, James
  Ferrell/3

Bay Hundred
Coll. Matthew Tilghman Ward, Dennis
  Barratt, Samuel Breerly, John
  Shurdin, Negroes: Henry, James,
  Dick, Ned, Joe, Isabel, Judith,
  Rose, Margaret, Frank, Phillis,
  Rachel, Peter, Pompey, Sam, Betty,
  Anthony, Sarah, George, Elice(?),
  Ben, Titus, Tom, Sue, Jack,
  Flora/30
Revd. Henry Nicols, Robert Roles,
  Francis Roles, Robert Applegarth,
  William Temple, Thomas Higgins,
  Philip Moses, Sue a Mulatto,
  Negroes: Robin, Jack, Belinda,
  Rose, Daphny/12
to Hugh Speddan, John Speddan, Edward
  Speddan, John Fraisher, Timothy
  Maddin/4
John Hopkins, Edward Hopkins, Thomas
  Laremore/3
to William Sparks, Nicholas Cummins/1
Francis Sherwood, Josh. Sherwood,
  Philip Sherwood, John Sherwood,
  Negro: Jemmey/5

James Spencer junr, Isaac Hall,
Edward Smith, Negro: Will/4
At Poplar Island to Charles Carroll -
Richd. Croxill, Negroes: Jemey,
David, Jenney, Frank, Scipio,
Moll, Sue, Jenny/9
William Nevil/1
Hugh Sherwood, Negroes: Jack, Judith,
Lidia, Dinah/5
Edward Callwell/1
Joseph Dawson, Thomas Foster, John
Corker/3
Alexander Jurdin, William Jurdin/2
Risdon Bozman, James Preesly, John
Hall, Negroes: Jemey, Sambo, Rose,
Jemey/7
John Auld, Charles Morgan, Negro:
Toby/3
Daniel Sherwood, Ditto junr, Negroes:
Terry, Jack, Bally, Ffidolla, Boa,
Prossey, Moriah/9
Thomas Ashcroft, William Husler,
Edward Hall, Richard Keighly/4
Daniel Venton/1
Charles Langley/1
Saml. Brooms/1
Daniel Mcdaniel, Negroes: Jack, Dick,
Jacob, Rosa, Margery, Frank/7
William Web Haddaway, Joseph Valiant,
Negroes: Mingo, Hannah/4
Edmond Bell/1
John Camper/1
John Leeds, Edward Wood, Negroes:
Christian, Jacob, Harry, Sam,
Caesar, Nero, Pompey, Dido/10
James Harrison/1
Andrew Orum/1
Edward Rymour/1
William Arnett/1
Thomas Lowe/1
George Collison, John Hawk, Gilbert
Jackson, Edward Ryal junr/4
William Lamden, John Mohaney, Dennis
Cockerill/3
Thomas Smith, Thomas Bradshaw, John
Kinderdine/3
Edward Elliot junr, Peter Haddaway,
Negro: Hannah/3
Nathaniel French/1
Richard Dawson, Ralph Dawson, Anthony
Suple/3

To John Lurty, Henry Smith, Negro:
Jemey/2
Edward Ryal/1
John Low, John Macneal, Negro: Paul/3
James Dawson, Jams. Dawson junr;
Joseph Redish, Negroes: King,
Peter, Will, Grove/7
Edward Collison/1
Joseph Harrison Junr/1
John Staines/1
John Nowland/1
John Kemp, Ditto junr, James Kemp,
Thomas Fly, John Craburn, Richard
Waldon, Joseph Andrew/7
Solomon Horney, William Rakes, Ralph
Willson, John White, Negroes: Jack
Pompey, Paul, Dido, Eby/9
Daniel Lambden, John Lambden, William
Tipler/3
Mary Wrightson, Jonathan Whiteacre,
Joshua Wrightson, James Hays/3
Thomas Howard/1
Laurence Porter/1
Francis Porter/1
William Kersey/1
Peter Hunt/1
Edmund Blades/1
John Richardson/1
Thomas Richardson/1
Philemon Plowman/1
John Poor/1
Anthony Vickers/1
John Porter junr/1
William Dun(?)/1
Thomas Adcock/1
Henry Jefferson/1
Alexander Sinclair/1
Bartholomew Roberts, Nicholas
Roberts/2
Robert Edgar, William Roberts/2
John Porter, Francis Porter, junr/2
Francis Cook, John Right/2
Thomas Lurty, Dennis White/2
Thomas Haddaway, John Lurty/2
Darby Bullen, William King/2
Elizabeth Haddaway, Negro: Dido/1
William Cummins, Thomas Cummins/2
Robert Dawson, William Dawson/2
The Widow Sarah Porter, Phil.
Porter/1
William Richardson/1
Thomas Studham/1

A List of Taxables in Talbot County 1733

Thomas Webster/1
Thomas Sherwood/1
John Harrington/1
Charles Spencer, Charles Jenkson/2
James Barron, John Connel, John
    Landsberry/3
William Hambleton, Phil'n. Hambleton,
    Negroes: Nero, Darlphew, Singo,
    Toalo, Peg, Limas, Hannah, Nan,
    Rose/11
John Hambleton, Thomas Bell/2
John Harrison, Thomas Seril(?),
    Negroes: George, Kate/4
William Harrison, John Rice, William
    Rice/Negro: Cherry/4
Joseph Harrison, Timothy Cocklin,
    George Taylor, Negroes: Moreah,
    Phillis/5
David Hughs, John Hughs/2
John Wiles, Thomas Wiles/2
Robert Harrison, Richard Nutterwill,
    William Denghby/3
Richard Herrington, William
    Herrington, Patrick Ryaly/3
Joseph Herrington, William Morsey/2
Joseph Hopkins, Steven Hall, Negro:
    Dick/3
Philemon Skinner, Negro: Tombo/2
Nathaniel Grace, Benjamin Lakins,
    Daniel Carmady/3
Robert Dodson junr, John Cammell,
    Hugh Macgeorge/3
Edward Elliot, Philemon Mccarty,
    William Addison, Negroes: Joe,
    Joan, Durham/6
William Angle/1
James Spencer/1
Peter Richardson/1
John Eccles/1
Joseph Jones/1
John Hunt/1
John Blackitt/1
Joseph Welling/1
John Greenfield/1
Richard Laremore/1
Robert Laremore/1
Thomas Blusar/1
George Haddaway/1
George Jefferson/1
James Ferrell/1
John Smith/1
Henry Swordin, James Ryal/2

Edward Bandy, Edward Bandy junr/2
John Fairbank, James Fairbank, Thomas
    Fairbank, William Fairbank, Benja.
    Fairbank/5
John Fairbank junr, Thomas Satchell/2
Peter Coalk(?), Abraham Pilkinton/2
Christmas Jones, John Jones,
    Christmas Jones junr, John
    Glasscock, Peter Corkerin/5
Daniel Briges, Charles Briges/2
John Ball, Arthur Carter, Hugh Ceeff,
    Thomas Ball/4
Robert Sands, George Collison junr/2
John Wrightson, Thomas Pears, George
    Ardell/3
to William Skinner junr, & a Negro/1

Bullenbrook Hundred

Hezekiah Mecottor, Ditto junior/2
John Higgins/1
Simon Ffisher/1
James Herbert, Charles Herbert/2
Joseph Withgott/1
Mary Bowdle, Patrick Berrey/1
John Sanders/1
William Robinson, Thomas Robinson/2
John Mecotter/1
Sarah Marsh, John Marsh/1
John Abbott, Edmund Marsh/2
Thomas Helsby, Francis Smith, Thomas
    Carnes/3
Richard Mekindly/1
Edward Brayning/1
Robert Welch, William Anderson, John
    Madden, David Sisk/4
William White, Richard White, Thomas
    Flemond, Richard Winford, Negroes:
    Cook and Moll/6
James White, Negroes: Pompey and
    Daff/3
Mark Noble, John Noble, Phenix a
    Negro/3
James Megraw, James Wilson belonging
    to William Thomas junr/2
William Thomas, Trustrum Thomas, John
    Stanfield, Patrick Elwood, Thomas
    Cockett, Negro: Jack/6
Daniel Mcdaniel/1
John Millar, Jonathan Millar/2
John Carr, Thomas Elliss/2

Mary Sales, John Stapleford, Francis
  Sheredine, Henry Joyce, Henry
  Walker, Negroes: Adam & Eve/6
John Edmondson/1
John Vaine, William Vaine/2
Owen Sullevan, Owen Sullevan junr/2
John Dulen, James Miller/2
John Latham/1
Joseph Bowdle, Thomas Bowdle/2
John Feaston, Henry Harris/2
Nicholas Higgins/1
Robert Cathcart/1
John Younger/1
Matthew Jenkins, Walter Jenkins/2
Barnabas Stapleford/1
William Ayers, Francis Chaplain,
  Negroes: Pompey, Sinkels, Moll/5
John Mullikin, William Mullikin, Hugh
  Lynch, Joseph James, John Walker,
  Edward Davis, Negro: Captain,
  William Skinner/8
Sarah Webb, Peter Webb, Joseph Webb,
  Negroes: Joe, Jack and Daff/5
William Mackey/1
John Dickinson, Negroes: Jack, Robin
  and Sall/4
Richard Barnett/1
James Barnett/1
John Barnett, Thoms. Salisbury/2
Thomas Barnett, Ditto James, John
  Burgess, Negro: Robin/4
Thomas Little, John Leach/2
William Little/1
John Flemond, John Flemond junr/2
John Hoult/1
Robert Buckley/1
James Chaplain, Alexander Robinson/2
Christopher Birchead, Negroes: Dinah,
  Grace/3
Anne Turbutt, William Lankford,
  Negroes: Tom & Grace/3
George Brinsfield/1
Silvester Abbott/1
William Arington/1
Mary Scott, George Scott/1
Amos Harriss, Edward Scott/2
Benja. Bullock, James Bullock,
  William Higgins/3
William Connelly, John Fahay/2
James Corkrine, Daniel Corkrine/2
George Ward, Thomas Williams/2
John Shaw/1

John Bullock/1
George Robins, Negro: Sambo/1
James Eldrack, John Eldrack/2
John Doniley/1
Simon Jeffords, Roger Jones/2
James Melton/1
Thomas Trayman/1
William Pennymore, Richard Barson/2
James Pruett/1
John Handsworth/1
William Seeny/1
John Pruett/1
Michael Kitts/1
Bryan Seeny, John Winford,
  LukeLunderkine(?)/3
Silvester Abbott, William Abbott,
  Saml. Abbott, Jonathan Abbott/4
Timothy Cartey, Thomas Cartey/2
At Solomon Sharp his Quarter,
  Negroes: Jams., Fanny, Tony/3
John Standley/1
Samuel Abbott, William Shannahan,
  Chars. Cheseldick/3
Samuel Abbott junr/1
Peter Lecompt, Anthony Lecompt/2
William Anderson, Andrew Hudson,
  Samuel Clark/3
David Jones, James Houlton/2
Joseph Harden, William Harden,
  William Love, Robert Harden/4
Edward Herbert, Edward Lee/2
Margt. Lloyd, Robert Wardelo,
  Negroes: Jack, James, Esther/4
At Mr. Fottrell's quarter – Matthew
  Chohune, Negroes: Joe, Toney,
  Lilly, old Lilly, Kitt and his
  wife, John Davison/8
Arthur Megrah/1
Francis Sutton, William Sutton/2
John Gaskin/1
William Richardson/1
William Carey, Florence Carey/2
William Harrison, William Jones, John
  Mitchell/3
Daniel Boyer, Francis Parratt, John
  Marr, Stephen Stickberry, Humphry
  Taylor/5
Thomas Delahay, Ditto junior/2
James Williams/1

A List of Taxables in Talbot County 1733

Susannah Powell, Howel Powell, Joseph
  Powell, Negroes: Tice(?) Dick,
  Pollipus, Hagar, Jubey, Beck,
  Bess/9
John Powell, Negro: Prince/2
John Glover/1
Joseph Bunton, Thomas Bunton, John
  Frost, Negroes: Oxford, Moreah/5
William Barker, Oliver Lee, Patrick
  Lenard, Negro: Tom/4
James Merchant, Ditto junior, John
  Merchant, Richard Barker/4
Lemon Jno. Catrope, William Catrope/2
Edward Hiate/1
Dennis Carey, Saml. Hambleton,
  Patrick Shehawn/3
Thomas Wiles, Robert Wiles, Michael
  Ryal, William Bear, John Carter/5
Edward Neal, John Carter/2
Francis Neal, Ditto junior, John
  Nelson, George Cole/4
Thomas Griffin/1
William Arderey, John Hardgraves/2
James Barnwell, Ditto junior/2
Joseph Bell/1
Joseph Dawson/1
Henry Henricks, John Henricks, Henry
  Henricks/3
Thomas Matthews/1
Joseph Nunam/1
William Austin, John Austin/2
William Fooks, John Walker, negro:
  James/3
William Taylor/1
Elizabeth Taylor, Samuel Cheserim,
  Negroes: Jams. Hannah/3
Rachel Turbutt, Danl. Stapleford,
  Negroes: Caesar, Cook, Joe, Jack,
  Sarah/6
Jeremiah Neal, Daniel Merick/1
Thomas Stuart, Negroes: Tom, Robin,
  Daphny, Hannah, Will/6
Wm. Harrison (of) Dover, Ralph
  Snagnett, John Clash, Alexr.
  Merick, Negroes: Joe, Pegg/6
John Davis/1
William Corkrin/1

Anthony Richardson, Jeremiah Nicols,
  Thomas Richardson, Robert
  Biglands, John Anderson, John
  Priereel, David Shehawn, John
  Small, Daniel Shahawn, Anthony
  Bacon, Owen Sullevan, Charles
  Griffin, George Andrew, Negroes:
  Tom, Stephen, Jack, Price, Ward/17
William Robins, Cornelius Shehawn,
  Negroes: Jack, Jams. Harry/5
William Jones/1
Thomas Bullon, Thos. Armstrong, Darby
  Dwier/3
John Stevens, Thomas Stevens,
  Negroes: Jamey, Peter, Dick,
  Hagar, Mark, Nan, John Proctor,
  Joe, Joe, Moreah, Dick, Sambo,
  Maria/13
Thomas Whittington, Thos. Taylor,
  Negroes: Cook, Dover/4
Capt Jams. Dickinson, Negroes: Joe,
  Sampson, Jack, Scipio, Leverpool,
  Cuffy, Jupiter, Susan, Sarah,
  Maria, Hannah, Rose/13
Revd Danl. Maynadier, Abner Parrott,
  John Walker, Cornelius Mulree,
  William Walker, John Carelo,
  Negroes: Toney, Mingo, Hannah/8
Julia Stephens, James Medain, Walter
  Mitchel/2
James Taylor/1
Solomon Birkhead, Negroes: Jack,
  Caesar, London, Bristol, Peter,
  York, Daff, Otho, Joyce & Jane/11
Thomas Edwards/1
John Cooper/1
Thomas Howard/1
James Delahay/1
John Abbott/1
Ann Brin, William Brin, John Lee/2
John Cliff/1
John James/1
William Howard/1
Peter Shannahane, Alexr. Mcleland,
  Christopher Silver/3
Dominick Kirven for George Cradock/1
John Hickson, John Abrahams/2
Dennis Morris/1
Thos. Humphrys/1
John Beasley/1
Robert Stapleford/1
Charles Banning/1

Edmond Carey, Solomon Hutchins, James
  Powel/3
William Mashall, Ditto junior/2
John Alexander, Timothy Lane, Matthew
  Kery/3
Philip Carey, John Macon, Richard
  Blaman, Roger Conner, Negroes:
  Sarah & Alce/6
Christopher Connelly, Thomas White/2
Joseph Williams/1
William Carey junr, Thomas Douglass/2
Robert Lowd, Charles Lowd, Thomas
  Conaway/3
Pearce Flemond, John Corkrine, James
  Corkrine, Thomas Samon, William
  Larkins, Negroes: Flora & Rose/7
Andrew Bankson, Robert Groves/2
to Nichs. Goldsborough, Saml. Martin,
  William Scott, Negroes: Benbo,
  Chester, Rose, Pegg/6
Howel Powell, Daniel Powell, Thos.
  Powell, Negroes: Governour,
  Wackra, Yam, Doll, Rachell/8
Samuel Dickinson, Ditto junr, Jams.
  Hutchinson, Jams. Lumbard, William
  Clark, Negroes: Jos, Will, Harry,
  Tony, Hercules, Kitt, Nero, Toby,
  Abraham, Peter, Jack, Dick, Mingo,
  Sarah, Daff, Betty, Alce/22
Samuel Platt/1
Richard Holms/1
Mary Holms, Henry Clark/1
Wm. Slaughter/1
Richd. Ecclestone/1
John Libbey, Ditto junr/2
Terence Connelly/1

Mill Hundred

Robert Goldsborough senr, Ditto junr,
John Goldsborough, Bryan Mackhugh,
Negroes: Portsmouth, Andrew, Job,
Dick, Lambeth, Jacob, Candlemas,
Joseph, Susan, Hagar, Esther, Denby,
Tom, Sampson, Daphny, Julia, Mercury,
Barratt/22
Tench Francis, John Ward, Thos.
Molison, Thos. Snelling, Negroes:
Frank, Boatswain, Will, Phillis,
Maria, Rachel/10
Ditto for John Toomy/1

Edmond Ferrell, Negroes: Doctor,
  Joe/3
Edward Harding junr, John Badfie/2
James Harvey, Thomas Davis/2
Mary Atwell, Angus Mcdaniel/1
John Carslake, Edward Carslake,
Richard Burk, Henry Gates, Benja.
  Start/5
Francis Pickering, Robert Pickering,
John Pickering, Michl. Crump, negro:
  Jenney/5
Matthew Kirby, James Kirby, Henry
Martin, John Hayly, Negroes: Jack,
  Diana/6
Thomas Atkinson, Joseph Atkinson,
Negroes: Jack, Bess/4
Thomas Cockayne, John Summerson,
Negroes: Denby, Sambo, Quastus, Bess,
  Peg/7
Jeffery Horney, William Horney,
Jeffery Horney junr/3
James Ratcliff, John Spencer/2
Francis Stanton, John Mallin/2
Ditto for George Clough/1
Thomas Gully, Joseph Stiff/2
Anthony Gregory/1
John Potts, Thomas Blanch/2
Thomas Chandler/1
Morton Ewbanks/1
John Brasscop/1
Henry Burgess/1
Jacob Falconar/1
Margery Smallcorn, Abraham Falconar/1
John Gough/1
Edward Hubanks/1
Jeremiah Thomas, Thomas Winchester,
Negroes: Toney, Will, Sam, Andrew,
Frank, Jacob, Bombro, Peter, Caesar,
Dick, Joe, Pegg, Sue, Bess, Sarah,
Maria, Crambo, Jenny, Old Kate, Young
ditto, Moll/23
Martha Ewbanks, Thomas Ewbanks,
Terence Grahams/2
Mark Williams/1
Edward Perkins/1
Richard Hopkins/1
Thomas Brown/1
John Quin/1
John Fellows, James Carnoway/2
Mr. Henry Nicols, Darby Barratt,
Negroes: Sam, Ned/3

John Ratcliff, Michl. Harper, John
Ewbanks, George Ewbanks/4
John James Junr/1
to John Kimble, Richard Kimble/1
Jams Merrick, Joseph Merrick/2
Michael Fletcher, Negroes: Dick,
Maria/2
John Humphry/1
Charles Sinclair/1
James Voss/1
Jonathan Shannahane, Enock Jackson/2
Minikin Freeman/1
John Freeman/1
William Clayland, James Clayland,
Robert Cushington, negro: Judith/4
Isaac Dixon, Negroes: Jack, Joe, Ben,
Ned, Nero, Luce, Rose/8
John Bartlett (smith), Ditto junr,
Joseph Bartlett, John Bryan, Richard
Bartlett/5
Isaac Maurling/1
Ditto for Wm. Jacobs/1
John James senior/1
Thomas Cranor/1
William Rakes/1
John Loockerman, Jacob Loockerman,
Ralph Dawson, Daniel Davis, James
Sharp, Negro: Davy/6
Robert Newcom, Duncan Stuart, John
Hackett, Negroes: Mingo, Judith,
Flora, Lydia/7
John Harrison, Jeremiah Cotton/2
Michael Stoker, Ditto junior, James
Stoker/3
Nicholas Bartlett/1
Ralph Pearson/1
Nichs. Clash senr/1
John Bartlett (Carpr), William
Bartlett, Negroes: Mingo, Jenny,
Kate/5
George Lenny, Nichs. Clash junr/2
Tamerlane Davis, Negroes: Ben, Wye,
Caesar, Thamar, Kate, Coco, Dab,
Joe/9
Elizabeth Davis, Robert Read, John
Mackmerry, Robert Betts, negro:
Rose/4
John Spencer/1
Joshua Hewett/1
William Hobson/1
Nathaniel Grace, Negroes: Phebe,
Judith/3

Henry Wharton/1
Thomas Greenhock, Ditto junior/2
John Valliant, William West/2
Edward Norrod/1
Richard Marshall, Ditto Junior/2
Richard Aldern, John Hange, John
Davis/3
James Marshall/1
Peter Smith/1
James Moor/1
Owen Mccarty, Patrick Mackway/2
David Matthews/1
Arthur Rigby, Philip Armfield, John
Newman, Negroes: Trummel and Daphny/5
William Ridgway/1
Joseph Hicks/1
William Harrison, Ditto junior,
William Lee/3
Maurice Orem, Robert Smith, Wm.
Hollyfield, Denton Carrol/4
Susanna Scott, John Scott/1
John Seymour/1
William Bennett, James Page, Thos.
Tennant, Negroes: Dick, Kate/5
Thomas Eaton/1
Richard Eaton/1
John Peck, Negro: Candace/2
Daniel Peck, William Blessett/2
John Nutwell/1
William Bandy/1
William Skinner senr, Thomas Skinner,
Lewis Matthews, Negroes: Mingo,
Pompey, Jacob, Bess, Susana/8
Saml. Chamberlaine, Henry Turner,
Negroes: Harry, Nan, Daphny/4
John Leonard, William Harrison/2
John Robinson, Ditto junior, Henry
Robinson, Thos. Robinson, Peter
Barber/5
Joseph Prout/1
Thomas Hopkins, Samuel Hopkins/2
Robert Williams/1
John Hopkins/1
Thomas Dickes/1
John Barwick/1
James Congdon/1
John Wise, John White, Negro: Sarah/3
John Achan/1
Frances Ungle, Negroes: Sam, Will,
Kate, Phillis, Jack, Dick, Jupiter,
Sharper, Flora, Eve, Rose, Maria/12

James Hurlock, George Hurlock, Robert Holms/3
Eliza. Meginny, John Meginny, Danl. Meginny/2
John Male, Ditto junior/2
John Watts/1
John Stanton, Robert Booker, Joseph Booker/3
Ralph Holms/1
John Waymouth, Ezekiel Murdick/2
Robert Harwood, Negroes: Will, Simon/3
Samuel Harwood, Negro: Mingo/2
Peter Harwood, Saml. Booth, Negroes: Tom, Maria, Tom, Pegg/6
Peter Harwood junr, Negroes: Hannah, Bess/3
To Henry Nicols, James Dwiggens, Negroes: Peter, Julius, Simon, Jenny Sabina/6
Thomas Spry, Christopher Spry/2
Dennis Hopkins junr, Joseph Denny/2
Richard Hopkins/1
John Mcmahawn, Thos. Mcmahawn/2
Peter Denny, Benja. Hopkins, John Robinson, Samuel Small, Negro: Lilly/5
James Hopkins, Jonathan Hopkins, John Clark, Negro: Rose/4
Nichs. Goldsborough, Ralph Kendrick, Negroes: David, Sam, Edith, Phillis, Cummy/7
John Floyd, William Hutton/2
John Neighbours, John Morris, Thomas Waller/3
Thomas Bartlett junr/1
James Bartlett/1
Thos. Bartlett senr, Samuel Bartlett, Alexander Leith, James Cartie/4
Jams. Bartlett (Carpr), Ditto junr, James Plunkett/3
To John Guy Williams, John Smith, Edward Harman, John Lloyd, William Moss/4
Edward Harding senr, Maurice Giddins, Joseph Smith, Negroes: Cambridge, Caesar, Judith, Daphny/7
John Sutton, Ditto junior, Richard Start, Benja. Merchant/4
Philip Feddeman/1
John Tibbels/1
John Booker, Lambeth Booker/2

The Wid. Alice Roberts, William Roberts, Andrew Roberts/2

Tuckahoe Hundred

Eliza. Millington, George Roberts, Negroes: Dick, Munday, Rose/4
William Thorp, John Thorp, Thomas Thorp, Isaac Thorp/4
William Barwick/1
To Edward Fottrell, Edward Barwick, Negroes: Tom, Plaister, Lydia/4
John Barwick/1
Edward Slaughter/1
to John Bradshaw, Xtopher Bradshaw/1
John Nickason/1
John Sprignal, Richard Hall/2
Thomas Thompson, Robert Moody/2
Charles Morgan/1
Jane Turner, Isaac Cox, Thomas Turner, Negroes: Davy, Judith/4
Samuel Morgan, Thomas Martindale/2
John Sancstone, James Sancstone junr, William Wood/4
Charles Warner/1
John Cullin/1
Oliver Millington, William Lane/2
James Thomas/1
Thomas Vickers/1
William Vickers, William Pickrine, Negro: Strange/3
Robert Stonestreet, George Penfold, Richard Sneed/3
John Vickers, Isaac Ruxe, Archibald Anderson, Negro: Sambo/4
Mary Brown, William Lahey, Negroes: Robin, Joe, Phillis/4
William Scott, Solomon Scott, Negroes: Kate, Alice, Moreah, Rose, Joney/7
To William Turner, David Turner/1
Thomas Uselton/1
Thomas Pratt/1
Jacob Wooters, Ditto junior/2
Michael Maloony/1
John Robins, Negroes: Preston, Sambo, Goodman, Jenny/5
Thomas Purnal, John Bannin, John Heelis, Negro: Phillis/4
William Frantom/1

28

John Camperson, Nathaniel Hull,
Leonard Hull/3
William Warring, Negroes: Caesar,
Nan/3
John Smith/1
Humphry Spencer/1
Samuel Broadaway, Jams. Broadaway,
Saml. Ditto junr/3
To Uriah Matthews, Ditto junior/1
John Leverton, Alexr. Codnar, Henry
Mason/3
Ennion Williams, Negroes: Simon,
Jack, Moreah/4
William Dudley, Nath'll. Ruxe,
Limbrick a negro/3
Xtopher Wise/1
John Herrington, Anth. Herrington,
John Ditto junr/3
Jacob Bradbury/1
Charles Gannon/1
Danl. Thompson/1
Xtopher Small/1
Thomas Parlett, Sarah (Senah?)
Parlett/2
John Rathel senr/1
Michael Kirby, John Cannady/1
William Kirkby, Stephen Bush/2
David Kirkby, Daniel Ward, John
Cuckow/3
Richard Kirkby/1
William Mitchell, John Dun/2
James Kindred/1
Simon Keld/1
Thomas Keld, Robert Caid/2
Caleb Clark, Robert Lowdar, William
Roberts, David Rothell, Negroes:
Nan, Jemmey, Caesar/7
Edward Clark, John Bank, Robert
Bessell/3
Thomas Turner, David Register/2
Francis Register/1
James Dudley, Jeremiah Smith, Joseph
Smith/3
Thomas Dudley, Jere. Byrell, James
Dee, Negroes: Jack, Patt/5
John Keld/1
Samuel Dudley, Isaac Wheely, Nehemiah
Higgins, Thomas Ball, Jenny a
Negro/5
Burtonwd. Alcock, Richard Williams,
Tom a Negro/3

William Lewis, William Batchelor,
John Batchelor/3
Charles Manship/1
John Burgess, Stephen Burgess, Henry
Manship/3
Richard Burden, Danl. Richardson,
negro: Burten/3
Samuel Duning, Edward Burk/2
Edward Nedels, George Morris, Joseph
Lawrence, Negroes: Jemo, Occary/5
John Tomlinson, Ditto junior, Henry
Tomlinson/3
Thomas Silvester/1
Edward Russam, Samuel Russam,
Negroes: Draper, Rose/4
James Berry, Negroes: Sam, Daphny,
Hannah/4
John Hutchens, Sampson Warring/2
Joshua Clark, Benja. Sylvester,
Michl. Anderson, Francis Petty,
John Best, Negroes: Oliver/6
Henry Buckingham, negro: Phillis/2
Susannah Slaughter, Thos. Turner,
James Roberts/2
Jams. Willson junr, Negroes: Nero,
Nan, Esther/4
William Willson, Negro: Lilly/2
Jams. Willson senr, negro Jack/2
Thomas Frantom/1
Thomas Willson/1
Isaac Dobson senr, John Morgan,
Daniel Mckan/3
William Carter/1
William Oldfield, Edward James /2
Katherine Russam, George Chambers/1
William West/1
John Rothel junr, James Lowdar/2
John Dicas (Duas?), James Hurlock,
John Laine/3
John Loveday, John Christian,
Negroes: Nan, Sarah/4
Aaron Parrott, Thos. Sylvester junr,
William Steal, Negro: Sampson/4
Edward Ozwell, John Williamson,
William Grace, Abel Grace/4
John Hollon/1
George Prouse, William Davis/2
Dennis Larey, Solomon Larey/2
John Eustace, Nichs. Bartlett/2
Joseph Turner, James Chambers/2
Andrew Bannin, Richard Bannin, John
Gares/3

Abraham Sherwin/1
John Grosier/1
Thomas Hutchins/1
Roger Bradbury/1
Joseph More, William More/2
James Powell, Thomas Taylor, Negro:
 Answer/3
Anne Dobson, Isaac Dobson, Shadrach
 Bodfield, Richard Sweels, Dan'l
 Martindeal, Negroes: Pompey,
 Dell/6
John Warford, William Warford,
 Jeremiah Ffloyd/3
Jonathan Tyler/1
John Chambers/1
Thomas Matthews/1
Robert Frantom/1
Anthony Booth/1
Robert Hunter, William Gannon/2
John Kennedy/1
William Shield, Negro Mingo/2
Catherine Buckingham, Howel
 Buckingham, Isaac Buckingham/2
Thomas Edge, William Edge/2
Robert Walker, Jacob Gore/2
To Robert Goldsborough senr,
 Nathaniel Clow, Negroes: Will,
 Peter, Billy, Simond, Jenny, Rose,
 Phebe Sarah/9
Rebecca Durden, Cate, Jack, Dugany/3
Henry Oldfield, Thomas Hall/2
Daniel Chapman/1

The number of taxable persons:
Island Hundred	433
Thirdhaven Hundred	432
Bay Hundred	337
Bullenbrook Hundred	470
Mill Hundred	391
Tuckahoe Hundred	289

Total in Talbot County - 2352

Kent County Cattle Marks

1659-1676, 1694-1726, 1732-1734

Found in the court records held by the State Archives.

1659   John Erickson Junr son of John Erickson, Andrew Ehlenas, Hasaida Hills, Edward Halls, William Richards

1660   Margret Hansone

1661   John Wedg, Regere Baxter for his children

1669   John Wallton, Richard More, Isaac Burgger

1670   John Winchester for his daughter in law Elizabeth Montrosse, Francis Pyne, Richard More, William Joyner, Vallentine Sutherin

1675   William Vaughan, Richard Fillingham, Samuell Tovy, Charles Bancks, Hance Hanson, Bennett Starres for a cow calf given by him unto Martha dau of Edward Chicken, Edward Chickin, Thomas Warren senr, Ellis Humphrey

1676   Thomas Williams, William Harris, William Frisby, William Trews, Abraham Messeter, Thomas Warren Junr

1694   Tobias Kelley; Isaac Harris; Rebecca dau of Joseph Sudler; Isaac Ashly; John Wade, Peeter Alaby; John Tiller
John Murphey of Kent Island gave unto John Gill son of Roger Gill a horse with mark.... and should said John Gill die then to Sarah dau of said Roger Gill
Lazarus Pether of Kent Co gives Rebecca Sudler a cow; Go: Sudler to have all male calves for looking after; should Rebecca die then to her sister Rachell
Capt John Copedge gives to Charles Eareckson son of Matthew and Dorothy Eareckson a yearling

1695   John Hurt; Thomas Dones

1696   John Johnson, James Wilson, Richard Mason (On Feb 17 1702 Richard Mason records that this description of the mark has a mistake)

1697   Robert Ingham, Phillip Hopkins, Elizabeth Kearsey, Richard Daniel, John Chaires, James Weyatt, John Underhill, William Austin, John Huer(?)

1698   Thomas Usher, Michael Miller, Tymothy Montsouir, John Sheapard, Richard Bishop, John Sutton

1699   Thomas Ruth, Phillip Hopkins, Robt. Ingram, Stephen Bordley, James Heath, Joseph Weeks, Mary Hunter, Anne Hunter, Danl Mulligin, William Glanvill, Peter Allaby

1700   John Hackett, Timothy Hurley, Stephen Bordley, Ffrancis Thomas dau to Jerimiah Thomas, Majr Thomas Smith keeps Mr. Nathaniel Evetts, Jno. Ally, Pattrik(?) Creagh, Jno. Griffith, Darby Hearne, William Tippen, Margaret Mason

31

1701 Cornelius Rice now of Easter Neck, Jno. Uneck, George Copper of Kent Co, Charles Ffloyd, Charles Hollingsworth Junr, Richd. Ffillingham, John Hackett, Patrick Bryan, Lucy Green wife to Henry Green, John Moore, Cornelius Crsley

1702 John Dowdall, George Hartshorne, Edmond Mackdannell, Charles Baker, John Shaw, Wm. Ford, Richard Burke, Robt. Maxwell, Ffrancis Collins, Richard Norcott
Jul 4 1702 Coll. John Hynson records that he gives to his grand son John Rogers one earling heaffer and to his granddau Eliza. Rogers one earling heiffer and to his grandson Edward Rogers one earling heifer and grand child Rachell Rogers one earling heafer and his grand child Mary rogers one earling heafer and his grand son Nathl Rogeres one earling heafter to be recorded with mark of their grandfather, Edward Rogers

1703 William Mackey, John Jones, John Woorth, Mathew Smith, William North, Capn Perrigrine Brown, Andrew Prewet, Thomas Ward, Charles Skinner, Samuell Taylor, Wm. Redding, Patrick Creagh, Fflower Walker, John Meraday Junr, Joseph Paines

1704 Anne Hamer, William Hamer, Thomas Beckly, Sarah Hamer, Jo'n. Fannen upon Mary Moors .. daughter to John Moor, Ffrancis Boxe, Thomas Weyatt, Edward Scott

1705 Wm. Boier

1706 Joseph Dorrington, Haunce Hanson, James Smith, Richard Laurence, John King

1707 James Alpen, John Barnet Sovereigne, Michael Willson, William Hanson, John Price, Zapher(?) Lewis, James Lewis, Capt John Dowdall, Col. Nathaniel Hynson, William Roberts, Mathew Piner, James Smith, John Lee who also records that John Lee of Swan Creek intermarried with the daughter of Henry Green

1708 William Duerly(?), Charles Neale, Hugh Perry, William Dycas

1709 John Williams, Simon Wilmer, Nicholas Moore, John Heading, Alexander Brisco, John Knowles, William Dicas for his son Edward, John Frogett, William Haynes, Richard West(?)

1710 Samuel Fovey(?), Oliver Mitchell, John Fulston, Richard Fulston, John Fulston
Oliver Mitchell gives a heifer to Hugh Wouth son in law to him
Thomas Pryor gives a mare to his cosin Thomas Powell son of Richard Powell

1711 William Blay, Zachariah MacDaniel, Doctor Richard Simonds, Nicholas Sinnett

1712 Hugh Perry in behalf of his son Samuel Perry, Rogert Canady, George Hanson, Charles Fitzpatrick, Henry Batthershell, Robert Ford, William Milbourne, Michael Miller

Kent County Cattle Marks

1713 Dominick Kenslaigh, Doctor Bartholomew Brown, Daniel Pirkins, John Hugg, John Huff records a mark of cattle for his dau Margret Huff

1714 John Ingram, Thomas Gore, Michael Miller in behalf of his dau Martha Miller, Charles Greendize, George Linegar, James Frisby, John Willis, Jacob Caulk, Thomas Ares, John Wright, Richard Davis, Alsip(?) Robinson, Alsip Robinson for his dau Rachel Robinson, Hoplan Williams, William Deans, Mary Orreal(?), James Frisby

1715 Elizabeth Shield, Rachel Shield, John Brooke, William Granger, Dennis Sullivane, Edward Comegys

1717 John Pryor, Isaac England, George Still

1718 Edward Sammon

1719 William Grewer, Samuel Clarke, James Wilcocks, William Deane, William Boyce Junr, Augustine Boyyce, Martha Middleton, Samuel Gooding, Thomas Rush

1720 John West, Robert Street, Henry Pearman, John Duncan, William Comegys Junr

1721 John Clayton, George Meray(?), Lambert Wilmer, George Debrular, Phillip Jones

1722 Jarvis Spencer, John Coward, Richard Fulston of Kent

1723 Robert Foreman, Mark Noble, Edward Roger, John Carvell, Abraham Redgrave, Francis Hill, Solomon Brward, William Ackland, William Beck, William Bradshaw, John Rogers, Elias Thomas, Matthew Beck

1724 John Macknemar, William Dicas, John Davice, William Kaindall, Francis Lewis, John Woodall, William Waltham, James Dill, John Lovegrove, Ishmell Bennett

1725 Henry Knock Junr, Henry Knock Scnr, John Prier for his son Thomas Prier, William Standley, William Smithers, George Skirven, Samuel Andrews, John Wilson, John Wilson Swan Creek, Mathias Day, Joseph Parsons, Thomas Boardley

1726 Nicholas Smith, James Kelly, Henry Evans

1732 John Newell Junr, Josias Ringgold, John Crittel, John Bradshaw, James Bond

1733 Cornelius Baian junr, Isaack Redgrave, Thomas Wells, Isaac Crow, David Hull, Doctor Jacob Glenn, Robert Speer, William Cornelius

1734 Joseph Mason, John Clarke, Benjamin Blackston

33

Cattle Marks – Somerset County

1666–1705

Accession number 7839-3 of the court records and Liber IKL of the Land records of Somerset County, held by the Maryland State Archives. Descriptions of the cattle marks are omitted here.

1665 George Johnson, William Plannor, William Whittfield, John Roads, William Boyd, William Collboorne, Ambros Dickson, Thomas Price, John Johnson, Elizabeth Curtis, Daniel Curtis, Henry Pedington, Mary Dickson, Sarah Dickson, Ambros London, Richard Britten, Robert Cattlen, Robert Cattlen, John Ffloyd, William Ellijott, Allexander Draper, Edward Ffurlong, Robert ..., John Richards, Edward Dickson, John Winder, William Taylor, Nicolas Rice, Thomas Shiall, Phillip Barre, Phillip Barre, George Linne, Mary Ivery, Elizabeth Barre, Grissegon Barre, William Will..son, Benianion Sumner, Thomas Ball, Margaret Ivery, Thomas Poole, William Lows, Elizabeth Munt(?), James Jones, William Collboorne Junior, James Dashiell, Elizabeth Dashill, Charles Balle, Thomas Tull, William Watons, Elle Ball, Nicolas Ffountayne, William Ffurnis, William Dusse, John Roach, John Crew, Robert Bignett, Cornelius Ward

1666 Daniel Boast, Richard Davis, George Smith, Sollomon Collboorne, Katharine Johnson the elder, Katharine Johnson the younger, Joseph Buse, William Davis, Henry Boston, Samuell Moore, William Jones, George Mitchell, Cornelius Johnson, Robert Harde, Christopher Nutten, Nehemiah Covington, Thomas Covington, Thomas Bloys, John Marsum(?) senr, John Marsum(?) Junr, John Hallon, Steven Elliott, James Davis, ditto James Davis (another mark), Gideon Tillman, Thomas Davis, Mary Barnabe, widow, John Rogers, Jonas Davis, Ffrancis Vincent, John Goldsmith, William Goldsmith, John ..., Capt. William Thorne, Roger Wollford, Edward Soutzerine(?), Levin Denwood, Thomas Denwood, Boven(?) Marlra(?), Edward Hazard, John Westlarka(?), John Marlett sonne in law to Jno. HoWestlarka(?) , Henry Miles, George Read, Thomas Winder sonne of John Winder, Richard Whitte, John Panter, George Andra, Randal Revell, Randall Revell (different mark), Mary Robbins, Ellin Robbins, Ellin Whitly, Richard Allen, Tho: Howard, Jeffery Minshall, Richard Munty, Peter Elzey, James Nicollson, John Manloe, Richard Stevens of Nissosomiso(?), George Booth, Edward Surnan, John Waken(?), Thomas Caire, Henry Heymore, Thomas Carnes(?), George Bell, William Cannedy, Thomas Manley, Richard Acworth, Thomas Manley, James Dawes, John Nellson, Henry Hutton, John Mackoffairk(?), Daniell Quillane, Anthony Johnson, John Hinge, John Townson, Thomas Gillis, John Gillis, Marke Manlove (Manlow?),Elyzabeth Manlove (Manlow?), John Cooper, John Hillard Senr, John Hillard Junr, Samuell Long, Masune Thomas, Ann Ingram the relict of Robert Ingram, James Carne, Jinkin Prise, William Cheaseman, Allexander Jemison, William Robbinson, David Spence, Allexander Mitchell, John Bun, Steven Horsi, William Greene, Christopher Nutten, John Peter Edward Dirkinson the sonne of Edward Dirkenson, Allexander Kinge, John Avery, Daniel Donnahoe, Cornelius Morris, Morris Liston, William Howard, Richard Ackworth

1667 John Ellis, Thomas Carnes, John Shipway, Richard Tull, Teage Riggein, Lawrence Henley, John Griffith, Martin Mooni(Moore?), George Day, Thomas Carroll (Carvell?), William Stevens, James Wooden, Jasper Lane, John

Harrison, Nicholas Hirtson(?), Dannarka Dennis, Isaack Hilliard, John Lawes, William Waters, Edward Whaley, Arthur Fframe, Jinkin Morris Martin Moore of Annamessex in Somerset County assigned over his right of mark to John Price, living in same place of the county.

1668 Edward Hazard John Sterling, Thomas Davis Carpenter, Edward Lewis Edward Hazard of Manoakin has sold his right to mark to William. Joseph Howes of Manoakin has granted mark of cattle to Joseph Huse

1669 Randall Minshall, Thomas Moolson, Elizabeth Groome, Jeremiah Hoopes, Patrick Robinson, Robert Johnson, John Paramor, Stephen Barnes, Rodi Patrick, Thomas Given, John King, William Doirnin(?), Edward Smith, Henry Bishop senr, Henry Bishop Junr, David Bishop, Thomas Selbe, William Bowen, Henry Morgan, George Hamblin, Samuell Jones, Samuell Jones, Samuell Jones, John Browne, Edward Davis, Gideon Tillmans, Jacob Sheltenham, Phillip Noarris, Samuell Jackson, Tho: Purnell, John Evans, John Kirbe, James Hinderson, William Bradshawe, Cornelius Morris, George Trehearne

1670 Thomas Dixon, Comfort Ffurnis the daugher of Wm Ffurnis, Sarah Ffurnis the dau of Wm Ffurnis, Edward Jones, Edmund Keyser, John Emmett, Thomas Wingod, William Prentice, John Johnson negro, John Johnson the soone of Johnson negro, Dennis Ffountaine and Merry Ffountain, George Haffurt, Robt. Hignitt Junr, James Hignitt, William Hignitt and John Hignitt the sonnes of Robert Hignett senr, Elizabeth Poole the wife of Thomas Poole, Rachell Poole, daughter of Thomas and Elizabeth Poole, John Poole the son of Thomas and Elizabeth Poole, An additionall mark of Richard Ackworth, Christopher Nutter (additional mark), Margaritt Prise the daugher of Jinkin & Martha Prise, John Prise the sonne of Jinkin and Martha Prise, Thomas Stanbridge, John P...., Sarah P... daughter of John Pe...., Walter Powell, Elizabeth Powell daughter of Walter Powell, Mary Powell daughter of Walter Powell, John King of Manoakin, John Bossman, William Bossman, John Renshawe

1671 John Triford, Robert Innes(?). Christipher Newgons(?), James Curtis son of Daniell Curtis, George Bossman, Edmund Beauchamp, Anne Surnam wife of Edward Surnam, John Jorman, Mathewe Jorman, Elizabeth Manlove dau of John Manlove, John Wootters, Teage Mishell, Ellis Empeou(?), Mickell Williams, Thomas Williams, Bridgett Nelson dau of John Nelson, Moyses Owen son of Thomas Owen, Thomas Miller, John Davis son of Thomas Davis Taylor, Elizabeth Davis dau of Thos. Davis Taylor, Joseph Cattlin sonn of Robert Cattlin, John Ffreeman

1672 Stephen Bond, Mathew Dorman, Andrew Whittington, John Anderson, Capt John Paull Marsh, John Cazara negro servant to Mary Johnson negro .. of Anthony Johnson decd with her said Mary's consent, John Jones son of William Jones of Manny, Mary Jones dau of Wm. Jones, Robert Houston, Richard Wharton, Mary Johnson relict of Anthony Johnson, Robert Crouch, John Winder, Daniel Hass(?), Edward Southrin, Phillip Askine(?), John Evans, Elizabeth Dixon, Alixander Williams, Daniel Moore, John Bound, John Hall, William Keene, Robt. Murdugh, William Scott, Robert Hignett Junr, James Hignett, William Hignett and John Hignett sons of Robert Hignett Senior, Samuel Jones of Anamessicks, William Ellemes(?), George Kallen, Thomas Dixon, John Kibble

Cattle Marks - Somerset County

1673 Robert Hodge, Elizabeth Avery dau of John Avery, Sarah Avery dau of John Avery, Mary Avery dau of John Avery, Abraham Heath, Vincent Shuttleworth, Mary Goldsmith dau of John Goldsmith, Dorithy Bundicke, Isaack Hillyard, Robert Blades, Richard Partridge, George Johnson, Henry Smith, Thomas Holbrooke, Thomas Roe, Thomas Roe, Mathewe Dorman, John Bu..., Anne Bradshaw dau of William Bradshaw, William Walstonne, George Phebins, William Leighton, Roger Phillips, William Giles, Thomas Sawell, Thomas Carey Senr, Richard Carey, John Winsor, Isaac Edmonds, Thomas Lampin(?), John Kirk, Grace Dixon dau of Ambrose & Mary Dixon, Alce Dixon dau of Ambrose and Mary Dixon, Robert Hopkins, Robert Millnor, John Webb, William Mullnor

1674 Ambrose Riggen son of Teage Riggen, Jankin Mark, Thomas Cox, Thomas Garrett entered by Wm. Canning, John Pearse, John Bulk

1675 Reynolld Douglas, William Ellgate, Capt. Thomas Jones, Maror (Major?) Thomas Brereton, Edward Bennet, William Brereton, Thomas Waller, Ralph Horsley, Richard Hazeldine, John Squire, John Webb
John Bulke of Somerset Co planter sells to Edward Evans of said county his mark

1676 Thomas Humphry, William Keene son of William Keene senior, William Walton, William Walton (another mark), Daniell Selbe, Robert Willson, Richard Samuell, John Glass, Christopher Nutter, John Jarrett, Solomon Turpin

1677 Phillip Wollaham, Thomas Walston, Peter Surnam, John Wright, Peter Wheples, George Downes, Robert Catlin Junior, Robert Catlin Junior, Edmund Beauchamp, Thomas Adams son of Philip Adams, Jacob Adams son of Phillip Adams, Margarett Jones dau of Wm. Jones, William Jones Senior, Wm. Jones Junior, Richard Boston, George Hopkins son of Robert Hopkins, Allexander Maddox
Robert Hodge of Somerset Co assigns his mark to Richard Lanes(?)

1678 Samell Handy, William Green Junr son of Wm. Green senr, Elizabeth Green younger dau of Wm. Green, Robert Paine, Richard Crockett, John Hust, John Hust, Thomas Dias, William Dias son of Thomas Dias, Isaac(?) Al....(?), Tobias Pepper - Henry Hall, Anne Hall, John Mackay and Thomas Smallwood, together - William Stevens, planter, Elizabeth More, William Sherman son of Joseph Sherman, John Crowley, Richard Buckland, Sam'll Jacob, Sam'll Davis, George Marsh, Robt. Cattlin Junr, Mary Hall dau of Charles Hall, Benjamin Sawser(?), Rob... Pope
George Hasbu.. assigns his mark to John Colebourne
John Squire of Somerset Co sells to Sam'll Davis of sd co his mark of cattle
Heifer given to Anne Jones dau of William Jones of Little Many from John Parker(?)

1679 William Hayman son of Henry Hayman, Phillip Adams Junr son of Phillip Adams, Thomas Smallwood, Anne Colebourne wife of William Colebourne Junr, Samuell Handy, John Shiles, Charles Williams, Elizabeth Jones dau of William Jones of Little Manny, Richard Shockley, Thomas Davis Ploughman, Sarah Marrett, Stephen Coston, John Carter, Donnan Kan...(?), Thomas Shilleto, Thomas Walston, Edward Wootton

36

Cattle Marks - Somerset County

A calf given by Edward Davis to John Shiles son of Thomas Shiles lately deceased of this county
Henry Boston of Som Co planter son and heir of Henry Boston senr, late of said Co, sell his mark to Thomas Leister of said co
Gift to Elizabeth Hamlin dau of George Hamlin a cow and calf by William Walson 24 Nov 1679
Gift to James Nicollson from George Parker

1680 Thomas Robeson son of John Robeson, Alce Beauchamp, Edmund Beauchamp Junr, John Beauchamp, Edward Sidbury, Daniell Selbe Junr, Thomas Purnell, Augustine Standford, John Ligerius(?), Samuel Furnis, Richard Tull son of Thomas Tull, John Tull son of Thomas Tull, Robert Collier, William Mathews son in Law to Daniel Dennis, Mary London wife of Major Ambrose London, Joy Hobbs son of Thomas Hobbs, James Ingram, George Banum, James Willis, Christopher Little, John Polk, Peter Parsons, Capt. David Browne, Capt. David Browne (another mark), Capt. David Browne (a third mark), Nehemiah Covington son of John Covington, James Sangsten, Thomas Laramor, Nicolas Toadvin, Roger Bersum(?), John Parsons, John Heath, Jacob Warring, John Bennett, Arnold Ffrancis, Nathaniel Doughertie
Gift of a Calf to use of Alce Taylor from loving friend Ffrancis Martin
Thomas Ball of ..., Somerset Co sell mark to Ben. Nesham

1681 George Jones son of Wm. Jones of Manny, Wm. Jones Junr, Benjamin Samson Junr, David Spence, Allexander Spence, Anne Spence, John Holland, Roger Bercum, Phillip Carter, Elizabeth Poole dau of Thomas Poole, Wm. Jones, Leonard Campison, John Moore single man of Anamissex, John Heath additional mark, William Ingle, Edward Day, Charles Hall Junr, Hugh Tingle, Thomas Cottingham, Edmund Beauchamp, John Davis, Isaiah Boston, Isaiah Boston, Robert Crouse, Mary Ffreeman dau of Joseph Ffreeman, William Moore Brasier, George Marsh, Walter Lane, John Lane, Manns Morris, Daniel Cox, Wm. Gullet, Landgen Goddard, Richard Karey (Karvy?), Jeremiah Hook, Edward Wale, John Crupper, John Cropper, James Weatherle, Samll Collins, Samuel Jackson, Anne Bound, Edward Ffowler, Richard Aldridge, Eliza. Williams, David Richardson, Thomas Relk(Polk?), Phillip Carter, Joseph Gray, Rowland Bevens, William Keenes, Joseph Crowder, Richard Pepper, Elizabeth dau of Tobias Pepper, Samuell Horsey, Samuel Jackson, Anne Bound, William Baker, William Dedulphus, John Askins, Dogett Beauchamp, Richard Warrin, Thomas Lester, Walter Taylor, George Harris, Thomas Standridge
Lawrence Henly late of Somersett assigns to Robert Hall of same co his mark
George Marsh of Somer Co assigns his mark to Thomas Leister,

1682 John Henderson, Richard Tull Senr, Richard Tull Junr, George Tull son of Richard Tull, Rachell Tull dau of Richard Tull, John Rickards Junr, John Ayleward, Josias Seaward, Charles Jones, John Gladstone, John Fferrell, Iris (Jns and other various possibilities?) Rogers dau of John Rogers, William Tomkins, Robert Smith, Gideon Tillman, Ffrancis Martin, Michaell Dishroon, John Gislin, Thomas Tyre, Thomas Horstman, James Round, John Tucker

1683 Richard Small, Richard Webb, Samuell Horsey, William Holsteine, Gil..(?) James, William Haller(?), John Taylor, Richard Chambers & Roger Burstuns(?), Robt. Bowdetsh(?), Edward Howard, Ann Vigerous dau of John Vigerous, Kersey Innis dau of Samll Innis, Ann Innis dau of Samll Innis,

William Giles Junr, Edward Webber, Thomas Hobbs, John Price, Allexander Thomas

1685 Ffrancis Allexander, Rebecca Hardy, Thomas Ackworth, David Harris, Richard Jefferson, Anne Mumford, Edward Smith Junr, Samuell Quellin, John West Merchant, Leonard Jones, John Wepworth(?), Thomas Potter son of Henry Potter, Elizabeth Potter dau of Henry Potter, Henry Leabon, Nicholas Tyler (two differenct marks), Pasque Burleigh, Robert Loe, Henry Hardy, Nicholas Cornwell, Thomas Pyle, Anthony Bell, William Colebourne Currier, John Webb & Isaac Williard, Randall Minshall & Tymothy Harney, John Starrett, John Macknitt, William Paterson, Archibald White, Edward Wright, Mary Hardy, Esau Boston

1686 William Harris, Samuell Marchment, Mary Turpin dau of Wm. Turpin, Elizabeth Turpin dau of Wm. Turpin, Sarah Turpin dau of Wm. Turpin, William Turpin son of Wm. Turpin, Adam Heatch, John Webb son of John Webb, Alce Wright dau of Wm. Wright, Bloice Wright, Judith Wright (her mark), George Newman, John Rickins, Rebecca Covington, Anne Sherley, Jeremiah Wright and Rebecca Wright children of Edward Wright, James Inglish, Samuell Cooper, Samuell Cooper (second mark), William Kennett, Mary Kennett, Elizabeth Kennett, Susanna Kennett, John Lane, John Wyne, Joseph Statin, Samuell Worthington, Capt. William Colebourne, Andrew Whittington, William Nelson, Tymothy Harney, Michaell Hannah, John Huett minister, William Stevens, Henry Lake, John Barber, Thomas Hillson minister, William Noble, William Traile minister, Hugh Tingle, William Harvey, Richard Cole, Edward Shipham, Edward Wheeler, Cornelius Mulka, Thomas William Blacksmith, James Langreene

1687 James Rawley; Richard Ffarewell; Henry Ayres; Nicholas Carpenter; Thomas Millman; Thomas Millman; Stephen Lusse; John Bennett; John Covington son of John Covington; Phillip Covington son of Jno. Covington; John Covington Senr; Jno. Browne of Senepuxen; Jane Dreden; John de Brulagh; William Skyn(?); John Murphie; senr; John Murphyie Junr; Thomas Murphie son of John Murphie; Anne Betts dau of George Betts which was the mark of Ffrancis Betts son of said George given to said Ffrancis by Wm. Whittfield, said Ffrancis being dead; William Lewis; John Trushaw(?); John Mahaun; Mary Bennett dau of Edward Bennett; Jane Bennett dau of Edward Bennett; Jonathan Cooper son of Sam'll Cooper; Richard Stevens; Richard Stevens; John Price of Somerset Co sells his mark to John Rock Cooper of said County; Mathew Scarbrough; John Rush; Samuell Handy Junr; William Handy; Edward Wheeler son of Edward Wheeler; Thomas Morris planter of Poponno; Thomas Camplin Senr; Robert King; George Glandenning; Samuell Heydon; Pheanix Hall; John Broughton; Mercy Ffountaine (his mark); Andrew Speare; John King; Richard Shockley; Archibald Holmes; Robert Givan; William Allegand

1688 Mary Jones dau of William Jones of Anamessix; Allexander Price; Randall Revell; John Royall son of Thomas Royall; William Vaugham; George Benston; Hugh Stevinson; Charles Ballard; Wm. Wheatly; Thomas Winder; Robert Butcher; Wm. Shollitto son of Mary Ellis; the subscriber assigned to his wife Mary Connor and both my daughters Eliza. Mary and Anne Conner my morks — Phillip Connor; Thomas Cary Junr son of Edward Cary; James Bratton; Edmund Dickeson; William Dencom; Margarett Scofeild widdow; Randall Revell; John Taylor planter; William Nelson; Andrew White; Hugh King; Benjamin Keizer;

38

Cattle Marks - Somerset County

Thomas Humphreys; Manns Morris; George Baily; Ffrancis Thomas; James
Strawbridge; John Strawbridge; John Parsons; Andrew Whittington; Richard
Chambers; Edward Craige; Henry Sasnett; John Pelty(?); John Wheeler; James
Given; James Smith; Gabriell Henery; Subscriber makes over his mark to
Anthony James now aged 12 years or there abouts a young heifer - Edward
Gould; Edward Gould; Edward Gould Junr; John Macclaster; John Macclaster

1688/9 Michael Holland; Moses Ffonton; John Ffossett; Roger Phillips;
Richard Jeferson; John Evett; Walter Talbot; Rodi Talbott (her mark); John
Robinson; Griffin Thomas

1689 John Browne; Richard Anterham; John Langford; Stephen Page; Alce Hill
Junr (her mark); Mary Johnson; Thomas Johnson Senr; William Clarkson; Edward
McGlamry; Sarah Keene; John Hine; James Hayman; Charles Hayman; Arthur
Hayman; Wm. Hayman; Thomas Everton; Mathew Wynn; William Keene; John
Ritchins; Deed of gift from John Vigerous of cattle to his children when the
oldest comes of age: Armewell Robert Vigerous, Anne Vigerous, Elizabeth
Vigerous, Mary Vigerous and Ffrances Vigerous; William Mason; Catherin
Anterham; William Clarkson makes over to Anne Langford wife of John Langford
and to her children a heiffer; William Law; James Smith; Lawrence Connor;
Abraham Emmett; John Emmett Junr; Josias Emmett; John Steel; David Miller;
William Owens; William Carey; Thomas Davis of ChriKetuk(??) county of
Nanfumum but formerly of Somerset County assigns his mark to Lewis Knight;
William White (3 different marks); Stevens White; John Browne, planter;
Allexander Prise & Rebecca Thomas the daughter of Lambert Thomas were
married by John Huett Minister of the gospel of Jesus Christ 29 Jan 1680
Cris... Prise son of Allixander Prise b of Rebecca his wife 5 Nov 1789;
Edward Ross; John Ffrizell; Lambert Thomas; Barbiry Dent; John Houlston;
John Rutter of Ronowokin; Ffrancis Thorowgood of Pocomoke; William Mead
Bricklayer; William Graham; William Warwick; Samuell Handy Senr; Thomas
Handy;

1689/90 William Bound; William Tisdald

1690 Thomas Beauchamp; Charles Bollerd; Edward Perkins; David Adams son of
Phillip Adams; George Adams; son ot Phillip Adams; William Catlin son of
Robert Catlin; Sarah Catlin dau of Robert Catlin; James Brookshaw; Hugh
Porter; Charles Kinsey; Ninian Dolap; Charles Loe; Joseph Benson; Robert
Polyk; Joseph Polyk; Teague Riggen Junr; Humphry Road; John Stoukley(?); John
Parker; Philip Parker; Charles Parker; William Wilson; Andrew Miller; Robert
Wroth; Mary Prise; Mary Prise; William Curre; Nathaniel Clark

1691 Samuel Richinson; James Davies; Henry Haylor (sic) ; Elizabeth Harney
dau of Timothy Harney; Phillip Askue; John Tull; John Bennet; Henry
Sasnett, John Johnson of Jericoe; Joseph Cearsy; Assignment from George
Haffurt of Somerset Co to John Colherne his mark; said Coherne and Joseph
Eames enter into partnership

1692 Martha Hughes; Robert Pirrie; Capt John King; George Hey; John
Ffletcher; John Tayler son of John Taylor of Animessex; John West Junir;
Elizabeth West dau of John West; Thomas West son of John West; George Noble;
John West; John Wine has assigned to John West his mark; Edward Perkins;

Alexander Mcculleth(?); Alexander Mcculleth(?); John Mccullock(?) (two marks; Edward Shippam; Archibald Smith; Thomas Pryer; Thomas Waller; Andrew Alexander; Edward Hordell; Edmund Collins; Matthew Wallis; William Wilson; Richard Waters; Thomas Waters; John Waters; Edward Harper; Marcy Ffountain and George Lane assign marks to Wm. Banister; David Shehe; Marsy Ffountaine (two marks); Joseph Boyce; John West, clerk records heifer given by Arnold Elzey, another given by Charles Ballard and another given by Randell Revell to Sarah Revell dau of the afsd Randall Revell and Sarah his wife; William Polke(?); Richard Davis Junr; William Davis; George Langdell; George Magee

1693 Henry Lynch whose mark was Wm. Davis's mark father to the said Lynch's wife; Bernard Ward; John Cary; Benjamine Idelett Junr (two marks): John Idelett (two); yearling heifer given to my grand child Mary Ingram with the increase of males to go to her father, James Ingram - Philip Askue; heifer given by me to Abraham Ingram son of James Ingram - Philip Askue; William Noble; gift to Wm. Noble of a heifer - Mary Streaks; William Browne; William Browne; Dennis Lane, dau (sic) of George Lane; Catherane Lane; Ambrose Braimaugh; Ambrose London of Somerset Co gives to above Ambrose Braimaugh a calf to be kept in custody of John Judrell; John Judrell; Thomas Sernam; John Cole; Mary Prise, widdow and relict of Robert of James Prise (two marks); John Jenckinson son of John Jenckinson; John Watt; Maj. Robert King; Bryan Kellegan (his mark was bought of Robert Hignett by sd Bryan; John Wale; William Poynter; Edward Slebews; John Saunders; Jeremiah Harrison; George Baines; David Dreddon; Thomas Dashiel (two); Philip Carter son of Philip Carter; John Ricketts Junr; Robert Stott(?); Samuel Johnson; John Rine; Adam Hatch Junr; Thomas Giddins

1694 Robert Jones; Patrick Conner; Richard Plunkett; Robert Patrie; gift to daughter Sarah feather bed and other and grand daughter Jane - Jane Cary; Jane McLaughan; John Cullin; William Wainwright; John Houston (two); Sarah Houlston; Jane Mulcah; Alexander Barrett; James Knox; Ambrose Riggen; James White; John Gillis; Thomas Young; John Rutter Junr; Richard Rutter; James Weatherly; James Weatherly; Thomas Price of Somerset Co assigns mark to Isaac Boston; Thomas Bromley; Esau Boston of Marumsco of Som Co assigns his mark to dau Bette Boston; Anne Bostin; Capt. William Coulborn and Robert Prentice their joynt mark; Capt. William Coulbourne & John Cowin their joynt makr; William Giles Junr (two); William Layton; Nathaniel Davis; Patrick Conner; John White of Anamessex; Thomas Clarke; James Davis servt. to Marsy Ffountain; Robert Catlin

1695 Stephen Dear; Hederak Odougherty; Thomas Parramore; Richard Ackworth; William Denson of Som Co assigns his mark to John West; Robert Carney; Noah Macclaster; John Evans of Smiths Island; Thomas Wilson; Edward Davis; John Meclaster; Neal Macoy; Gregory Murmurenough; Daniel Long

1696 Thomas Tull Junr; Richard Slevens (Stevens?); John Evans; Mary Prise records mark for her granddaughter, Mary Ward, dau of Cornelius Ward; Mary Adams of Som Co bestows to her son Abraham a ewe and sow; records mark for Abraham Adams son to Philip Adams; Anne Adams dau of Philip and Mary Adams; given to Edward Benbridge by his aunt Mary Winster a cow - mark recorded by David D. Jenckins the childs father in law; mark of John Coleson late of this co on creatures given to John, Margrett and Anne Coleson son and daughters to the said John Coleson - William Mackmullen; Edmund Howard fifh son of son of Edmund Howard; John White of Dam quarter; Randall West son of John West; William West son of John West; Robert Catlin assigns over to Edmund Munlavell a mark

1697 Solomon Hitch; gift of mark to my daugher Mary Cary the wife of Thomas Cary - Robert Crouch; Edward Wheeler; William Ellis; recorded for my dau Hannah Huckley(?) a cow and calf - John Huckley; Henry Bishop the mark belonging to his father John Bishop; Jeremiah Townsend; John Evans; Dent Gray; Matha McClester; Edward Isenott(?) Junr; John(?) Ellis(?); John Garsons; John Fisher

1698 George Rawley; Charles Williams of Sea Side; Sam'll. Davis planter; Thomas Ellis; James Callwell; Thomas Shaw; Thomas Horseman; William Grear (two); William Kibble; John Webb senr of Som Co gives to Colebray Wilson and Rachel Wilson daughters of George & Jane Wilson a cow and calf; Richard ...; John McCloster; Peter Dent; Richard Boston; Records a yearling for Jean Murfe...(?) from friend Dennis Driskill; heifer for John More given by Robert Downs; John Cottingham; Charles Cottingham; James Dickinsons; for my son John Megroly(?) - Mary Megroly(?); Isaac Boston junr; Robert Crouch junr; James Dashield; Daniell Jones (two)

1699 Robert and Samuell Owens; Henry Acworth; Daniell Long; David Long; John Salter; Mary Applestone; recorded marks for son Nathaniell Waller and heifer and daughter Mary Waller a heifer(?) iron pott left her by her father deceased; and dau Sarah Waller an iron pott; for son John a calf and dau Laurawa a heifer, dau Joane a heifer, dau Hannah a calf, dau Mary a yearling, dau Naomi a calf - John Harrett; Daniel Walter; Thomas Walter; John Brittingham (two); Henry Walter; Thomas Winder of Northumberland Co, Va, assigns his mark to James McMurrie of Som Co; Robert Twilley; Robert Twilly; John Clarke the son of Edward Clarke; Thomas Wilson junr (two); Henry Ffreekes; Thomas Evens(?); Thomas Wilson, Nanticoke; Thomas Lucas

1700 Thomas Ffarnall; John Pitts; John Edmonds assigns his mark to Ralph Milbourne of Pocomoke; Phillip Selby; Godfrey Russell; John Odear; James Hayman; John Candry; Robert Wrath (?); Robert Tyrar; Londan Wilston; Nehemiah Holland; John Abbitt; John Roah junr; John Carrokin; Jeffery Long; Mary Culling cow given to her by Thomas Tull; Andrew Smith; Mary Culling

1701 Jones Ricketts; William Nelson; John Gunby; heifer given to dau Alce by Thomas Stockwell; John Dredon; Ann Terrieher; Peter Surnam; Wm. Phillipson; Dorathy Venables; John Pageman(?) junr; James Murrah; Isaac Ernshire (Ironshire?); Thomas Powell; Darby Riggin; heifer given to Elizabeth Roach from her ffriend John Roach Senr; Robert McQuillin; Walter Lane

1702 Jacob Adams; Robon Harris; Elizabeth Layfield; Thomas Collins; Ffrances Deards (her mark); Phillip Graverner; William Graverner; Thomas Graverner; William Richards; Wm. Richard junr; David Wallis; John Walter; Thomas Ralph Junr; James Spence; John Davis; Ffrances Thomas (her mark); John Larramore; John Collins; Dogel Beauchamp; ... Beauchamp (her mark); James Crasson(?); Surkick(?) Coleman; John Lewoc(?); gift to my dau Sarah Davis a mare coalt and cow - Thomas Davis; Benjamin Woiloc; Robert Dashiele; Ralph Doe; John

Cattle Marks - Somerset County

Waters (two); James Odougherty; James Collier; Robert Collier; Edmund Beauchamp; John Beauchamp sonn of ut supra; Wm. Beauchamp sonne of ut Supra; Isaac Noble; John Noble; James Adams; Hugh McCollogon

1703 John Waltan; John Disharoone; Jonathan Sheares; Richard Parr; John Roberts; Ephraim Polke; Margret Green; Stephen Smith; Robt. Crockett junr; Charles Wharton; John Lokear; John Longodon junr; John Taylor son of Walter Taylor; William Beauchamp; Thomas Beauchamp; Anthony Goldsmith; for my dau Ffrances Elzey a cow - Peter Elzey; for my dau Elizabeth Elzey two cows and calves - Peter Elzey; David Linsey; Jonathan Cottingham; John Holder; cow given to dau Mary Dorman - Henry Dorman; For Mary Dorman a sow and shoats; her father is Henry Dorman; Ann Hye; William Poalke; William Richards; Wm. Richards junr

1704 John Davis and Coll Ffrancis Jenckins Esq; for my dau Catherine Roach heifer - John Roach junr; Enoch Griffin; Joseph Would(?); for my two sons John Swillivane and Timothy Swillivane ewes - Timothy Swillivane; for the use of John Daniell & James Kabble(?) son of Daniell Kabbles(?) - John McCarlore; John Phillips; John Hodgin; William Goddard; John Hall; for my sonns David Wallis 20 head of cattle of my own mark and furniture - Matthew Wallace; I record for my youngest sonne Richard Wallis a bay mare - Matthew Wallace; William Peemer(?); Anderend Derickson; for my sone Thomas Royall a cow and - Thomas Royall for my sonne Lewis Jones a mare - Samll H. Jones Senr; John Hall; Lowe Jones; for my dau Elizabeth Phillips her mark - John Phillips; for Charles Loe(?) heifer - Wm. Clarkson; Bryan Snee; Naomi Snee alias Knee(Rwee?); for my son Thomas Hill two cows - James Hill; Richard Stockley junr; William Scott junr; Job Truett; John Sawer

1705 George Boseman; John Hall; Thomas Jones; John Beavens; Benj. King; Daniel Jones; George Gayle; John Shors; Jeremiah Harris; for my dau Mary Phebus a mare - Geo. Phebus; David Linzey; Jonathan Cotingham; Samuell Taylor; Joseph Porter; Robert Wilson

Talbot County Marks of Cattle

From Court Records of Talbot County, 1741-1750/State Archives, Accession # 9060. All entries are for markes of cattle, hogs, geese, turkeys, dunghill fowls

1741 - Andrew Orem, Elizabeth Bush, Level Morgan
1742 - Samuel Sharp, John Lowe
1743 - William Richardson, Henry Lowes, William Thomas, Thomas Ashcroft, Holland Edmondson
1744 - John Exley, James Benny of Talbot Co, Elizabeth Edwards, Thomas Clark
1745 - Jonathan Gibson, Joseph Atkinson
1748 - Samuel Atwell
Jan 23 1750 Peter Denny

1750 Notices: Edward Spencer Doude has taken up a stray bay gelding
William Brown Vickers has taken up a stray mare
Solomon Larey has taken up a stray horse

Overseers of Roads - Dorchester County

Complaints of overseers in August 1690 Court

From Dorchester County Judgement Records, held by the State Archives,
1690-1692.

August 1690 Court/Complaint of John Makeele Junr, overseer of the high ways
in Fishing Creek Hundred, that ... Mills, Mr. Pollard Man, David Jones, Mr.
Clark, s Edward, Thomas Nooner, Cornelius his negro, William Hill planter,
John King servant to John Branock, Walter at Mr. Woodwards and Rich Thomas -
would not attend the clearing of the highway being summoned by the said
overseer. (The above named persons were summoned to appear at the Next
County Court.)

August 1690 Court/Complaint of John Lecompt, overseer of his majesties
highways in Little Choptank hundred that Thomas Cook, Mr. Edward Cooke,
William Willoby, Thomas Killman, Henry Wheeler Junr, Cornelius Armington,
William Warner Major, Henry Trippe, Henry Beckwith would not attend the
clearing of the highways. (The above named persons were summoned to appear
at the next County Court.)

1702 - 1713
Excerpts from the Appointments of Overseers of Roads, Talbot County
1702-1713: Maryland State Archives/Accession # 9093-2

John King of St. Michaells River overseer Road from Coll. Lloyds bridge to
Miles River Fferry ... to Capt. Davis's bridge and from thence to Carters
bridge and ...Capt Davis's bridge to the road that leads from York Towne to
Donchaster
Wm Skinner overseer of the road from Edgar Webbs to Richd. Ffeddemans bridge
Robert Clark - of road from Richd. Ffeddeman's bridge to Ralph Elstons senr

19 Jan 1702 John King of St. Michaells River - of road beginning from west
side of Coll Lloyds bridge keeping Maine road to the north side of Carters
bridge ... to Court house and from court house till it intersects road from
Col. Loyds bridge to Carters bridge and also to beginning the east side of
Capt Davis's bridge ...
Jacob Gibson - road from Donchester Towne along maine road to Miles River
ffery and from ...
Wm. Hadden - of road beginning from North End of Moses Harris bridges till
it intersects the road there ...to Court House to Carters mill branch and
from three bridges til it intersects a road by the Bever damms ....to Race
ground by the court house
Daniel Baker - of highways north end of Moses Harris's bridge to the North
side of Wye Mill branch and from Zebbs(?) Crooke Branch to Thomas Emersons
... Indian bridge and from there to Fisher Roade(?)
John Green - of road ... North side of Wye Mill to Chester Mill ... St.
Pauls' Church ...
Thomas Yewell road from ... Wye Mill branch ... to North side of Wye bridge
... to north side of Beaver damm branch to Wm. Courseys plantation and
thence to Mill branch
Matthew Smith Junr - of road from Beaver damm to Wadeing place marshes and
to Richd Bennetts ...
Richd Jones Junr, Wye, of road to Arthur Emmory's Plantation ... Beaver
damms to Wadeing place ... Chester Mill ... to Richd Tilghman
John Keld - of road ... three bridges to Tuckahoe bridge and from Wooters's
Mill to Three bridges
Thomas Lewis - of road from Chester Church to John Wellingtons

Court held at Towne of Yorke 16 Mar 1702
John Hunt overseer in the stead of Robert Clarke late of this county
Robert Jadwin in place of Thomas Ewbanks, from Choptank Roade to Wooters's
Mill

Court at Town of York, 15 Jun 1703
Walter Quinton - of road from Clement Sales's to Robert Grundy's landing
William Sharpe of road from Thomas Taylors to Howell(?) Cove(?)
William Hatfield of road ... from Wye Church to Tuckahoe bridge
Wm. Warner in stead of Daniell Baker

Mar 26 1703
Daniel Sherwood in stead of Wm. Skinner

Overseers of roads - Talbot County

William Webb in stead of John Wrightson

Sep 19 1704
Thomas Bennett - of road from his dwelling plantation to John Dawsons
John Worby - of road from Edward Satterfoots to John Kelds roade and from
Robert Grundy's to Wootters's Mill
Robert Noble in stead of William Warner

Nov 21 1704
Robert Redgister Junr in stead of Robert Jadwin
John Henrix - of road from Dover into Choptank Road
John Baggs - of road from Rich bottom untill it intersects the maine road
Thomas Buckingham - of road from Beaver Damms to Kings' Towne

Mar 20 1703
Edward Tomlin from Wye Mill to Chester Mill and from St. Pauls church to
where it intersets said road by the bridge

Nov 21 1704
John Long in stead of Ambros Fforad - from Allemby Bridge to Wm. Stadk(?)
and from Clemt Sales's to Crock's bridge
Ennion Williams in stead of Wm Webb late decd
Benja. Ball in stead of John Hunt late decd
Oliver Milington of road from Wye Church to Robert Grundys'
Anthony Wise in stead of Edward Latham
John Booker in stead of Peter Harwood
John Nabb in stead of Richard Jones Junr late decd

... 13 1704
Wm. Stevens of road from Tho: Taylors to Howell Powells
Peter Tharp of road from Clovis point to Peach Blossom
John Dawson in stead of Thomas Bennett late decd
Thomas Booker in stead of John Booker late decd

March 20 1704
Andrew Skinner in stead of John King

Nov 1706
Davis Arey from Tuckahoe bridge to Mr. Grundy's Mill and from Tuckahoe
bridge to said Grundys and from the mill towards said Grundys till it
intersects the Queen Anns County

Nov 20 1705
John Roe in stead of Robert Noble

March 18 1706
Vincent Hemsley in stead of Andrew Skiner
John Ross in stead of John Rue
Joseph Gregory in stead of Wm. Hudden

Mar 18 1707
William Dixon from Coll Smithsons Bridge to Pitts bridge

45

Overseers of roads - Talbot County

Nov 16 1708
William Finney instead of John Ross

Nov 16 1708
William Ffarrell from Choptank road to Southbeys Mill in stead of Dennis
Hopkins Junr

June 20 1710
Richard Dudley instead of Thomas Buckingham

Mar 21 1709
John Tibballs instead of Anthony Wise, from Rich land at the head of Dawsons
Creek to the north east syde of Coll. Thomas Smithsons bridge, ... to his
plantation ... St. Michaels river fferry ...

Nov 29 1710
Arthur Rigby in stead of John Dawson
William Ares(?) from White.. church to William Dickenson's Dwelling
plantation
Jacob Wooters instead of John Keld (John Keld was overseer in stead of David
Arey)
Philip Sherwood from Richd. Ffeddeman's bridge to Choptank Island

Nov 21 1710
Henry Ffritz instead of John Long from Allumby's bridge to Port of Oxford

March 20 1710
Danl. Sherwood - of road from Richd. Ffeddeman's bridge to Oxford fferry
Thomas Lockwell - of road from The Rich Bottom along the upper Road to Kings
Creake bridge ...
Thomas Price - of road from old Court house til it intersects the road that
leads from the Three bridges to Carters bridge
Jacob Gibson - of road from the South syde of Thomas' Hopkins' plantation to
Miles River ferry and from said ferry along by Andrew Kinnamonts plantation
to the head of Leeds Creeke
Richard Bruff - of road from Wye Towne along the ferry Road to South part of
Thomas Hop..'s plantation and from Coll. Loyds bridge to the head of Leeds
creek

Jun 19 1711
Griffith Evans instead of Henry FFrith, of road from Sherwood's Bridge to
the port of Oxford
John Robinsons instead of Walter Quinton, of road from Clement Sales's
plantation to the Parsons Landing and from the White Marsh Church to William
Troth's branch

.. 19 1711
William Clayton - of road from Moses Harrison's bridge to Wye Mill and from
Wye Church to Thomas Emerson's plantation and from thence to Randalls Mill
Henry Daley in stead of Jno. Sherwood, from Pitts bridge to Sherwoods bridge
and from New Market to the Revd Wm. Glenn

Overseers of roads - Talbot County

Aug 21 1711
Daniel Sherwood - of road from Oxford ferry to the Little bridge on the west
end of Edgar Webbs plantation and from thence to Ffeddemans bridge
Henry Baley - of road from Sherwoods Bridge to the Little bridge between the
great Meeting house and Pitt Bridge ... to the bridge ordered to be made
over the head of the Tred haven creek ... from new market to Revd Wm. Glens
dwelling plantation
William Arnett - of road from the bridge to be made over Tred haven creek to
Miles River ffery
James Loyd - of road from south syde of Wm. Eubanks plantation through the
swamp, to the head of Leeds creeke

Mar 18 1711
William Arnett as above
John Morgan - of road from Moses Harriss's bridge to John Kings bridge along
back of Majr Genrll Lloyds Forrest plantation
John Henrix from Dover to the Court House at Pitts Bridge
John Brin instead of Daniel Powell, of road from Abbotts Mill to White Marsh
Church and from Abbotts Mill to road that leads from Peach Blossom to Dover
... to Walter Quintons ...
John Watts - of road from Swetmans Mill to Mudie Branch and from Randalls
... to Thos. Emersons and from thence to Wye Church
Thomas Adkinson - of Road that issues out of the ... Carters bridge along
Madam Carters plantation and ... that neck to plantation of Jacob Abrams
... Parkers Bridge ... road that goes to Coll. Ffinleys

Aug 1712
Arthur Rigby from Dawsons ... Rich Land to Edgar Webbs ...

Nov Court 1712
John Sherwood instead of Henry Bay ... from Sherwoods Bridge to Pits Bridge
... Tredhaven Creek Bridge and from New Market to ... Rev Mr. Wm Glen's
dwelling plantation
John Henrix - of road from Dover to Court House at Pittes Bridge and to
Clear the road Round Mr. Phi. Hemsleys Lotts at sd Court house
John Stevens instead of Willis Stevens, from Thomas Taylor to Howell Powells
William Arnett - of from Dawsons Rich land to Court House and ... to road
that leads from ... Smithsons to Miles river Fferry
Thomas Bowker from Edward Latham to Miles River Fferry ... and from Edward
Lathams to Edward Hardins(?)

Aug Court 1713
Thomas Hopkins instead of Richard Br...
Willus Thompson instead of Jacob Wootters

Nov Court 1713
George Bowes - to clear and make a road from Majr Robt Grundy's ... to
Wooddenhawk Branch (the nearest and streightest way and with as little
prejudice may be to the Inhabitants in those parts, to the County Court
house
Peter Harwood - to make a road from this county Court house until it
intersects road that leads from Majr Robertt Grundys Mills to Wood... branch

47

Petitions from Archives of Maryland

1. 1689-90 Kent county in the Province of Maryland. Address to His
Majesty. ... We your Majesties most loyal, dutiful and protestant Subjects
in these our Addresses humbly crave by your Princely care and prudence to be
freed and enlarged, and that the Government together with your Majesties
favour and a lasting Settlement may be again restored to the Right Hon'ble
Lord Baltemore which will make him and us happy, and give us new occasion to
bless God, and pray for you Maj'ities life and happy Reign.
    Signers: Wm Frisby, Henry Coursey, Robert Burman, Philemon Hemsley,
Simon Wilmer, William Peeke, Josias Lanham, Thomas Ringgold, Tho. Smyth,
Griffith Jones, Josh. Wickes, Jno. Hynson, George Sturtem, Lambart Wilmer,
Gerrardin Wessels, Richard Jones, Philip Conner.

2. 1689-90 Talbot County in the Province of Maryland – their Address to
His Majesty. To the Kin and Queen's most excell't Maj'ty... we abhorr and
detest the falsehood and unfaithfulness of John Coade, and other his
Associates and Agents, who first by dispersing untrue Reports of prodigious
Armies of Indians and French Papists invading us did stir up unjust
jealousies and dismal apprehensions in the less cautious sort of people of
this Province .. and disposed the people to mutiny and tumult, made a
further insurrection, and extorted the lawfull Government from the Lord
Prop'ry ...
    Signers: Tho: Smithson, Thos. Hopkins, Ro. Gouldsbrough (Two other
copies in the same words, but addressed to the King alone, are signed by the
following person:) John Hawkins, Will. Coursey, Ric'd Macklin, Rich. Jones,
Daniel Glover, Robert Macklin, Robert Kent, William Tonge, Rich. Tilghman,
John Chaiers, John Johnson, Nathaniel Pucker, John Nabb, John Lamb, Joseph
Lambert., William Conners, Hugh Sherwood, John Newman, Ralph Darson Sing'r,
W. Hambleton, John Yonn, Richard Seddeman (Feddeman?), Henry Frith, Henry
Odcocke, Henry Price, Richard Parnes, George Bowell, James Smith, Samuel
Taylor, William Hackit, Thomas Wetherby, John Whittington, Francis Shephard,
John Hambleton, Michael Harbet, Robert Norest, Charles Hollinworth, Andrew
Hamilton, Jno. Swaine, James Murphy, Charles Cartwright, Robert Harrison,
George Corson, Thomas Evans, Mich'l Turbutt, Charles Robinsons, Ralph Dawson
junr, Zerbuable Wells, Joseph Green

3. To his most Sacred Majesty – The humble Petition of the Inhabitants of
Cecill County in the Province of Maryland. 18th Nov'er 1689. ... that the
Lord Baltemore may be restored and sent back again unto this his former
Government, under whome we doubt not but we may live a quiet & contented
life ...
    Signers: St. Leger Codd, Casp'r Agust. Herman, Gideon Gundry, J. Wroth,
Isaac Caulk, York Yorkson, Georg Beestone, Thomas Billton, Daniel Smith,
John Darby, Wm Nowell, George Warner, Thomas Beakston, Robert Randoll,
Georg. Stevens, Geo: Oldfield, Wm Chamberlaine, Henry Eldest, Rob: Crook

4. Address of the Inhabitants of the County of Somersett. Nov'er the 28th
1689. To the King and Queen most Ex't Maj'ty. ... wee resolve to continue
... in the Profession and defence of the Protestant Religion and your
Majesty's Title and interest against the French and other Papists that
oppose and trouble us in soe just and good a cause not doubting but your
Majestys wisdom and clemency will afford unto us all needful suitable Aid
and Protection for securing our Religion, lives and liberty under Protestant

Governor and Government, and for enabling us to defend our selves against all Invaders...

Signers: John Huett, Wm Coulbourne Junr, Thomas Wilson, Henry Philips, John Parsons, Thomas Shild, Thomas Stivenson, James Knox, John Browne, Wm Alexander, Randolph Revell, Peter Elzery, James Smith, Epraem Wilson, Thomas Smith, John Knox, Thomas Wall'r, John Knox, Thomas Wall'r, Alexander Knox, Alexander Procter, John Renshaw, James Conner, William Wilmot, Micayah Sadler, John Chanceleer, John Smoche, Nicholas Cornwell, Robert Cade, John Miller, Adam Spence, Tho. Midgley, John Baron, John Deale, Martin Curtis, Clement Giles, Robert Johnson, William Bowen, Devoraux Diegas, Robert Simson, Edward Evans, Hugh Jingle, John Coltston, Richard Warren, Mathew Jones, Richard Hill

Calendar of Maryland State Papers

5. (After 1713 Nov 10) Christ Church Parish, Kent Island. Petition to Gov. John Hart and the House of Delegates.

The church has been without an incumbent for nine years, being incapable of maintaining a minister; the petitioners have employed one moiety of the 40 (lbs. of tobacco) per poll toward building a new church and one moiety in procuring a lecturer of good life and conversation; the 40 lbs. per poll is not sufficient for him to maintain his family; since the church is now finished, the petitioners pray for liberty to dispose of the 40 lbs. per poll during the vacancy.

Signers: Vall(entine) Carter, Thomas Marsh, John Carter, Isaac Harris, Nathaniel Connor, Thomas Godman, Thomas Jones, William Elliott, Sa(mue)ll Eagley(?), Jacob Blangey, Marmaduke Goodhand, James Evans, John J. Corken (?), Phil(ip) Connor, William Brown, Matthew Eareckson, Charles Connor, John Sutton, Charles Stevens, James Sudler, Thomas Jackson, Peter Deney, Alexander Towlson, Thomas Rouse, Robert Porter, Thomas Woollahand, Samuel Thorlow, Robert Blunt, Timothy Carthey, Matthew Griffi(t)h. See Arch. of Md., XXIX, 239-240.

6. 1721 Jul 13. Various Indian Tribes, Somerset County. To Gov. Charles Colbert and the Upper and Lower Houses of Assembly. Petiion concerning the sale of strong liquor to the Indians: poor Indians have been ruined by liquor in spite of laws to the contrary; ask that no liquor be sold the common Indians; chief men to be allowed a restricted amount.

Signatures with marks: Indian Panquash, Indian Winomatoakem, Indian Mr. Nanoy, Indian Asick, Indian Mianita, Indian Sawamack, Indian Powinixus, Indian Chinramack, Indian Alexander, Edmon Noll, Indian Will, Indian Wittangebott, Indian Witaricon, Indian Pettor, Indian Basteby, Indian Mr. Rango, Indian Robin, Robin Sockrockett, Indian Mr. Bearatt, Indian Peetor, Indian Gorge. Interpreter: Luoss Disharun

7. (After 1737 Mar 3) Upper Chesapeake Bay. Petition of various inhabitants and grain traders to Gov. Samuel Ogle. By a recent Act of Assembly the head of the Chesapeake has suffered to the grievance of farmers and traders, but to the vast profit of Pennsylvania; the petitioners pray that the said law may be repealed.

Signers: John Veazey, John Ryland, William Walmsley, Isaac Caulk, John Beedle, John Penington, Jr., Thomas Been, John Mareen, William Beaston, J. Ward, Jr., John Holland, John Jones, William Knaresbrough, J(oh)n Campbell,

William Pearce, Pereg(rine) Warde, John Baldwin, George Veazey, Jeremiah
Gridley, Robert Mareen, John Ryland, Sen., Henry Penington, Sen., John
Chamberlin, Barnet Vanhorn, Jacob Ozier, Peter Overstock, J. (?) Penington,
Jr., Richard Smith, William Mercer, Peter Cooper, Thomas Spencer, John
Carrington, William Pennington, John Beetle(?), Jr., Benjamin Torry, Thomas
Pearce, John Cooper, Thomas Pearce, Jr., John Wallace, Edward Beaston, John
Cox, Phillip Cazier, Robert Croker, John Lovering, Samuel Beck, Benjeman
Parsans, Daniel Whalles, John Wethered, James De Hart, Richard James, John
Bennet, D(av)d Witherspon, Aug(us)t Bayne, Robert Penington, Thomas Kees, J.
Penington, Peregrine Frisby, Mathias Daye, William Ellis, John Wallace,
William Lavin, Richard Wethered, Gid(eo)n Pearce, Edward Mitchell, Richard
Scise(?), John Denning, James Woodland, William Catton, Porter Jorensine(?),
Phillip Holbeadger, Dannelle Brian(?), Edward Furron, Thomas Sinnett, Philip
Jobson, Thomas Haughton, Thomas Hynson.   On verso: Mar 3 1737, Levin Gale,
brig Brereton, Henry Smith, m(aste)r, John Williams, Robert Henry.

8. 1738 May 9. Sundry Inhabitants on the Sea Board side of Sommert County.
To Gov. Samuel Ogle and the Upper and Lower Houses of Assembly.   Petition
for permission to export their surplus of wheat and Indian corn.
    Signers: John Smith, Sergt. Smythies, Michael Godwin, John Watson,
William Burton, Thos. Robinson, Joshuah Robinson, George Howard, George
West, Nehemiah Howard, Leonard Johnson, Wm West, Thomas West, Thos Cary,
John Short, Bebbins Morris, Tho: Fletcher, Sam'l Hopkins, David Johnson,
Alex'r Burrell, Edm'd Cropper, Wm Campbell, Thos Harny, John Rickets, Tobies
Rickets, Rich'd Hickman, John Idolett, Wm. Collins, Moses Chaille, Jr., John
Selby, John Newbold, Thomas Mishell, John Purnel, Isaac Marshal, Richard
Holland, William Whailie, Wm Jones, Nath: Cropper, Jno Massey, John Johnson,
Dan Wharton, Bowd'n Robins, Thos Robins, John Fassitt, Thos. Purnell, Jenken
Murey, Joseph Porter, Jno. Scarborough, Geo. Selby, Math: Wise, Jno Hopkins,
Josiah Hopkins, Philip Selby, Daniel Sturges, Saml Porter, Edward Franklyn.
On verson: "Read and Rejected, signed per Order - J(ohn) Ross, Cl(erk),
Up(per) Ho(use)." See Arch. of Md., XL, 174

9. 1738 May 11. Inhabitants of a Part of Talbot County. To Gov. (Samuel
Ogle) and the Upper and Lower Houses of Assembly. Petition for the erection
of a new parish; they can support a church and they will not reduce the
revenues of any other parish by lessening the membership; the new parish
will begin at Anthony Richardson's wharf and following the main road to the
county courthouse, along the main road from Oxford to Wye Mill, thence to
the road between Talbot and Queen Anne's Counties, on to Tuckahoe Bridge and
along Tuckahoe Creek and Choptank River to the beginning.
    Signers: Jos. Parrott, Sim(o)n Kelld, Stephen Burgess, James Benrry, John
Benny, Thos. Russum, Thos. Turner, John Chambers, Thos. Mathews, Michael
Kirby, David Kirby, Rich'd Kirby, Sam'll Morgan, Charles Morgan, Wm. ...,
Peter Russum, Wm. Frampton, Thos. Frampton, Robert Frampton, Anthony Booth,
Charles Gannon, Charles More, Joshua Clark, James Millis (M.), Sam'll
Broadaway (M.), George Dulin (M.), Isaac Dobson, Jr., Joseph Horner, Dan'l
Chapman (M.), Anthony Gregory (M.), Lambert Clayland, Isaac Dobson, Thos.
Kelld, Jacob Williams, Joh. Robins, J. Goldsborough, Samuel Dudley, Thos.
Dudley, John Kelld, John Burgess, William Robins, Edw'd Russum, George
Palmer, Lambert Sheeld, Edmond Ferill, George Boswick, Rob't Boswick.   On
verso: "By the Upper H(ouse), 11 May 1738. Read and Rejected. Signed per

Order. (John) Ross,Cl(erk) (of the) Up(per) Ho(use)." See Arch. of Md.,
XL, 153

10. (Before 1740 May 23) Petition of inhabitants of St. Peter's Parish,
Talbot County. To Gov. Samuel Ogle and the assembly. The parish is so
large that many people are almost deprived of the Gospel; the 40 (lbs. of
tobacco) per pole would make an ample living for two incumbents; the
petitioners therefore pray that an act may pass to divide the parish, said
act to go into effect upon the death of the present incumbent, Rev. Daniel
Maynadier. On verso: May 23, 1740, read and rejected by the Upper House.
Signed: J(ohn) Ross, clerk. Signers: Thomas Bozman, Thomas Bullen, Thomas
Martin, Thomas Metcalfe, John Hickson, Joseph Bell, George Prouse, Thomas
Loveday, Lambert Clayland, Edward Nedels, T. Parker, James Farrell, William
Adams, Thomas Dudley, John Keld, John Batchelder, Stephen Burgess, James
Thomas, Charles Manship, Richard Dudley, Denis Larey, Abraham Sherin, Herey
Oldfield, Olever Lee, Daniel Ward, Daniel Maynadier, John Sherwood, Samuel
Dudley, William Mullikin, Thomas Browning, Edward Oldham, Samuel Abbat, John
Jones, Isaac Dobson, Andrew Baning, David Rather, Nathaniel ..... See
Arch. of Md., XL, 478

11. (Before 1741 Jun 1) St. Luke's Parish, Queen Anne's County. Petition
of inhabitants to the Governor (Samuel Ogle) and the Assembly. Many
inhabitants are so remote from the church that they can have little
advantage from it; the petitioners therefore pray that a chapel of ease may
be built in Tully's Neck; a parishioner has given two acres for the purpose
and the petitioners have subscribed to the building; the person making the
grant, Nathaniel Scott, informs the Assembly of this fact in a signed
statement appended to the petition; the exact location of this land is
given; it is part of a tract called Partnership; the witnesses are Richard
Hynson, James Earle, James Knotts (M.).
     Signed: William Montague (M.), Richard Mason, Charles Storey, Edward
Satterfield (M.), James Earle, Baldwin Kemp, John Miller, James Knotts (M.),
John Atkonson(?), Richard Hyunson, Michaell Hussey, Henry Kemp, Solomon
Scott, Benjamin Sylvester, Fairclough Wright, Edward Godwin, Jeremiah
Jadwin, Charles Lemar, William Jumpe, Thomas Hussey, William Maradeth, Jr.,
Nathaniel Knotts, James Hamilton, John Kenderdine (M.), Solomon Hinesly
(M.), Nathaniel Scot, Jr. (M.), Laurence Copland (M.), William Countess,
Charles Bradley, Art(hur) Hold (rector), John Dempster, James Brown, Thomas
Hackett, John Collins, N(athaniel) Wright, Nicholas Sherlock, Thomas Betts,
Robert Sumpter (M.), Thomas Lee (M.), Thomas Glanden (M.), James Ailer (M.),
James Blades (M.), Arthur Emory II, Joseph Merchant (M.), John Loyd (M.),
John Young (M.), Jacob Boon, J(ames?) Boon (M.), J(ames?) Berwick (M.),
George Elliott (M.), Charles Lemar, Jr. (M.), Thomas Wheeler, William
Satterfield (M.), William Kemp, John Hutcheson, Absalo(m) Swift, Abner Roe,
John Young, Jr. (M.), Joseph West (M.), Henry Mason, William Young, John
Young, Richard Swift (M.). See Arch. of Md., XLII, 165

12. 1748 Aug 31, Sep 16. The Inhabitants of Coventry Parish, Somerset and
Worcester Counties. To Gov. Samuel Ogle and the Council. The pettitioners
have been denied the liberty of the church and the chapel of ease by Capt.
John Williams, Capt. John Dennis, Capt. Sampson Wheatly, Samuel Adams,
William Duett, Collins Adams, and William Smith, vestrymen and wardens of

the parish; they pray that they may have free acess to the Gospel at the
discretion of Rev. Nathaniel (Whitaker, rector).

Signers: Thomas Lambden, Daniel Young, John Blades, Benjamin Blades,
Joshua Atkinson, Jr., Henderson Baker, Soll(omo)n Gray, Robert Layfield,
Teague Riggen, Benjamin Sharpe, Charles Walston, Robert Lamberson, Robert
Lindow, Jacob Boston, John Henderson, Peter Reading, Joseph Schoofield,
Jonathan Sturges, James Tayler, William Bennit, Elias Lamerson, Thomas
Newton, Samuel Cooper, Dantford Townsend, Henry Landing, Thomas Walston,
Sen., John Sheldon, Joseph Vitt ---, Joshua Atki(nson, Sen.), James
Atkinso(n), Saul Townsend, Thomas Barns, Marshal Townsand, William Donoho,
Samuel Lamberson, John Seby (Selby?), Peirce Riggen, Whittington Johnson,
Absolom Foard, Stephen --- earn, Francis Ottwell, Jeremiah Smith, William
Duks, Darby Riggen, Peter Taylor, William Walston. Printed in Arch. of Md.,
XXVIII, 450-451.

13. (After 1745 Aug 28) Vestrymen, Churchwardens, and Principal
Inhabitants of Coventry Parish, Somerset County. To Gov. Thomas Bladen and
the Upper and Lower Houses of Assembly. Petition against the request of
less than one-third of the parish for permission to build another chapel of
ease; they now have a parish church, a chapel of ease, and a temporary place
of worship in their parish; most of the parishioners have not heard of the
request sent to the Assembly; the parish may be divided very soon and the
40,000 lbs. of tobacco they now pay will become a burden.

Signers: Sam'l Adams, Jam's Trehairn, Will'm Duet, Edw'd Cluff, William
Turpin, Wm. Adams, Charles Roach, Collins Adams, John Howard, Walter
Brinningum, Sam'l Long, Thom's White, Wm. Catlin, Thom's Schone, John
Teckare, Solom'n Tull, Rich'd Tull, John Pollock, Joseph Pourter, Will'm
Pourter, John White, Henry White, Jam's Porter, John Pourter, John Fleming,
Wm. Fleming, John Fleming, Jr., Rob't Mitchell, Joshua Fleming, John Cahoon,
Sam'l Cahoon, Southy Whittington, John Waters, Wm. Waters, Kirk Gunby, John
Dennis, John Waters, Jr., Robart King, Isaac Mitchell, Sam'l Handy, Sam'l
Mathews, Will'm Cassey, John Dennis, Jr., Michael Cluff, Littleton Dennis,
John White, Will'm Adams, Jr., Gedden Tilmon, Dav'd Dreadon, William
Coulbourn, Sr., Sam'l Coulbourn, Henry Potter, John Kellam, Solom'n
Coulbourn, Rob't Geddes, Solom'n Coulbourn, Jr., W'm Allin, Michal Hollond,
Michel Hollondy, Jacob Adams, Will'm Wood, George Tull, John Starling,
Nobold Tull, Henry Starling, Dav'd Bird, Jam's Gunby, Joseph Starling, John
Gunby, W'm Williams, Isaac Moore, John Wheatler, Joseph Bird, Thomas Moore,
Thos. Bird, Dav'd Adams, Stephen Moore, W'm Adams, Thos. Adams, Arm(strong)
Starling, John Williams, W'm Hodert, Ambr's Dixon, Sampson Wheatly, John
Davies, John Broughton, Jr., Thom's Madax, Will'm Braughton, Alexan'r Madux,
Bruff Braughton, John Breaston, Sam'l Coursey, Walter Bloyce, Jacob Cullin,
Jonathan Summers, Thos. Summers, Jam's Ward, George Summers, Benj'n
Langford, John Summers, David Sumers, Benj'n Summers, Rich'd Summers, Lazrus
Summers, Thos. Banston, John Tompson, Edw'd Banston, Edw'd Banston, Jr.,
Jacob Banston, Laz(ru)s Banston, Edw'd Beachamps, Thos. Beachamp, Henry
Scholdfield, Hountain (Fountain?) Beachamp, Mercy Beachamp, John Beachamp,
Benj'n Banston, Rob't Taylor, Henry Scoorfald (Scoolfald?), Jr., John
Clifton, Phillip Adams, Jr., Rob't Taylor, Jr., Stephen Horsy, Sr., Rob't
Boyer, George Weatherby, Ralph Milborn, Ralph Milborn, Jr., Hope Adams,
William Milborn, Phillip Adams, Sr., Teague Mathews, Isaac Adams, George
Adams, George Adams, Jr., Edw'd Dikes, Sam'l Mathews, W'm Mathews, W'm

Mathews, Jr., John Horsey, Thos. Evans, John Evans, Isaac Banston, Isaac
Banston, Jr., W'm Evans, Elas Taylor, Soloman McCredey, Isaac McCredy,
Nehem'h Tilmon, John Roach, Joseph Bell, Arche'd White (?), W'm White,
Step'n Handy, Sam'l White, Jam's Tull, John Zavary(?), Sam'l Ward, Sr.,
Joseph Langford, Pussy Langford, Whilly (Whitty?) Mathews, Thos. Bell, John
Perkins, Mich'l Perkins, John Mathews, Isaac Mathews, Jonath'n Mills, Ezeke.
Mathews, John Ellit, Jonath'n Tull, Edw'd Rook, John Pitcher, Chas. Riggin,
Cornea(lu)s Riggin, John Riggin, Jam's Bayne, Sr.(?), John Elis, Nath'll
Roach, Bell Madux, Alexand'r Madux, W'm Stevens, Jam's Bairn, W'm Mills,
Fran's Steuart, Jno. Beauchamp, Henry Lawrence, John Mcclea(n), David Gogin,
Edw'd Scanlon, Jno. Riggen, Jona'n Riggen, Solo. Coulbourn, Jr., W'm
Coulbourn, Benj. Coulbourn, Isaac Coulbourn, Josh'a Tull, Rich'd Hall,
Nath'l Daugherty, Rob't Kensey, Smith Horsey, Ezekiel Hall, Sam'l Handy,
Henery Miles, William Miles, Henry Miles, Jr., Chas. Hall, Dav'd McDonald,
Jos'a Hall, Step'n Tull, Rich'd Tull, Benj'n Grumble, Thos. Moor, Thos.
Walston, W'm Walston, Thomas Tull, Jr., Hen'y Landen, Absa(lom) Foord, Thos.
Sommers, Jr., Sam'l Sommers, Dan'l Dies, William Olsen, Obed(iah) Outen,
John Ellet, Jacob Cullen, Chas. Bannister, Thos. Tyler, John Tyler, George
Hopkins, John Hopkins, Dan'l Hogg, Hen'y Horseman, Will'm Paul, Jno. Evans,
Jno. Evans, Jr., Will'm Hopkins, Thos. Evans, Richard Evans, Job Parks,
Arthur Parks, Geo. Hopkins, Jr., David Tyler, John Scot, Rob't Scot, Henry
Land, Thos. Land, Rand(olp)h Land, Potter Land, Stephen Daugherty, Peter
Daugherty, Jno. Daugherty, Jr. See Arch. of Md., XLIV, 24.

Land Records of Cecil County, Book 1, folio 153

Petition of Several friends of the county ... that the meeting house by the
Rode Side att the head of a branch of Steel pone Creek may be entered or
Regystered in the County Records..." George Warner, James Barber, James
Kelly, Mathew Pope, Jno. Beck, James Coursey, Wm. Bailey, Edwd Beck. 27th
of 9th mo 1696.

Somerset County Court papers of Somerset County
1722

Petition for ferry over An... River: Tho. Humphry sen, Adam Hitch, ...
Hitch, John Hitch, Solomon Right, John More, Phillip Records, Rich.
Nicholson sen, Rich. Nicholson Junr, George Huchons, Thos Bartolles, Tho.
Byrd, Wm. Elgey, Cris Price, Rich. Acworth senr, Jos. Maclester, Rich.
Ryder, ..., James Caldwell, Thomas Gordon, John Roach sen, John Roach
Junior, Benjamin Hookes, Henry Todvine, Rob. Grian(?), James Watherlee,
James West, John ..., John Richards senr, John Richards Junr, Robert Downs,
Thomas ..., Alexr. Adams, Tho. Humphry, Moses Driskell, Jno. Handy,
Heatherley(?), Joseph Pemberton, Franis(?) Longlake(?)

Kent County Court Petitions, 1739-1742

taken from Kent County Court records, Accession # 8766, Liber J.S.

1. Petitions for licenses to operate taverns, houses of entertainment, ordinaries, convenient houses:
1739 James Wallace of Kent Co who kept a tavern in Cecil County; Thomas Davis who hast taken a Convenient House in Chester Town; Elizabeth McCurrel(?); Ebenezer Reyner - to keep a tavern; William Purnall who hath taken a house in Chester town for keeping a house of Entertainment; John Bennett for house of Entertainment
1740 To have license renewed: James Wallace; Ebenezer Reyner; Hugh Oneal(?) to keep an Ordinary; James Purnall to keep tavern in Chester Town; Samuel Massey for a lycense; Edward Jones to renew lycense
1741 Thomas Atkinson to renew lycense; John Graham residing in the place were the late James Wallace decd, kept ordinary - that he be granted a license; Samuel Massey - to renew license
1742; For licenses: (including renewals): Thomas Atkinson, Ebenezer Reyner, Daniel Bryan, John Graham, Benjamin Woodward, George Clarke, Ann Oneil, Daniel Perkins, Gideon Pearce; Mary Clark wife of George Clark of Chestertown - to renew her husband's tavern license

2. For a house for worship in Chester Town for the protestant dissenters of the Presbyterian persuasion upon a lot of land # 100 - James Wright, Thomas Williams Junr, James M'Clean, William M'Clean

3. For a main road from Joseph Gleave's plantation at the mouth of Morgans Creek to ... Bridge - Marvin Potter, James Moore, Chris Bellican, Saml. Mansfield, Robert Mansfield, Hugh Wallace, Jos. Gleaves, Nathaniel MacClanahorn, Theophilus Randall, John Hindrixon, Mary Forbush

4. That the main road passing from Chester town over the mill damm of James Harris is thought dangerous and hazardous and pray that the road be made to pass below the dam - James Harris, Robt. Dunn, Chas. Smyth, Thomas Walker, James Ringgold, Thomas Maslin, James Smithe, Jose. Nicholson

From Dorchester County Judgement Records - 1734

Petition of John Anderson - "never known to be of quarrelsome manner," endorsed by James Woolford, Tho. Howell, Tho. Woolford, Jacob Loockerman, Solomon Edmondson, William Grantham, Robert Wing, John Stewart, Geo: Griffith, Cha. Dickenson, John Brannock, John Robson, Edwd Allford, Wm Gunn, Eben White, Isaac Nicolls, Wm Trap, James Peterkin, John Stevens Jr, John Woolford, Wm Kennerly, Peter Taylor Hodson, Thos Hicks, John White, Thos Airey, Tho. Ennalls Senr, Richd Willis, J. Ennalls, Henry Tripp, Adam Muir, John Hooper, Thos Nevett, Walter Campbell.

Levy Book for Kent County - 1722

Court Session for 20 Nov - 15 Dec 1722
(Edited and re-arranged, in some cases placed in alphabetical order)

1. Payments for sitting as a Justice:
Coll. Edward Scott; Capt. St. Leger Calder(?); Mr. Lambert Wilmer; Dr. John
March; Mr. Marmaduke Tilden; Mr. Simon Wilmer; Mr. Thomas Ringgold; Mr.
Abraham Redgrave

2. Payment for attendance as pettit Jurymen (rearranged alphabetically):
Samuel Berry; John Blackiston; Thomas Boon(?); James Bowyer; Thomas Boyer;
John Brooks; John Clayton; Richard Davies; John Davis; William Dunn; John
Fannen; Robert Green; Charles Grindage; Fredrick Hanson; Vincent Hatchison;
John Huff; Nicholas Joce; Thomas Joce; John Jones; Peter Jones; Rue Jones;
Henry Knock; John Mauny(?); Robert Meek; Arthur Miller; George Murphy;
Charles Newman; Thomas Pinar; Franics Read; James Reyley; Nicholas Reyley;
Edward Rogers Junr; William Simcock; William Simpson; Charles Smith; Charles
Stewart; James Thomas; James Tibbatt; John Walls; Hopton Williams;

3. Daniel Dyer for Jane Black, board one year ... 1000
To Rachel Body son and of(?) John Ashlle(?) one half the Charges for trouble
    and disgrace and Mambrance of child ... 900
To John Young for maintaining Mary Chambers child till March Court 1721- 500
To John Beach - two Grand Jurys ... 1000
Thomas Nutt a poor man for maintentance of John Ripp to be allowed to Thomas
    Browning ... 600
John Cleaves for keeping Isabell Landers Child ...
James Watson for keeping Sarah Chaddocks a young child, 3 months ... 300
Thos. Thackston for provideing for Ann Bust a poor woman ... 120
Christopher Knight for his wife being lame and he not able to maintain her
    ... 500
To Mr. Samuel Wallis for burying Sarah White ... 200
Wm Cookson for burying Honour Haley ... 200
Jane Bleuet for Cloaths to be allowed to Coll Edw'd Scott
James Smithers for keeping Jane Harrin (Harriss?) almswoman ... 1200
Timothy Maddin a poor man ... 1200
William Hopkins a poor man ... 1200
Thomas Massey for keeping Mark Ayres an orphan child being lame ... 600
William Edwards a poor man ... 130
Nath'l Ricketts for maintaining Rowland Pew a poor man ... 1200
Edward Hoskins a poor blind man ... 1200
John Pickett a poor man ...
Daniel Flinn for keeping John Dunnahaws lame son ...
William Trew for maintaining Francis Hall a poor man
Dr. Thomas Williams for means administered to John Wrin a poor man as (per)
    account ... 200
Mr. Simon Wilmer - takeing care of and burying the same ... 150
Eliz'a Meeks a poor woman ... 500
William Balladine a poor man ... 500
To John Young on acco't of William Wran(?) for maintaining his child had by
    Mary Chambers ... 500

55

4. Bounty for killing squirrels and crows (re-arranged alphabetically):
Aron Alford; Isaac Ashly; John Ashly; Arthur Barker; Francis Barney; Joseph
Basengay; Edward Beck Junr; Christopher Bellikin; Edward Berke Senr; John
Blackiston; Predux Blackiston; Benj'a Blackledge; Augustin Boyer; William
Brewar; John Brisco; John Brown; John Brown, Easter(n) Neck; Joseph Butler;
Benjamin Butler, assigned to Mr. Gideon Pearce; Dennis Carter; Thomas
Christian; John Clark; John Clayton; John Clove; John Cloves; Peter Cole;
William Comegs; James Course; Richard Crouch; Wedge Crouch; Edward Crow;
William Crow; Henry Davis; Phillip Davis; Richard Dawson; Matthias Day;
George Debruler; William Dicas; William Dunn; Robert Dunn Junr; Benj'a Eley;
William Emory (4 wolves heads); Daniel Ferrill; Daniel Flinn; Francis Lamb;
Capt. William Frisby; Charles Gafford; Robert George senr; George Gleaves;
Samuel Goodin; John Green; John Greenwood; John Greenwood Junr; Charles
Griffith; George Griffith; Michael Hackett; Vincent Hatchison; Thomas
Hebron; John Hendrickson; Oliver Hickenbottom; Robert Hodges; John Huff;
Emanuel Hurst; Thomas Hynson; Nicholas Joce; Griffin Jones; Peter Jones;
Thomas Jones; Benj'a Kelly; Nath'l Kennard; Henry Knock; George Lanagar;
Samuel Larrance; Josia Lenham; Francis Lewis; Daniel Mackonakin; Thomas
Mahon; Dr. John March; Nicholas Massey; Thomas Massey; Arthur Miller;
Michael Miller; William Moor; William Morris; James Murphy; Roger Murphy;
John Myers; Stephen Myers; Charles Newman; James Noreman; Samuel Norris;
John Oliver; Daniel Pearce; Gideon Pearce; Isaac Perkins Junr; Thomas Pinar;
Andrew Price; Richard Price; John Pryor; Robert Randall; Thomas Rasin;
Joseph Read; James Reyley; Nicholas Reyley; Benjamin Riccar(?); Nathaniel
Ricketts; Phillip Ricketts; Elias Ringgold; Thomas Ringgold; William
Ringgold; John Rollison; Glanvill Ross(?); Joseph Rye; Richard Scagg; Edward
Scott Junr; Edward Skidmore Junr; Mrs. Mary Smithers; Phillip Spearman;
Jarvis Spencer; Thomas Thackston; Capt. Samuel Thomas; William Thornton;
William Treszar, assigned to Thomas Jerom; John Trew; John Turner; John
Twigue; Samuel Wallis; John Walthom; Peter Watkins; John Webb; George
Wetherly; Daniel Whaley; Owen Whaley; Samuel Wicks; John Wilson; John Wilson
Junr, Sassaffr'a; John Wilson Senr, Sassafras; John Wilson, Taylor; Humphry
Younger

5. Other payments:
To Mr. Michall Howard Clk of In... (Instruments?) Criminal Servt fees ...
    1500
To Mr. Augustine Thomson for Cedar towards building a bridge over the head
    of Chester ... 500
To William Ringgold Coron'r (per) acco't ... 500
Coll. Richard Tilghman, Chancellors fees as (per) acco't ... 2000
James Smith, criminal (court) serv'ts fees as (per) acco't ... 2067
Francis Hill, Cryor Crimminal Court serv'ts fees as (per) acco't ... 415
Coll Nath'l Hynson 7 Leveys over charged last year at Andrew Hamptons that
    the forty (per?) pole is not allowed by the minister. James Smith
    promises to refund the same next year. ... 846
Benj'a Griffith one Levey overcharged last year ... 120
Dr. James Cruckshanks, Do ... 120
James Smith for Cleaning the Court House ... 300
Gabriel Johnson for building a bridge over the Cyprus Branch - 50000 & 500
    towards timber cedar ... 5500

Levy Book for Kent County - 1722

Total (paid) 59933

6. Debts due to the County - the Sheriff is to Collect the Ensueing year vizt

Peter Green for Elizabeth Lock which the County paid and was not delivered up when free ... - 729

Mr. John Austin and ... administratrix of William Smith for Cathrin Poor as afd - 261

George Gleaves and John Johnson mercht for Mary Batemens fined 3 pounds

John West fined 100 lbs tobacco for not keeping Clear the roads half thereof to the County - 50

John Massay as afd - 50

John Jones (Sasfras) as afd - 50

Jones Jones Irish as afd - 50

Mr. James Wilson for Magraret Oagle which the County paid and was not delivered up when free - 360

Thomas Garnett for Patrick Macneal as afd - 275

Thomas Ayres for Sarah Sellwood as afd - 534

Nicholas Barefoot for Rachel Body as afd - 840

Mr. Wm Ringgold for Ann Sanders as afd - 376

Samuel Berry for Eliz'a Goodman as afd - 334

Thomas Cook for Mary Neal - 273

Mr. John Johnson admr of Mr. Thomas Bown for Mary Bryan as afd - 186

John Gale for Stopping the high way fined 500 lbs of tobacco half thereof to the County - 250

Mr. Gideon Pearce for Cash paid by Henry Davis for being Drunk - 5 pounds

Dr for Cash paid by John Huff for Do - 5 pounds

John Roffs bail and to County for Sarah Hopwood 1400

Mr. Williams Haggathy for 11 oaths 360

Thomas Massey for Elizabeth Hinsons Molatto Child Sold to him - 600

Court held 19 Nov to 23 Nov 1723

7. Names of Pettit Jury men (whose names do not appear above):
Abraham Ambrose; Maurice Cartey; William Dean; Laughlan Fflinn; Arthur Fforeman; Roger Hales; Richard Kennard; Thomas Kinard; Josiah Lanham; Francis Meeks; William Smithers; John Taylor; Henry Trulock; John Twigg; John Wallis; John Woodall

8. Those receiving bounty for squirrels and crows, (whose names do not appear above):
William Apsley; Martha Áskins; Joseph Barney; Christopher Bateman Junr; Caleb Beck; Edward Beck; Joshua Beck; Matthew Beck; Vivian Beck; Christop Bellican; Benjamin Blackston; John Blackston; Francis Bodeen; John Body; Thomas Booth; Austin Boyer; James Boyer; William Boyer Junr; William Boyer Senr; William Bradshaw; Alex'r Briscoe; Marg't Brooks; John Brown Mercht; William Brusard; John Carvill; John Cole; Thomas Cole; William Comegys Jnr; William Comegys Senr; Jeremiah Covinton; Edward Cozens; George Davis; John Wilson Enock; Henry Evans; Daniel Farmer; Gilbert Ffalconar; Arthur Fforeman; John Cooper Forrest'r(?); Isaac Freeman; John Gale; Robert George; Samuel Gooding; Bowles Green; John Green Senr; George Griffin; Joseph Hall; William Hall; John Haly; Hense Hanson; William Haults; Oliver Higgenbottom;

Roger Hix; Edward Holliday; Henry Hosser; John Hurt; Morgan Hurt; Thomas
Hynson, E'r Neck; John Ingram; John Johnson Attry; John Johnson, Attorney;
John Jones (M. Creeck?); Nicholas Jose; James Kear; Richard Kennard;
Ffrancis Kinsay; Josiah Lanham; Francis Lewis at hirce?; Geo. Lineger; John
Macnemara; William Massey; Luckenor Midleton Senr; John Moore; Robert
Murray; John Nanswyn; Maurice Nodike; Ralph Page; Benjamin Palmer; Richard
Peacock; Isaac Perkins; William Powell; Andrew Price; Abraham Redgrave Senr;
James Reily; John Ridson; James Robertson; Edward Rogers Junr; John Rolph;
John Sapp; Wm. Sapp; William Savory; Edward Scott Junr; Richard Sewell;
William Shield; William Slipper; James Smith (Langfords ...); James Smith up
Chester; John Smithers; William Smithers; Thomas Strong; Ashbury Sutton;
Jno. Taylor(Cyprus); John Tharp; Ffrancis Thomas; Ffrancis Thomas (miller);
Andrew Tolson; John Twigg; George Warner; Joseph Warner; John Warren; John
West; George Wetherly; Samuel Wickes; George Wilson; John Wilson assigned by
Josiah Crouch; John Wilson Senr (Sass); John Wilson Junr Do place; William
Woodland; Joseph Young assigned by Josiah Crouch

9. Other payments:
Mr. Laughlan Fflin for keeping a fferry at old Town - 3000
Thomas Browning for maintenance of Jno Ripp by Order of the court - 1200
Mr. William Ffrisby for Claudius Rogers - 221
Claudius Rogers a poor man - 1200
To Jane Bluets board one year - 1000
Mr. John Earle for makeing Shelves for the Records and a Writing table and
    Benches in the Court House - 2000
Benj'a Griffin - 24
Daniel Whaley for maintaining & burying Thomas Nuts - 500
To Do for Supply of his mother in Law Nutts (Nulls?) - 500
To Coll Edward Scott for Cloathing Jane Bluett - 900
George Wethersly do - 20
To Mr. Gid'n Pearce for John Peter Zenger for the Body of Laws 1721 which
    was ordered to Thomas Wilkins but if the Court Should be oblidged to pay
    the same again then to be reimbursed - 500
To William Ketch for maintaining and burying James Connaway - 600
To James Wyatt for Cloathing Elinor Broke the Ensueing Year - 600
William Baluntine a poor blind man - 1000
William Hopkins a poor man - 130
William Edwards a poor man - 500
To Mary Roberts a poor woman - 600
Zacharias Brown a poor man - 130
William Brockett a poor man - 600
To Mr. James Smith for takeing care of Catharin Poor in her sickness and
    burying her - 200
Eliz'a Meeks a poor old woman - 500
William Trew for maintaining Ffrancis Hall - 1200
To Dan'l Fflin for keeping and burrying John Dunnahaws Son - 1000
John Pickett a poor man - 600
Edward Hoskins a poor blind man - 1200
To Nathan'l Ricketts for maintaining Rowland Pew - 1200
Thomas Merey for maintaining Jane Harim (Harrin) a lame woman - 1200
Christopher Knight for his wife being lame - 500
Mr. James Smith Clk for Crimin'l fees as per accot - 813

Levy Book for Kent County - 1722

Mich'l Howard Esqr. Clk of Indictments Do - 500
Ffrancis Hill Cryor Do - 270
John Wilson in full of his act agt Claudius Rogers a poor man - 500
To Mr. James Smith Clk for a large Record Book - 500
To Mr. Ffred'k Hanson Sher Crimin'l fees as per accot - 1045
To Mr. James Smith Clk for Special Services - 500
To Ffrancis Collins for maintaining Ann Connar's Child the Balt'r(?) - 200
Thomas Macknemara for keeping Thomas Usher a poor man 145 months - 1400

Talbot County Levy Court - 1724

Talbot County Judgements , PF No. 4, Accession # 9098-3

1. For petit jurymen: William Aires; Ffrancis Armstrong; Richard Barrow;
Perry Benson; William Brown; Richard Chance; Samuel Cockayne; Cornelius
Davis; David Davis; William Elbert; Wm. Ferrell; John Gaskin; Richard
Harrinton; John Harrison; Wm. Harrison, Miles Creek; William Holmes; James
Hopkins; Thomas Hopkins; James Horney; Jeffery Horney; Edmund Marsh; Edward
Needles; John Peck; John Price, Dover; John Robson; Gabriel Sailes; George
Sailes; William Shield; Thomas Spry Junr; Wm. White Bullingbrook.

2. (Costs of the court)
John Bradshaw for criminal servants fees as per acct
Phillip Ffeddeman for criminal servts fees, for cleaning the court house and
for making up the Leavy
Robert Goldsborough esqr, Robert Hugh, esqr, Mr. John Bullen, Mr. Daniel
Sherwood, Thomas Bozman, as Justices
Mr. William Clayton, Mr. William Skinner, Mr. Nicholas Goldsborough for
attendance in the County Courts
Edward Elliott sheriff for fees
John Sherwood Coroner
Michael Howard for criminall servts fees
George Shannahane for Grand Jurys allowance
Coll. Richard Tilghman Chancellor; Joshua George prosecutor assigned against
Danll Coyne servt to Geo. Cooper (and) Richard Dorman(?) servant to Wm
Furner

3. Ffrancis Ffaulkner, Geo. Robins by assignment of John Briun(?) for
squirrels heads omitted last year; John Ffanning a poor man; Thomas
Alexander, Judith Valliant for keeping ferry over Third haven; Henry Bullen
for ditto over Choptank; Richard Bruff for ditto over Saint Michaels River;
Doctor John Bullen for keeping James Fferrell as usuall; Daniel Boyer for
keeping the orphan of Israel Moore 5 months
Henry Bayley for keeping a bastard child of Alce Case
Henry Bayley for building a new bridge over Peach Blossom
Francis Pickering for keeping Ffrancis Dickman seven monthns
For cloaths for the sd Dickman to be laid out to the best advantage
Thomas Gould a poor man; Jane Duhurst a poor woman; Wm. Clayland for grand
Jurys
Tamerlin Davis for building Carters Bridge
Thomas Ashcroft for keeping a bastard child of Eliza. Lasley 5 months

59

Talbot County Levy Court - 1724

Thomas Ashcroft for keeping Eliza. Stoker a poor woman as usuall
For squirrel heads: William Elston; Isaac Molin
John Kinneran an old man, to buy him cloaths
Mary Lord orphan of James Lord to buy her cloaths
Roger Hunter for keeping Jno. Booth
Wm. Clayton for an old negro Tax this year

4. Wm Cole Constable of Island Hundred, Loftus Bowdle constable of Third
Haven hundred, William White, constable of Bullingbrook hundred, James
Colson constable of Mill Hundred: for suppressing the frequent meeting of
negroes according to act of Assembly

5. Fines
Wm. Ratcliff for Jane Hattersons a fine; Mary Stevens a fine; John Barwick a
fine; Robt. Sand a fine; Mary Thornton a fine; Thos. Perkins a fine; Anne
Holt a fine; John Marr a fine; Jno. Bodfield for Ann Staffords fine
John Ffeaston for swearing 2 oaths
John Peck for being drunk
Stephen Esgate for being drunk and swearing 2 oaths and one curse
Darby Derragin 2 oaths at one time and two at another
David Jones one oath
Wm. Harris Irish Creek one oath
Arthur Connar 7 oaths
Alexander Ray 3 oaths
John Bradshaw one oath
Thomas Maid 5 oaths
Edwd Raly 3 oaths & one curse
Margrett Lowder 5 oaths
Alce Thompson wife of Daniel Thompson 25 oaths & curses
Eliza. Shaw now wife of Christ'r. Moore for 6 oaths & curses
Edwd Elliott - fined
One oath from David Mathes paid by Jno. Sherwood to Sher.
By the Sheriff for Tobacco per last year for Mathew Skillett

Levy List of Somerset County - 1724
Held by State Archives, Accession # 20398-1

By Ephraim Willson for C. McDonnald - 320
Larzarus Maddux for Ann Woods - 600
Merrick Ellis for Mar'tt. Jervice - 1000
Thomas Holbrook for Mary Ash - 1031
Thomsa Holbrook for Geo. Godman - 600
Isabealla Bryan for Cols. hous(?) Laird(?) - 300
John Bartlett for Jane Dashell(?) - 600
John Ricketts for Mary Roberts - 337
Patrick Mellaley for not doing his duty on the road - 100
John Hurst for ditto - 100
Wm Jones Senr. for ditto - 100
John Medcalfe for Breach of Sabboth - 100
Wm Eskridge for one oath when Constable - 120
Wm Miles for several oaths - 390

Levy List of Somerset County - 1724

Benjamin Esome(?) for 3 oaths - 150
Roger Nicholson Junr for 3 oaths - 150
Richard Tiler 1 oath - 30
Solomon Yearly against(?) Turpin oaths, Jeremiah Wright security, 300
Thomas Hugg 11 oaths - 600
Henry Spear 4 oaths - 218
John Willson 5 oaths - 270
Jeffery Long for Catherine Ryne - 75
Merrick Ellis for Ann Shiles for fornication - 600

November Court Minutes and Papers of 1724 Recorded by Thomas Hayward, Clerk.

Levy List of Somerset County - 1725
Accession # 20398-2

Payments made to (payee rearranged in alphabetical order): John Adkenson; William Ainsworth an object (of charity?); Henry Ballard for inquisitions; George Benson; Peter Benton; William Booth; Isaac Boston for Elizabeth Boston an object of charity; Thomas Brown of burrying Comfort Newman; William Burton; Charles Calvart to be disposed of by order Capt Planner; Merrick Ellis for a drum head Cesiah Mackew (Mathew?); George Clifton; Daniel Cordery for Pocomoke ferry; Stephen Costin; Richard Crockett for ferry over Wickamico; George Dashiel; Samuel Davis for a wolf's head; William Davis, Seaside, for keeping his sister, Elizabeth ...; John Dennis Junr; William Denston a poor man; Daniel Derrum; Lewis Disharoon for interpretting of Indians; Mathew Dorman; Samuel Dorman for Sarah Brown; Elianor Elliot an object of charity; Col Arnold Elzey for cloathing Elizabeth Jervis; Capt Levin Gale; Robert Gant; William Groom for keeping ferry over Indian River; Ebenezer Handy 1 tax his servant being a runaway; William Handy for repairing the stocks; Thomas Harney; John Harper; Thomas Hayward; Abraham Heath; Thomas Hill; Nat Hopkins Senr; Revell Horsey; George Hutchins for ferry over Wickamico; Abraham Ingram; John Johnson; Peter Johnson for Adria Davis; Martin Kennett; William Kennett Junr; Marg't Leach; Joseph Lewis; William Samuel Long; William Macleny (Mackeny?) for Pocomoke Bridge; Mary Martin for taxes overcharged her husband by Mr. Adams; William Merchamant, Cryer; Robert Mitchell for Elizabeth Kelly; John Murray for keeping Isaac Jackson; Wm. Painter for an object of charity; John Parker for Pocomoke Bridge; Isaac Piper; Maj. Planner taking care of William Newman; William Pointer; Wm. Richardson for his negro woman; John Scarborough for keeping Carebra Webb; John Scarbrough for his negro being tax free; Robert Scott; Samuel Tayler Senr; George Taylor; Ester Taylor an object (of charity?); Ralph Tilman; Charles Townsend for keeping Elizabeth Willis; George Tull; Elizabeth Walers

Payment to jurymen (rearranged in alphabetical order)
Thomas Adams; Samuel Alexander; Edward Beachamp; Lewis Beard; George Benston; John Bivans; James Boucher; William Bratton; Thomas Brereton; James Caldwell; John Caldwell; Alexander Carlyle; Richard Chambers; Thomas Collier; Thomas Collins; Daniel Cordery; Charles Cottingham; John Dennis Junr; John Dennis Senr; Col(?) John Donelson; Merrick Ellio; Moses Ffenton; John Ffleming; Peter Ffrazer; John Fleming; Robert Givan; Thomas Gordan;

61

Ebenezer Handy; William Handy; Robert Harris; James Harris; Edmond Hough; Joseph Houston; Capell King; William Lane; Ffrancis Lanke; James Lindow; Robert Martin; Capt Joseph McClester; Robert Miles; William Miles; Robert Mills; Robert Mitchell; James Mumford; Thomas Peale; Joseph Pemberton; Isaac Piper; Christopher Piper; William Piper; William Pointer; John Pope; Charles Rackliffe; Underwood Rencher; Randall Revell; Edward Rownd; James Rownd; John Scarborough; Capt John Scott; George Scott; Robert Scott; William Selby; Philip Selby; Henry Sisfeild; Adam Spence Senr; William Story; James Strawbridge; John Sutton; Giddion Tilman; Charles Townsend; John Townsend Senr; John Tull; William Turpin; Joseph Venables; Joseph Wailes; Thomas Walker; John Walters; William Walton; John White, Marumsco; Southy Whittington; Thomas Williams, Annamessex; Cannon Winright

Fines

Catn(?) Dyall for swearing 5 oaths; Joseph McClester; George Bounds breach of Sabboth; Tobias Burk one oath; Capt Joseph McClester for William Robertson; Thomas Dashiell for Bridgett Lowder; Michael Holland for Mary Bolitha's taxes; Thomas Pointer and William Pointer for Ffrancis Pointer - fine for fornication; William Mathews for Jno. Taylor; Capt James Lindow for Ann Bartons child; Samuel Tayler for taxes not returned; Robert Mitchell for a mulatto; Thomas Collier for Jane Nutt; William Adams for Elianor Collins; William Robertson; Thomas Dashiell for Bridgett Lowder; John Hayward for fornication; William Hudson for fornication; Elie Gray; Mary Pardue for fornication; William Chamberlaine for fornication; Michael Holland Junr for Mary Bolithe; William Langford for fornication; Honor Norgate for fornication; Capt James Landow for Ann Bartons child being a mulatto; Jacob Hall for fornication; Ffrancis Watson for fornication.

Queen Anne's Court 1728 - 1729
Queen Anne's County Court held 26 Nov 1728 at Queens Town/Levy List

Present: Mr. James Earle senior; Mr. Wm Turbutt, Mr. Augustine Thompson, Mr. Arthur Emory, Mr. Solomon Clayton, Mr. Andrew Price, Mr. John Carter, Mr. Thos. Hynson Wright and Mr. Humphery Wells (Justices of this court)

Payments to petit jurors and others for attendance at court:
Christopher Birch; Richard Blunt; James Brown; Thos. Burk; Wm. Campbell; Richard Carter; John Chaires; Thomas Chaires; Nath'll Cleave; John Cobreath; Edwd. Cockey; James Countis; Wm. Coursey; Thomas Davis; John Earle Denny; John Downes; John Emory; Arthur Emory jun; Richard Fisher; Thomas Fisher; Marmaduke Goodhand; H'm(?) Granger; John(?) Hamer; Jno. Hamond; Thos. Hamond; Robert Jerman; Rich'd Keys; John Lain; John Lane; Walton Neville; Charles Oneal; Wm. Osburk; Charles Price; William Ratcliffe; Thos. Redford; ... Roe (of Tuckahoe); John Salisbury; Thomas Silvester; Thomas Tannard; Edmund Thomas; Trustram Thomas; Trustram Thomas Junr; Charles Vanderford; Robert Walters; Robt. Walton; Joseph Weeks; Peter Wild; Thomas Wilkinson; William Wrench; John Wright; Robert Norrest Wright; Solomon Wright; Solomon Wright senr

John Higginson for keeping Ferry at the Wadeing Place of Kent Island the year last past ... 5000

To Mr. James Calder per assignment of Thos. Willmore for part of one allowance for keeping Ferry over Chester River opposite to Newtown the year last past 955

To Thos. Willmore (part) for keeping ferry over Chester River opposite to New Town(?) the year last past 845

...Knight for keeping a poor old woman named ...Eackelsmith the year last past & burying her 550

To Mary Allchurch a poor old woman

To Sarah Robertson a poor old woman

To Will'm Shorter a poor old man

To John Clemons for keeping Wm. Burk a poor man

To George Hutchison a poor old man

To Doctr Walton Carmichall for visits to and Phisick administered to Jane Leath a poor old woman

To John Clemons for keeping Jno. Bolt the year past and clothing him

To Elizabeth Wilkinson a poor old woman

To Doctr Jno. Brown for endeavoring to cure a poor orphan Girl named Mary Carman of a sore legg

To Wm. Mason for keeping a certain John Clossy(?) and burying him

Rose Mahone a poor old woman

Jno. Downes for the maintainance of Elizabeth Lloyd a poor old woman

John Hawkins Hambleton for keeping orphan child named Charles Newnam six months

Simon Davis who Lately married Katherine Wright widow the year last past for his & her maintainance of a certain Jane Leith a poor decriped woman the year last past

For wolf heads: Daniel Boulton and Edward Skinner for one each; Wm. Matthews 8, James Knotts 4

Carpender Earle for one grand jury in Sep 1728

Francis Barnes for two grand jury allowances

Jos. Higginson for making ditch or drayn...the wading place marshes from a pond adjoyning to the third Causeway on this side the said Wadeing Place

Francis Barnes for keeping and maintaining Wm. Burk a poor lunatick man 8 days

Andrew Prewit for maintaining the ...?

Carpenter Earle for cleaning and sweeeping the Court house

Edward Tobin, overcharged last year

Francis Barnes one grand jury

Thomas Silvester for repairing Tuckahoe Bridge

Daniel M. Camley for maintainance of Sarah Sweet a poor Object of Charity

William Turbutt for maintaining a poor woman

Bedingfield Hands the remaining part of tobacco due from this County to said Hands for purchasing ... 7668 tobacco and also 673 tobacco for shipping charges on the said ...

Ann Lodge a poor woman

Rich'd Tilghmam clk of this co for criminal servants fees

Wm. Price for repairs done to the Prison of this county

Carpenter Earle Cryer of this court

John Reading for bleeding of Wm. Burk

Doctr Walter Carmichall for administring medicines to Michael Aley a poor Prisoner

Edward Wright for insolvent taxables

Queen Anne's Court 1728 - 1729

Philemon Lloyd Esqr. for criminall servants fees and ...
Edward Wright for one whole election of delegates
Edward Wright for imprisonment fees of Wm. Burk a poor distracted man
Edward Wright Sheriff of this county for criminal servants fees
John Emory for cleaning the arms of this county
Robert Jones, Coroner for three inquisitions on the bodys of James Goulding a salor of Capt. Samuel Becks, a person unknown, and a negro of Esq. Lloyds
To ditto for an inquisition on the body of Samuel Dyre
To ditto for ditto on the body of Child of Wm. Scandrett

Service in preventing the tumultious meetings and other irregularitys of negroes in this county: James Brown, then constable of Town hundred; Matthew Eareckson, in the lower hundred of Kent Island the year last past he being constable of said Hundred; John Collins constable of Island Hundred; Thomas Curtis Constable for Wye Hundred; George Jackson Constable of Worrell Hundred; James Evens constable of the upper Hundred of Kent Island; John Andrews constable of Town Hundred

Credits to inhabitants of Queen Anns County: in the hands of Edward Wright sheriff .... (various sources of revenue, including following), By Elizabeth Beech her fine for fornication 600

The 1729 Court (4th Tuesday in Nov)

Payments for counting tobacco plants made to:
John Baggs; Robert Blunt; Edward Brown; Rich'd Brown; Rd. Carter; Rd. Carter; Thomas Chaires; Hercules Cook; Wm. Crupper; George Cummberford; Thomas Curtis; Simon Davis; Thomas Davis; Wm. Dawson; John Emory junr; William Gough; John Hamer; Peter Hinesly; Wm. Hopper; Michael Howard; George Jackson; Joseph Jackson; John Johnson; Jonathan Jolly; Thomas Jump; Simon Knox; Wm. Meredith; Walter Nevill; Walter Nevill; James Ponder; Charles Price; William Scandret; Francis Spry; Wm. Starky; Joseph Sudler; Christopher Tillotson; John Tillotson; Alexander Toalson; John Walton; Robert Walton; Joseph Weeks; John Wells; John Wells; Robert Wharton; Edward Williams; James Williams; John Wright; Edward Wright junr

Bounty paid for wolves heads to: John Keys, Solomon Wright by assignment of Thos. Falkner for part allowance for seven wolves heads, Thomas Falkner for remaining part.

Bounty paid for squirrel heads to (re-arranged alphabetically):
Edward Adolly; Henry Ailer; George Aires; John Ally senr; Richard Arrington; Sarah Ausiter; William Austin; John Auston; John Baggs; Jacob Baily; Wm. Bannen; John Barker; James Barkhust; John Barmingham; James Barwick; John Bath; Susanna Baynard; Thomas Baynard; James Bell; Wm. Bell; Richard Bennett, Esq.; William Bennett; David Berry; James Berry; William Bird; William Bishop; James Blades; John Sayer Blake; Phillch'r (Philadelphia?) Blake; Richard Blunt; Samuel Blunt; John Bolton; Wm. Boon; Thomas Bostick junr; Daniel Boulton; James Bowers; Charles Bradly jun.; Phillip Brady; Francis Bright; Andrew Brown; Edward Brown; James Brown; Matthew Brown; John

64

Bryant; William Bryley; Richard Buckley; Thomas Bullen; Thomas Burck; William Burroughs; William Burroughs junr; John Bushnall; Joseph Butler; Edmund Cahall; William Campbell; Robert Camper; John Camperson; John Carradine; Andrew Carrow; Hercules Carter; John Carter; Richard Carter; Stephen Cats; James Chaires; Joseph Chaires; Matthew Chelton; Edward Chetham; John Clayland; Benjamin Cleave; Nathaniel Cleaves; John Clemons; Joseph Clift; Maurice Cloak; Benjamin Clouds; John Cobreath; Edward Cocky; Thomas Coleman; Richard Collins; John Collins junr; Nathaniel Comegys; Charles Connor; John Cooper junr; William Cooper; Henry Costin; Richard Costin; Henry Councill; James Countis; Henry Coursey; John Coursey; William Coursey; Henry Covington; James Cross; Robert Crump; William Crupper; Nicholas Cummings; John Curtis; Katherine Davis; William Dawson; Lewis Deford; Thomas Delanaway; John Dempster; Joseph Deroachbrune; Lewis Deroachbrune; Thomas Deverix; Thomas Dods; James Dolton; Charles Downes; John Downes; William Driskill; William Eagle; James Earle junr; James Earle sen; John Earle; Joseph Earle; Doctr. W. Edwards; George Edwards; John Ellickson; George Elliot senr; John Elliot; Joseph Elliot; William Elliot; Roger Elstone; John Emory junr; John Emory senr; James Evans; Thomas Everitt; John Evins; Francis Falconar; John Falconar; Thomas Falkner; William Farmar; John Farrowfield; Phill Fedeman; William Fenton; Andrew Finley; David Fitzpatrick; John Fitzpatrick; Robert Floyd; John Forcum; Peter Forcum; William Ford; Francis Foreman; Andrew Foster; Thomas Frye; Thomas Gale; John Gibs; William Gilgo; Thomas Glandin; Thomas Godman; Thomas Godwin; William Godwin; Marmaduke Goodhand; James Gould; Robert Gouldesborough; John Granger; John Green; Henry Green junr; Jonathan Greenwood; Matthew Grieves; John Hackett; Thomas Hackett; Thomas Hadley; John Hall; William Hamor; John Hamour; Thomas Hampton; William Harbert junr; John Harris; Coll. Ernault Hawkins; John Hays; William Hemsley; Florence Hendrickson; James Hines; Nathaniel Hinesly; Peter Hinesly; James Hollday; John Hollingsworth; Thomas Hollingsworth; George Hollyday; Thomas Honey; William Hopper; Joseph Howell; Michael Hussey; Archibald Jackson; George Jackson; Mary Jackson; Bartholomew Jennings; Robert Jerman; Thomas Johnings; Henry Johnson; Peter Johnson; Henry Jones; Henry Jones; Richard Jones; James Jordan; William Jump Junr; Thomas Jump senr; William Jump senr; Bolen Kemp; Richard Kemp; James Kensey; Richard Kerron; John Keys; Richard Keys; Africa Kirkham; James Knotts; Nathaniel Knotts; James Lane; John Lane; Timothy Lane; Thomas Langley; John Larwood; John Layton; Richard Leach; William Lee; John Legg; Charles Lemar; John Leonard; James Linch; John Loyd; John Madden; Robert Mahern; William Mansfield; James Manson; Joseph Mason; Matthew Mason; Richard Mason; Jac.(?) Massy; Edward Mayner; Timothy Mayner; John Meconnickin; William Mecors; John Meeds; Thomas Meeds; William Meeds; Sophia Meredith; William Meredith; Isaac Merrick; John Merriday; James Millis; David Mills; John More; Jeremiah Morse; William Mountecue; John Mumford; Thomas Needles; Thomas Nelson; John Nevill; Walter Nevill; Daniel Newnam senr; John Nicholson; Thomas Nuton; Patrick Obryan; Robert Offley; Charles Oneal; William Osburn; William Owens; William Parker; James Parnes; Thomas Parsons; John Pedry; Robert Phillips; Richard Phillips junr; Richard Phillips senr; William Pinder; James Ponder; Henry Poor; Jeremiah Poor; Mark Anthony Pouch; Thomas Powel; Thomas Powel (double Creek); James Powell; Elizabeth Prat; Andrew Price; Charles Price; Henry Price; Thomas Price; George Primrose; William Primrose; Edmund Pryor; William Purnall; Judith Raymond; Stephen Rich; Benjamin Riddle; Benja. Ridger; James Ringgold; John

Johnson Ripley; James Roberts; Franc. Rochester; Edward Roe; John Roe; John Roe; Thomas Roe; Richard Rogers; John Rowles; John Russum; Mable Ruth; Thomas Ruth; Thomas Ruth senr; Edward Satterfield; Andrew Saunders; John Saunders; John Saunders; William Scandret; John Scott; Nathaniel Scott; James Scotton; John Scotton; Richard Scotton; Richard Scrivener; Thomas Seaward; Patrick Senton (Sexton?); Charles Seth; John Seymour; Maurice Shehane; William Shepherd; William Sheppard; Nicholas Sherlock; Thomas Shoebrooks; James Silvester; Thomas Silvester; Lawrence Sinclar; Edward Skinner; James Slaney; Maurice Slaney; Robert Small; Casparus Smith; George Smith; John Smith junr; John Soans; Joseph Sparkes; Joseph Sparkes; William Sparkes senr; John Sparks senr; Francis Spry; William Starky; Thomas Stevens; James Sudler; Joseph Sudler; William Summers junr; Thomas Swan; Stephen Sweatman, John Swift; William Swift; John Tayler; John Taylor hardiner; Gilbert Teat; Edmund Thomas; Thomas Thomas; Trustram Thomas; Trustram Thomas junr; Augustine Thompson; John Thompson; John Tillotson; Alexander Toalson; Thomas Towers; James Townson; Walter Toy; Joseph Tryall; Charles Vanderford; George Vanderford; William Vanderford; Wm. Vickers; Godfry Viney; Daniel Walker; William Walker; John Walton; Robert Walton; John Ward; Elizabeth Watson; Francis Watson; William Watson; Timothy Webb; Joseph Weeks; Humphry Wells; John Wells; Richard Wells; Robert Wharton; John Wheatly; William Whidbe; John Wicks; John Wiggins; Peter Wild; Henry Wilkinson; Thomas Wilkinson; Henry Willcox; Edward Williams; Matthew Williams; James Willson; John Willson; Mary Willson; Robert Willson; John Winchester; Ephraim Winn; John Woodall junr; Phillip Wooters; Richard Wooters; William Wrench; Ambrose Wright; John Wright; Robert Norrest Wright; Solomon Wright; Thomas Hynson Wright; Edward Wright junr; Nathaniel Wright junr; John Wright of Kent Island; Edw. Wright senr; Ruth Wyat; Solomon Yewell; Edward Young

For care and servide in suppressing the tumultious meetings and other irregularities of the negroes in this county: Matthew Erreckson,, Constable of the lower hundred of Kent Island; John Brown, constable of Worell Hundred; James Bell, constable of Wye hundred; Jno. Carpenter, constable for Town hundred; Jno. Roberts Constable of the upper hundred of Kent Island; Rd. Keys, constable of Island Hundred.

Robt. Jones for grand Jury duty
Wm. Parks for printing the laws made October Assembly 1728 and the law made July Assembly 1729
Accidentall allowances:
Francis Bright for keeping a young child of Eleanor Moors ten months
Matthias Drura for keeping Wm. Burk a poor distracted man one month
Martha Kelly a poor woman
John Brown for going on a message to Mr. James Earle's for the Justices of this court - 50
John Higginson for keeping the Ferry over the wading Place of Kent Island, and the Causeway over the Marsh as on this side next to Queens Town in repair
Christopher Birch for keeping and maintaining a poor old man named John Bolt
Wm. Langley for keeping the ferry over to Newtown
Wm. Carman for keeping the ferry over Chester River to Old Town

Joseph Chaires for keeping in her sickness and burying a poor woman named Eliza. Whiley

Doctr. Wm. Edwards for administering medicines to and burying Ann Jewel a poor woman

Matthias Drura per assignment of Wm. Burk a poor man ordered to be allowed in this present levy the sum of 300

Mary Allchurch a poor woman

Mark Hargadine for keeping in his sickness and burying a certain Robt. Hutch

Mrs. Catharine Davis for keeping and maintaining Jane Leith a poor old woman

John Downes for keeping and maintaining Eliza. Lloyd a poor woman

James Hobbs for keeping and maintaining a poor child, a mere Idiot

Solomon Clayton for his wife her keeping and maintaining a certain Ann Merchant & child ten weeks past

John Taylor of Kent Island for keeping and maintaining Wm. Shorter a poor man

Augustine Thompson for the use of Andrew Prewit, a poor old man

Rose Mahane a poor woman

Henry Lock a poor man

Jane Jenkins a poor old woman

John Wells Coroner for two inquisitions on the body of a child and the other on Richd. Edwards, a Servant

Daniel McCamley for keeping a certain Sarah Sweet poor old woman

Joshua Clark for building a bridge over Choptank River - 3000

Jno. Emory for cleaning the arms of this co(un)ty

John Hawkins Hambleton for part of his allowance for keeping Joseph & Benj. Newnam the last year omitted to be allowed him in the levy last year

Robert Jones for four Inquisitions on the body of a child of Jos. Emerson, James Gill servt.of John Wright, Thos. Smith, & John Ryley servt. to Edwd. Chetham

Thomas Hynson Wright for keeping and maintaining Jane Wassey (not Massey) & her child ten months

Major Wm. Turbutt for keeping Alice Showers a poor woman four months and burying her

Edward Wright Sherr. for criminall servts fees

Elizabeth Beech her fine and summoning grand Jury - 3960

Mary Earle for cleaning and sweeping the Court house

Richd. Tilghman for fees due from this county as per acct filed

John Emory for fees from this county and small repairs to the Court house windows as pr acct. filed

John Soanes for deficiency in Squirrill heads last year

Rd. Tilghman junr for convenicneys made for securing records

Edwd. Wright Sherr for mistake in counting up the last levy list in prejudice to the said Sherr

Sarah Robertson a poor woman

Cecil County Militia - 1740

Box 1, Folder 4 of Colonial Wars Cecil County, 1740
To his Excellency Samuel Ogle Esq.,Governor of Maryland
In Obedience to yur Excellency ....

(When this book was assembled the sheets were placed out of order. The below text reflects the correct order.)

Troopers under the Command of Captn. John Baldwin, Vizt.
George Veazey, Lieutenant; Thomas Dane(?), Cornett; John Lusby, Quarter Master; Corporals: William Beaston; John Pennington Robert Porter; Phillip Stoopes; Hugh Terry; John Betts(?); Walter Scott Junr; Charles Scott; William Pearce; John Da..ge; James ...; Char...; W...; ...; Thom...; Jo...; ...; Jo...; Benj...; Otho ...; John Ba..an(?); Henry Pennington Jun.; William Bateman; Phillip Cazier; Thomas Savin; Thomas Bard; Richard Houghton; John Pennington; Jacob Evertson; Evert Evertson Junr; Jacob Hozier; William Ellis; William Savin; James Hughes; Richard Pennington; Anthony Lynch; Bartholomew Smith; John Ryland Junr; John Moser(?); Robert Wamsley; John Bette(?) Junr

Foot Company under the Command of Capt Edward Jackson (Vizt.)
Robert Story, Lieutenant; Henry Jackson, Ensign; Neall Carmichall, Sergt; William Ewing, Sergt; Thomas Miller, Corporal; John Read, Corporal; Tobias Long, Corporal; Christopher Tutchstone, Corporal; John Johnson; Edward Brimfield; John McGlaughlin; William Devall; John McTear; Reed J... Hunter; Samuel ...; Jo...; B...; ....; John ...; Sa...; ...; Robert ...; Hugh ...; David McCra...; Robert McCleary; James Navell; Mounts(?) Justice; Joseph Ritherford; Samuel Davie; Richard Davie; William Holly (Kolly?); Joseph Clift; Richard Titbald; John Osburn; Joseph Young; Benjamin Dickson; James Coulter; James Green; Anthony Dickson; William McKewn(?); Thomas Neall; Adam Armstrong; Charles Digson(?); Patrick Kelly; James Walker; Richard Harrison; James Harrison; Joseph Crosswell; Samuell Crosswell; James Broad...; George ...; Isaac ...; Laugh...(?) ...; ...; ...; ...; Matthew ...; ...; Daniel ...; William ...; John Crosswell; John Mitchell; George Lashley; James Bond; William Callwell; Robert Dickson; John Callwell; William Orre; James Finley; James Kennedy; Marty Machend; John McFadden; John Young; James Campble; Archibald Campble; John Currier; Randall Marshall; Robert Patton; Peter Justice; Thomas Tonney (Tomey?); John Clark; Roger Perryman; William Brown; John McClelen; Thomas ..llett; Thomas ...; Sam...; ...; Th...; ...; ..; ...; J...; Thomas ...; Ephraim Jo...; Jacob Johnson; Randell Death; Edward Death; James Death; John Death; Thomas Henney; William Jones; Jonathon Hartshorn Junr; Benjn. Hartshorn; Thomas Hartshorn; Robert Lashley; John McKenney; Enoch Enouchson; Benjamin Collver; William McDowall; Nathan Boys; Jedediah Alexander; Robert Morgan; Samuel Crawford; William Crawford; John Manery; Hugh McAlaster; Samuell Calwell; James Crommy; Nathaniel Ewing; George Gall...; William ...; Carle..(?) ...; ...; ...; Ro...; John...; Andrew...; Archibald ...; Joshua ...

Troopers who were under the Command of Captn. Thomas Johnson deceased (Vizt.)
Nicholas Hyland, Lieut; James Alexander Cornt.; Edward Johnson, Quartr. Master; Corporals: John Kankey; William Barry; Robert Holey

Cecil County Militia - 1740

James Veazey; Peter Boyer; Michael Lunn; William Wallis; Samuel Jones; John Ricketts; Thomas Edwards; Thomas ...; Sam...; Ja...; A...; ..; Thomas ...; Jose...; ..; Joseph ...; John Long; Nathan Baker; Henry Baker; John Starrot; Moses Latham; William Nelson; Robert Williams; William Dixon; Moses Andrews; William Bristow Junr; William Maffat; Samuel Bond; Michael Wallace; Hugh Lawson; Alexander McConel; John Alexander; Joseph Alexander; Theops. Alexander; David Patterson; Richard Foster; John(?) Ferrel; Robert Patterson; William Danniel; John Barry

Foot Company under the command of Captn John Veazey (Vizt)
John Pennington, Lieut; Thomas Ward, Ensign; Volentine Silcoh, Sergt; Michael Ruly, Sergt; Corporals: Benjamin Childs; Edward Morgan; John Robertson Junr; Joshua Meakins; James Price; William Morgan
Alphonso Cosden; John Wagoner; Thomas Turk; John Brown; Thomas Mercer Junr; Michael ...my..on.; James ...; Wil...; J...; J...; Ric...; John ..; D...; Olive...(?) ...; Robert ...; William Price; Robert Price; John Golet; James McFarrel; James See; William Whittom; Thomas Crisp; Thomas Sanders; Charles Huston; John Childs; Nathaniel Childs; George Childs; Thomas Etherington; Henry Hendrixson; Robert Roberts; Alexander Thompson; Thomas Wallace; Dennis Mehanney; Samuel Savin; Mathias Phippen; John Clark; Thomas Scurry; John Campble Junr; Richard Presley; Robert Scurry; Joshua Campble; Anthony Lynch; Charles Seaet(?); Henry Fowler; William Price Junr; Bryant ...; Isaac C...; Thomas ...; John ...; ..; ..hn ..; ...; ...; Mathew ...; John B...; Jeffery ...; Joseph Price...(?); Nathaniel Alexander; Edward ...gan; Barthol... Parsley; Thomas Severson Junr; Thomas Severson; James Morgan Junr; William Cole; Mathew Bulley; William Pickard; Edward Murfey; John Urin; George Robertson; Thomas Cox; John Kimber; Henry Cox; Peter Numbers; Otho Otherson; John Wood; John Wallace; Barth'w. Edrington; Andrew Price; John Money; James Cetch; David Cole; Joseph Ryley; Dennis Sillivane; John ...; Thoma...; Sc...; W...; ...

Foot Company under the Command of Capn Zebulon Hollingsworth,(Vizt)
Andrew Barry, Lieut, Refuses to serve; Moses Alexander, Insigne; Sergts.: William Currer; John Jones; George Bristow; Walter Sharp; Corpls: Jacobas Poulson; Simon Johnson Junr; John Phillips; Thomas Phillips
Thomas Wallace; Mathew Hodgson; Richard Nowland; Andrew H...; Allen Ro...; Robert ...; John L...; Olive...; Robe...; John ...; William ...; Mathew ...; John Ritche; James Ritche; Robert Ritche; Mathew Hopkins; William Henry; Nathaniel Moore; John Null; Robert Null; David Slone; Thomas Killgore; Robert Evans; Mathew Wallace; John Jodghead; John Wallace; David McKendley; William Balley; John Moke(?); George Welch; Gaven Clubege; William Irvin; James Armstrong; Oliver Johnson; Peter Johnson; Thomas Rite; John Alexander; Andrew Alexander; William Queatt (Queall?); John Mills; Jona...; Robe...; M...; S...; J...; John...; Jo...; Joseph ...; Jame...; John ...; Thomas Ph..(?); Nathaniel(?) Da...n; Joseph Thompson; William Young; Hugh Ross; James Carter; Adam Short; David Pain; David Rees; Francis Gardner; Richard Lewis; Hugh Morgan; David Hampton; Peter Brown; John Parker; Robert Carlile; John Carlile; Urias Anderson; William Daniel; John McCarter; Samuel Jackson; Peter Campble; William Phillips; Rubin Phillips; William Manson; John Irvin; James Hafe...; James Nowland; James Nox; William Smile...; Thomas ...; James P...; Samuel ...; Richar...; Henry ...; James ..; Joseph ...; Andrew ...; William Ram...; Mathew Arther(?); William Caughthran; Abraham Homes; John

Stinson; James Kees; John(?) Hambleton; Robert McKey; James McKey; Anthony
Ross; Robert Miller; Thomas Roberson; Robert Morrison; Mathew Irvin; William
Mont; David Care; William Wood; Robert Gordon; William Armstrong; Thomas
Armstrong; William Boyds; John Burns; John McCune; Hugh Were; John Were;
David Leech; James Stuart; Edward Clark; Charles Stewart; Robert ...;
Rober...; Joh...; W ...; Joh...; Geo...; Amos ...; James ...; Daniel ...;
John Compton; John Surgen; John Gray; Patrick Milton; John Hartness; Robert
Hartness; John Sith; Edward Patterson; Irvin Patterson; John Gardner; James
Smith; George Thompson; George Sair; William Hoddge; John McMaster; James
Burns; Robert Edmondson; Benja. Winsley; John Winsley; Nathan Pickels; John
Littles; William Gilletson; Martin McHaffey; Archibald Armstrong; William
Hall; Phemi Hodgson; Archibald Jackson; Archibald G...; James B...; Calip
Cann...; John ...; Dani...; Edwa...; Thomas ...; John Nealey(?); John Rutter
Junr (Senr?); Samuel Whitton; Francis Oens; Robert Milburn; Benjamin Maudin;
Jacob(?) Johnson Junr; Nicholas George; John Wescote; John Corsine; Edward
Veazey; Thomas Ricketts; Thomas Hitchcock; Thomas Parkerson; Joseph More;
John Hitchcock; Samuel Brown; Samuel Philips; Richard Foster; John Mainly;
Jacob Johnson; William Sluby; Benjamin Taylor; John Vancoslin(?); James
Anderson; Peter Poulson; Powel Johnson; Jobes ...; Rich...(?); Ga...; ...;
Simon..; James...; Thomas ..; Johannas ...; Thomas Veazey; John
Mitchel; Edward Condon; Isaac Foster; Elias Everson; James Leake; Mathias
Seal; William McClver; Lazerus Grainger; William Jemson; John Jones; William
Jones; Thomas Crouch; Richard Parsley; John Care; Richard Roach; John
Midleton; Peter Peco; John Kiteley; Philip Kitely; James Orton; Jeffery
Beasly; James Pearce

Troopers under the command of Capt. William Rumsey (Vizt) William Knight,
Lieut; Benjamin Slyter, Cornett; John Holland, Corpl; Peter Bushsell, Corpl;
Andrew Zelissow (?), Corpl; William Price, Corpl Alexander Armstrong; Enock
Jenkings; Abraham Allman; John Tilton; Thomas Beaston; Thomas Bolding;
Richard Taylor; Lawrence Lawrenceson; John Hamm; Peter Poulson; Ma...;
Rich...; Wi...; Ja...; W...; Pe...; Will...; Rich...; Ja...; Thomas ...;
Richard ...; John ...; Thomas Price(?); Andrew Alexander; Thomas Ebthorp(?);
Edward Rumsey; Thomas Stewart; Adam VanBebber; Cornelias Eliason Junr;
Richard Foord; John Bravard Junr; Peter Lawson; John Husband; William Chick;
Henry McCoy; William Harper; John Segar Junr; Joseph Alman; Joseph Looman;
Francis Ozier

Foot Company under the Command of Captn Peter Byard (Vizt.)
James Bayard, Lieut; Samuel Bayard, Ensign; Jeremiah Larkins, Sergt.; Thomas
Reynolds, Sergt; Jacob Harper, Sergt; Robert Patton, Sergt; Nicholas Wood,
Corporal; Richard Reynolds, Corpl; Jacob Hamm, Corpl; John Wood, Corpl; John
Lathem, Corporal; Steven Julien, Corporal; Samuel McClery, Corporal; John
Oglsby, Corporal Richard Franklin; William ...; Joh...; Ja...; ...; Den...;
Willia...; Thomas ...; Sam...; Thomas ..; Abraham Hug...; John Ford; William
Bowen; James Lyon; John McCrery; Richard Stevens; Ruben Roads; John Wood;
John Hunter; Thomas Stewart; William Cook Senr; Cornelius Wooliston; Abraham
Anderson; James Castro; John Chick; Philip Lancaster; John Whitehead; James
Hattery (Hallery?); Patrick Harris; Federick Elberry; John Barron; Enoch
Jenkins Junr; John Oglesby; William Oglesby; Richard Bowen; Thomas Moore;
Aron Moore; Philip Elwood; Richard Hukill; Richard E... Senr(?); John
Jenkins; ...; Thomas C...; ...; William ...; Thomas ...; Thomas...; William

...; Francis Jo...; Richard Elwood Junr; Edward Clark; George Hampton; William Crow; James Craige; William Craige; Andrew Rider; Nicholas Vandergrift; John Gullick; Robert Glenn; Hance Patton; William Pitch; Hugh Gullery; Alexander Bolding; James Smith; James Foster; Thomas Norman; Jacob Alexander; Charles Haltham; Alexander Scott; James McCurrey; John Nash; Samuel Nash; Isaac Gray; James Cowadon; Thomas Morrane; Elias Eliason; Stephen Julion; Alexander Waddle; John ...; Jo...; J...; Ch...; Dan...; John ...; Jo...; John ...; Alexander...; James Read; Henry Miller; Mathias Fellows; Thomas Bird; Edward Armstrong; Joseph Chick; John Barnaby; James McKitterick; John Killpatrick; David Mierick(?); John Hunter; John Veazey; James Taylor; Benjamin Lancastor; Samuel Seagar; Samuel Hughes; Charles Ford; William Moore; John Wood; Hugh Wood; Marten Alexander; William ...; Jonathan Melone; Henry Simmons; Aron Latham; George Oglesby; James Ford; Robert Wood; George Cozine; John McH...; John R...; Roberet ...; Samuel ...; George...; Jo...; Thomas ...; Isaac ...; John Harpe...; Thomas McCo...; William Bedle

Men without Commanding Officers Vizt. ...John Welch; John Welch Junr; Robert Welding; James Wilding; Charles Welding; John Ranzer; James Porter; James Jones; William Pennington; Henry Cox; Thomas Pennington; John Cooper Junr; Alexander Black; David Ricketts; William Ricketts; Benjamin Benson; Edward...; Jon...; Mi...; Wi...; Isa...; Willi...; Dani...; H...; John ...; William Jame...; Robert Croker; Henry Pennington; Daniel Maclean; Thomas Owen; John Maclean; John Jane(Fane?); John Jones; David Jones; John Loftus; John Coppin; John Price; John Artige; Nicholas Donell; Daniel George Junr; William Davis; Jeremiah Gridley; Richard Pennington; Manuel Blackford; Charles Mahony; Thomas Bean; Richard Smith; John Arnold; John Calk; John Christopher; John Coxill; Robert Pennington Junr; John Pennington; William Catch; Richard Chandl...; Matthew P...; Jacob Pen...; James P...; Benjam...; John ...; Edward ...; Andrew...; John Cha...; William Cham...; John Chambers Junr; John Shelley; William Bateman; Abraham Hollings; Patrick Tool; George Holton; William Richardson; William Mercer; Cornelius Vansant; John Bellarman; Nathaniel Bohannon; John Yorkson; William Sanders; William Marten; Richard McCary; Charles Johnson; William Sterling; William Pennington; Alexander Galaspy; Math'w. Steel; Math's. Dunahoe; John Ashford; William Ridge; Benjamin Ridge; James Ridge; Joseph Gray; Nathaniel Sapping; Hartly Sapping; Cornelius Vanhorn; James ...; Jame...; T...; Jo...; B...; Pet...; John ...; Ph...; Joseph ...; Thomas ...(it could be Ryland); Evert Evertson; John Hendrick; John Jone(sic); John Samson; John Dun; Walter Hill; Bryan Cradock; William Willson; Henry Ball; John Trase; George Rees; George Lewis; John Ball; William Smith; Barnet Vanhorn; William Burgess signed Jno. Webb(?)

An Act passed by Assembly on October 28, 1678 for the payment of the follow-
ing named persons, living in Dorchester and who had served in the campaign,
or aided the troops sent against the Nanticoke Indians: Capt. Thomas
Taylor; Lieut. John Ross; Cornet, Maurice Mathews, John Brooks; Wm.
Haselwood; Wm. Willoughby; Wm. Betts; John Alford; Robert Thornhill; John
Thomas; John Nicholas; Wm. Robson; James Mosley; Rich. Callenhaugh; Rich.
Tubman; Rowland Morgan; Philip Aherne; John Pope; John Savage; Thomas
Bowman; John Fish; Jonathan Waite; John Wallice; James Egg; John Richardson;
Lewis Griffin; James Dalton; Henry Johnson; James Fielding; Robert Evans;
Charles Hutchyson; John Hudson; John Curtice; John Causey; Capt. Henry
Trippe; Lieut. Edward Taylor; Ensign Edward Pander; Francis Tarcell; Richard
Owen; Wm. Law; Thos. Veitch; John Plummer; Laurence Woonett; Wm. Watson;
Matthew Hood; John Denaire; Mark Mitchell; Samuel Finch; John Snooke; James
Nowdell; Philip Gunter; Thomas Taylor; David Fortune; Edward Cheeke; John
Lawrence; Wm. Marchent; Stephen Pardue; Jos. Casten; Thomas Collens; Charles
Morgan; Richard Tucker; Andrew Pruett; Alexander Dowell; William Spuriway;
George Sprouce; Cornelius Lurden; Patrick Harwood; Wm. Walker; Alexander
Fisher; Henry Plummer; William Cheesman; Thomas Cloughtane; John Foord; John
Yate; Capt. Anthony Dawson; Lieut. John Mackeele; Ensigne John Dawsey;
Edward Hyde; Wm. Polovey; Corporal Lewis; James Haile; Thomas Symmonds;
Edward Newton; John Newton; John Waterly; Thomas Phillips; Wm. Evans; George
Hargissone; Rowland Vaughn; Philip Sutton; Henry Harvey; James Duell; John
Pollington; Wm. Beard; John Lunn; James Perle; Henry Newbell; William
Taptico; Wm. Berry; John Clark; Robert Robertsone; Stephen Bently; William
Messhier; Thomas Long; William Hares; Richard Thomasine; Francis Floyd;
Darley Cohoone; Wm. Mills; Joseph Reeves; John Stamward; Rich. Dudson; John
People; Bartholomew Ennalls; Henry Bradley; Daniel Jones; John Kirke; James
Peterkin; John Pierson; Oliver Gray; Wm. Robsone; Richard Holland; John
Hudsone; Henry Beckwith; Stephen Gary; Wm. Stephens; Wm. Dorrington; Daniel
Jones; John Richardson; John Steward; John Davis; William Daysone; Wm.
Willoughby; Thomas Flowers; Henry Turner; Raymond Stapleford; Frances
Tarcell. From Archives of Maryland.

"A List of The Several Troops of Horse and Company of (Foot?) belonging to
the militia in Dorchester County"
Held by the State Arhives, Box 2, Folder 5, Colonial Wars, Dorchester
County, List of Officers
Capt Francis Hayward's Company, officers and soldiers, 88
Capt Thomas Travers's Company, officers and soldiers, 80
Capt Henry Ennall's Company, officers and soldiers, 88
Capt James Brown's Company, officers and soldiers, 98
Capt James Woollford's Company, officers and soldiers, 99
Capt Peter Taylor, late deceased's Company, officers and soldiers, 140
Capt John Hodson's Company, officers and soldiers, 90
Capt Henry Traver's Troop, 38
Capt John Eccleston's Troop, 44
Capt Henry Hooper's Troop, (?)
Capt James Insley's Troop, 44
Capt Roger Hooper's Troop, 48
Capt William Grantham's Troop, (?)
Capt John Brown's Troop, (?)
Capt Levin Hick's Troop, 4_

Dorchester County Militia

Capt Thomas McKeel's Troop, 50
Capt Charles Dickinson's Troop, 52
Capt Thomas Wing's Troop, 42
Capt John Robson's Company, officers and soldiers, 80
 Total   1260

Queen Anne's County Militia
Box 1, Folder 11, Colonial Wars, Queen Anne's County, 1732
"May it please yr Excellency
In Obedience to your Excellency's Commande relating to the Militia of Queen
Anns County I humbly inform that there are in the said company county four
Companys of foot Soldiers and one Troop of Horse. The Troop commanded by my
self; James Earle Junr, Captain; Lieutenant Solomon Clayton, Cornet.   The
first Company of foot commanded by Lieutenant Colo Emant Hawkins, Wm
Elliott, Lieutenant, James Hutchins, Ensign.   The second Company of foot
commanded by Majr William Turbutt; Lieutenant, vacant; W. Meredith, Ensign,
declines to serve.   The third Company of foot commanded by Capt Edward
Wright; Lieutenant, vacant; Ensigne, vacant.   The fourth Company of foot
commanded by Captn Andrew Price; William Jump, Lieutenant; Ensign, vacant.
And upon advising with the Field Offices I humbly propose William Hemsley to
be Lieutenant and William Coursey, Ensign of Majr Turbutt's Company, John
Collings Lieutenant and Nathaniel Cleave Ensign to Captain Edward Wright's
Company and Thomas Rowe to be Ensign to Captain Andrew Price's Company.   I
humbly beg Leave farther to inform your Excellencys that Queen Anns County
is capable to raise another Company of Foot soldiers which would be an Ease
to the Inhabitants upon the Upper Parts of Chester and Choptank Rivers who
are now obliged to come a great way to attend musters and recommend
Augustine Thompson to be Captain, James Gould Lieutenant and James Brown
Ensign of such Company.   All   which is humbly ...(obliterated)...

February 22th Anno Domini 1748 - A True and perfect List of soldiers,
belonging to Captn James Brown's Company in Queen Anne County Feb 22, 1748/9
Box 1, Folder 29, Colonial Wars, Queen Anne's County
Cap'n James Brown; Lieutenant John Hackett; Clk. Rd Gould
Sergents: Trustram Thomas; William Soward; George Dobson; John Raley
Corprells: Thomas Mountseir; Thomas Teate; Thomas Parrarow; James Findley
Common soldier's   - Jacob Alguire; Stephen Andrews; William Bennett;
William Birch; Benjn. Blower; Matthew Baley; Henry Baley; Peter Baley;
Thomas Barnett; Christopher Brown; John Burk; Jacob Bell; Daniel Corker;
John Colgon; John Coleman; Wm Coyne; William Coleman; John Caddenhead; Thos.
Carman; Thomas Deans; Thomas Devrix Junr; Emanuel Deaven; John Forbush;
Frances Foreman; Daniel Ford; John Fouracres; Wm Gregory; Edward Gregory;
Matthew Greaves; Thos. Greaves; Thos. Goodman; John Hollingsworth Junr;
James Hambleton; John Holding; Wm. Hanecey; Thomas Hindsley; John Higgins;
John Hollingsworth; John Hart; John Haley; James Horsley; Abbot Johnson;
John Johnson Junr; Wm Kelley; Timothy Lane; Henry Lizenbe; Alex. Lee; Thomas
Lee; William Lee; Anguish Love; Henry Lembert; John Offley Collins; Thomas
Nooth(?); John Moor; John Moor Junr; Edward Mansfield; James McCoye; Patrick
Mohaney; Timothy Mangudge; Benjn. Newnam; John Nevill; David Nevill; John
Nevill Junr; Charles Nabb; Charles King; Robert Offley; Samuel Phillips; Wm.
Ponder; Vilet Primrose; John Primrose son of George; Rd. Ponder Junr; James
Ponder Junr; Daniel Ponder; John Parsons; Wm Pinder; Ephraim Ponder; James

Ripper; Gilbert Reed; William Reed; John Smith; John Smith; Thos. Soward Junr; Daniel Soward; John Soward; Isaac Soward; James Sparkes; Joseph Sparke; Daniel Smith Joyner; John Simkins; Frances Shepard; Benn. Sparkes; John Sparkes french; Edwd. Sparkes; Phillemon Birch; Ben. Hines; Thos. Griffith; Collins Hamer; Thomas Tippings Junr; Henry Tippings; Richard Vanderford; Charles Vanderford; John Sertain; Matthew Wickes; Stephen Wickes; Thomas Williams; George Webb; Wm Wyatt; James Willson; Henry Wilkinson; James Wilkinson; Thomas Wilkinson; John Wooddall; John Marshell; Walter Parland; Joseph Elliott Junr; John Hammet; Edward Colgon; James Carman; James Kelley

A List of the Names of the Several Officers and men Enlisted in the upper Hundred of Kent Island in Queen Anns County under the Command of Joseph Sudler this 6 day of Febru'y of Anno Dom. 1748
Box 1, Folder 30, Colonial Wars, Queen Anne's Co. (Upper Hundred of Kent Island)
James Sudler Lieutenant; Marmaduke Goodhand Ensign;
Serjeants: Thom. Tanner; Ricd. Carter; Joseph Evans; John Stevans
Corporals: William Baxter; John Legg Junr; Saml. Oburn
Frances Bright; Thoms. Barnes; Joseph Sudler junr; Nichs. Clouds; Edwd. Brown junr; Marmd. Goodhand junr; Vallentine Downey; Soloman Gilburt; John Gilburt junr; Thoms. Benton; William Jeffers; John Meconekin; Emanuel Meconikin; Peter Davis; John Legg the 3d; Edmd. Benton; William Joyner junr; Dobs Joyner; Absolam Joyner; Benja. Walters; Charles Chambers; Charles Conner; Frances Wollowhand; Richd. Goodman; John Wells; James White; John Rue; Richd. Chambers; Thoms. Chambers; Vall Carter junr; Henry North; Josias Soloway; Elias Meconikin; Anthony Williams; Nath'l Merideth; William Price; James Wright; Jeremiah Mose; George Asgood; Benja. Walton; Brown Wells; James Merrideth; John Rigby; Thom. Surcom; Joner Goodhand; William Dainty; Joseph Dayley; Thom. Harvey; Meths. H. Meeds; Richd. Carter junr; Thom. Price; Benja. Tanner; William Toomey; Valln. Downey junr; William Downey; Henry Haxter; Morriss Kiney; Molbrough Hunt; Andrew Belgrave; Thos. Connor; Absolem Davis; Nathl. Connor junr; Benja. Blunt; James Hutchings; Thoms. Rolph; John Rolph; John Brother; William Mullett; Saml. Street; Morriss Kerney; William Willson; William Mullett; Wm Legg; John Jackson; Thom. Parsons; Robt Pring; Robt Faning; Howel Jones

A List of the men in the Lower Hundred on Kent Island - 1749
Box 1, Folder 31, Colonial Wars (Queen Anne's Co) (Lower Hundred on Kent Island) Capt Blunt (1749)
Thomas Marsh Leftenant; Sergens Edward Cockey; John Winchester; Thomas Elliott; John Eareckson 3d
Corpls. Andrew Thohon(?); Allexr. Toulson; Jacob Carter; Benjamin Toulson
Armir: Richard Small
William Hamton; Henry Weeding Junr; John Smyth; Peter Corneliues; Jeremiah Grimes; Edward Tholow; Samuel Tholow Junr; Thomas Hamton; Charles Eareckson; Phillip Coppage; John Briant; Charles Collier; Henry Carter; Robbert Harvey; Charles Cockey; John Merideth; Nathaniel Conner; Joseph Toulson; John Eareckson Junr; Robert Blunt Junr; John Toulson; James Bryant; Benjamin Earikson; William Taylor; John Tholow Junr; Thomas Legg; Richard Lain; Jonas Willit; Isaac Winchester; Daniel Nickolson; Kemperson Harvey; William Orsburne; Thomas Warren; Jacob Pain; John Granger Junr; Richard Blunt Junr;

Queen Anne's County Militia

Thomas Pearce Junr; John Pearce; Thomas Horney; Mathew Earrickson; John Johnson; John Chace; John Elliott Junr; Edward Cockey Junr; Charles Basnett

The Roll of the Late Deceased Capt John Collin's Company - 1749
Box 1, Folder 32, Colonial Wars (Appears to be a company from Queen Anne's County, judging from the surnames)
Baldwin Kemp, Lieutenent; John Colens, Ensign; Thos Delanaway, Drommer; John Hamelton, Sargent; James Knotts, Sargent; Richard Hineson(?), Sargt; Edward Goddwin, Sargt.; Thos. Meleayed, Corpr.; John Miller, Corpr; Wm Stanton, Corpr; John Kenderdine, Corpr; Wm Serosberry; Charls Irins; Thos. Prat; Stephen Bush; Thos. Kemp; Thos. Donowho; Robart Smith; Robart Ratlief; Wm Ratlief; Vincent Hines; Wm Kurk; John Reynards; Henry Reynards; Richard Reynards; Wm Wilkenson; Thos. Wilkenson; Robart Knotts; James Clark; Edward Tarbutton; Wm Heartshorn; Wm. Deford; James Findly; Thos. Tippins; John Bird; Natthaniel Hines; Richard Kemp; Thos Newtun; James Barwick; Nathaniel Coventun; John Sewell; Nathaniel Curties; Nathaniel Knotts; Wm Tarbutton; Nathaniel Scott seanor; Solloman Scott; John Parker; Nathaniel Scott juner; Wm Emory; Jonathan Evans; Wm Saterfield; Thomas Delanaway juner; Edward Saterfield Junar; Solloman Scott junor; John Scott junor; John Young; Wm Young; Charles Murphy; John Oldson; Solloman Sinnet; Wm Permar; Philemon Thomas; Wm Ricketts; Wm Shepard; John Hucheson; George Seymor; Wm Mirredeath; John Deford; John Mansfield; Joseph Stevens; Thos Hinsly; James Permar; Lawrance Coplen(?); James Harris; Elexander Downey; James Davison(?); James Daley; John Daley; Edward Young; Wm Vockary; James Baker; Stephen Yoe; Thos. Yoe; James Pratt; John Coventun; John Starkey; Solloman Jons; Walter Colens; Danial Walker; John Hurd; Peter Hurd; Walter Edwards; Benjn. Thomas - Nathaniel Wright Clark

Feb 18 1748/9. A list of soldiers under the Command of Capt. Andrew Price
Box 1, Folder 34, Colonial Wars, Capt Andrew Price, Feb 18 1748/9 (Appears to be a company of Queen Anne's County)
Nethanel Knots, Liftenant
Vincent Price Insine
Sargants - James Pane; Willm Banning; Robt Hardassol; John Cooper Junr
Corporls - Vaughn Jump; James Kirckham; Solomon Eagle; John Willson
James Cannon; Thos Russam; James Gows; John Eubanks; Francis Orrel; John Meeds; John Morgan; Edward Cahell; John Anthony; James Evins; James Hicks; George Bell; John Russom senr; John Russom Junr; Henry Eagle; Wm Webb; John Clemmons; Charles Cammel; Wm Greenhawk; Thomas Purnerl; Thomas Climer; Robart Dwigins; James Landon; Jeremiah Floyd; John Flemon; Thomas Meeds Junr; Sharpless Cooper; Thomas Payne; Abner Tharpe; Joseph Tharpe; Wm Penny; John Mackneal; John Summers; John Pulling; Thomas Townsley; James Gray; James Kenting; Thomas Bush; Martin Mading; Wm Cooper; Thomas Steward; James Willson; Thomas Cox; Daniel Wheatley; James Bayley; Wm Wheatley; John Bartlet; James Swon; Thomas Swan Junr; John Young Junr; Abraham Jump; Peter Jump; Abel Chilton; Matthew Chilton; Thomas Roe; Evin Swoon; John Swoon; John Baker; James Cahell; Wm Purnerl; Wm Roe; Robart Turner; John Cahell; Thomas Martindil; James Silvester Carpenter; Francis Climer; James Lane; Otho Higgins; Richd. Wooters; Jonathan Wooters; John Wooters; Patrick Bane; Thomas Selvestor; Wm Draper; Thomas Towers; Wm Fisher; James Weeb; Wm Knots; John Knats; John Knats; John Nutter; Richd. Cooper; Joseph Longfellow; Aron Sanders; Robart Floyd; James Selvester; Benjamin Selvester; Wm Selvester; Wm

Skinner; Thomas Evins; Thomas Craner; Thomas Longfellow; John Cliff; David Selvester; Hery Pollock; John Peperdine; Micheal Hursey(?); James Wooters; Solomon Jump; Robart Bond; Thos Stanton; Jacob Wooters; Thos Jump Junr; Henry Fedemon; Thomas Banard - A True Copy of the List by me W. Robinson, Clrk

An Account of The Severall Officers and Men Enlisted of Capt. John Emory's Company Feb'y The 6th 1748 (Appears to be a Queen Anne's County Company) Box 1, Folder 37
Mr. Charles Price, Lieutenant; Mr. Arthur Emory Ensign; Mr. Phill Green, Sergeant; Mr. Aaron Yoe, Serjeant; Mr. Anthony Harrington, Serjeant; Mr. Barton Francis Falconar, Corporall; Mr. Amos Jarman, Corporall; Mr. John Ray, Drummr.; Arthur Emory junr, Clk
William Hall; Thomas Fisher; John Darrington; Stephen Jarman; John Falconar; John Falconar junr; Mark Hargadine; Mark Hargadine (this name given twice); John Phillips; Peter Rich; Thomas Dodd junr; George Dodd; John Green junr; Francis Arnott; Benja. Davis; George Jeffers; Thomas Mitchell; Thomas Goordon; James Rod; James Farrowfield; Thomas Gad; Charles Baker; Samuel Pratt; Richard Emerson; John Gordon; James Chambers; Edward Hill; John Goordon; John Williams; Williams Smith; Henry William; Mathew Griffin; John Sweatt junr; Edward Sweat; Thomas Kemper; George Hopkins; John Plowman junr; John Barnicklow; Christopher Wise; Daniell Baker; Mathew Bent; Samuel Rose; Michall Tool; John Knowles; William Scully; John Croney; James Jordon; Isaac Tharpe; John Tharpe; Ogle Tharpe; John Fisher; John Rakes; John Pemberton; Simon Keld; John Flint; James Flint; Thomas Morton; John Morton; Benja. Falconar; John Harden; John Brewer; Ezekiel Mordick; William Carter; James Plowman; Jeremiah Vincent; John Cox; James Dowden; William Egle; Phill Dulanaway; Mark Harman; John Woods; John Foster; John Churchell; Benja. Harden; James Calackhone; James Camron junr; John Emerson; Thomas Porter; James Ayler; William Meeds; John Hargadine; Henry Pratt Wye; Nicholus Rakes; Francis Falconar; Edward Hall; George Friend; Laynerd Topp; John Clark; John Ball; Peter Barwell; John Taylor; David Deen; Joseph Ellis; James Reaves; Sampson Warren; James Barns; James Moody; John Peperdine junr; William Drew; William Scully; Elisha Mannering; Henry Pratt; James Gors; James Linch
    - A True List   by John Emory

A List of Trooper's names belonging to Mr. Thomas Hynson Wright Company - 1749 (apparently a company of Queen Anne's County)
Box 1, Folder , 38 , Capt. Thomas Hynson Wright
William Coursey, Lieutenant; John Downes, senr, Cornett; John Downes Junr, Quarter Master; Richard Costin, Corporall
William Greenwood; Benjamin Kerby; William Elbert; Henry Jacobs; Thos Carradine; Nathan Wright (3); John Cole; James Emery; Thos Embert; Thomas Emory; William Dawson; John Nab; John Kent; James Carradine; Thomas Jackson; John Welsh Junr; Thomas Ringgold; John Elliott; Edward Clayton; Nathaniell Tucker; Trustram Thomas (3); James Downes; Hynson Downes; Henry Downes; John Hall; James Chaires; Christopher Cox; John Vanderford; Joseph Jarmon; Hancock Jones; Charles Downes Junr; Ambrous Kinimont; Vallentine Green; John Downes son of John; Samuell Wright

An Account of the Several Officers and Men enlisted in my Troop February 8th 1748. - Wm Hopper (Apparently a company of Queen Anne's County) Box 1, Folder 39 John Davis - Lieutenant; Thomas Hackett - Cornet; Matthew Dockery, John Tilotson - Quarter Masters; Edward Brown, William Pryor - Corporals William Carman; William Godwin; Thomas Obryon; William Robinson; George Smith; James Kersey junr; Thomas Meradith; Millington Sparks; John Sparks; Caleb Sparks; Ernault Hawkins; Joseph Chairs; John Pickeron; John Meradith junr; John Sott(?); Benj. Whittington; George Primrose; Tho. Pecock Betts; William Newnam; John Commegys; William Scott; William Campbell; John Keys junr; Anthony Roe; Vincent Benton; Francis Rochester junr; William Ricketts; Charles Raley; Johyn Davis junr; Henry Rochester; Daniel Smith; William Pratt; Morgan Brown; James Hamilton junr; Absolom Sparks; William Whorton; Thomas Lee; William Powel; Robert Smith; Matthew Hawkins; Thomas Price; William Meads; John Hamer; Thomas Mooth; Robert Hawkins; James Gold; Beynard Tillotson; Thomas Baley junr; Edward Wright; Benja. Thomas; John Brown (son Edwd.); Nathaniel Wright junr; William Wrench; Henry Wrench; Christopher Routh; Thomas Ringold; Thomas Obryon junr; Benj. Roberts; Joseph Elliott; Thos. Elliott Hutchins; Joseph Sudler junr; George Wells; John Hall; John Prat; Samuel Pratt; Henry Wiliams; Lawrance Hall; John Davis

Somerset County Militia
A List of the officers and men belonging to the troops under the Command of Capt Thomas Gilliss, June 30th 1732 Box 1, Folder 13, Colonial Wars (Somerset County?) Capt Thomas Gilliss, Charles Ballard, Lieutenant; David Polk, Cornet; Clement Dashiell, Quartermaster; William Winder, Francis Allen, Corporals. Henry Lowes, Levin Gilliss, William Addams, Michael Dishroon, John Dishroon, William Dishroon, Jonathan Bounds, William Kibble, Charles Leatherbury, John Leatherbury, Robert Leatherbury, Nehemiah Covington, Thomas Pollet, William Poollet, Jonathan Poollet, William Cottman, Isaac Dashiell, Thomas Dashiell, Joseph Piper, Robert Chambers, James Traherne, Meridlin(?) Hobbs, Stephen Hobbs, Benjamin Hobbs, Underwood Rencher, William Davis, John Crouch, Jacob Cawdry, Ahab Costen (Coster?), Thomas Hulbrook, Joseph Vannables, Ezekiel Humphris, John Ballard, Benjamin Cottman, Thomas Toadvine, William Harris, John Fowler, George Addams, Richard Phillips, Joseph Jones Bounds, Elias Bayley, Joshua Turpin, John Dorman, Benjamin Cottman, Nicholas Evans, Stephen Addams, Joseph Allen, William Rencher, Thomas Crouch - Louther Dashiell, Clerk

A List of Capt John Handy's Troope - 1749 Box 1, Folder 14, Colonial Wars (Somerset County?), 1749 William Nelson, Lieut; Douty(?) Collier, Cornet; Robert Collier Junr, Quarter Master; William Giles Junr, Corpl.; Jos: Nicholson, Corpl; James Dashiall,Corpl; Henry Dashiell, Clk, March 20th 1749 John Shiles Senr; John Nicholson; Evans Collier; Mitchell Dashiell; Rodger Nicholson; William Winright; Jesse Dashiell; Jms. Shiles Junr; Thos Dashiell; Jas Winright; John Goslie; Wm More; Wilson Rider; John Evans Junr; Joshua Jackson; Daniell McIntier; John Wailes; Geo Collier; Stephen Winright; Ezekiel Dorman; Geo: Bennet; Levin Larramur; Thos Willin Junr; Dan'll Henderson; John Willin; Robert Willin; Edward Bennet; John Beard;

Somerset County Militia

Joshua Humphris; Thos Russell; Matthew Kemp; Robert Hurdy; Graves Bourman; Thos Bird; Levin Willin; John Davis; John Leatherbury

A List of Soldiers bairing Armes under the Command of Captn William Jones, Danell Jones, Ensn, Thoms Jones, Cleark - Somerset County
Box, Folder 15
John Addams, George Jones, Sergts
Isaak Noble and Joseph Ellis and William Roberson, Corpls
Robert Malone; Peter Serman; Michael Dishroon; Jacob Morris; Joseph Morris; Clement Christefar; Mathew Goslin; John Ginkines; Haraen Radish; William Ellis; William Suilivan(?); Jarvis Ginkines; Timothy Colliers; John Mealy; Danaell Dalany; Smith Bruerton; Geo. Baly; Jonathan Standford; Thos Colliers (Colliens?); John Morris; Hen Kinnidy; William Booth; John Bruerton; Samuel Bruerton; Ezekiel Hilman; Luke Fosque; Thomas Stanford; Benjamin Mitchell; George Pullit; Edward Sirman; Isaak Sirman; John Hilman; John Williams; Thomas Fowler; James Wilkins; George Toadvine; David Mils; Jacob Crouch; Pirkins Vanables; Thomas Gordy; Richard Stpen Bounds; William Adley; David Ginkins; Hen Fraysher; Ambros Riging; Jacob Lolles; Joshua Sirman; John Hails; William Baly; William Swillivin(?); George Shane; John Vance; Alexander Fullerton

A List of the foot Company of Soldiers under the Command of Captn William Lane
Moses Mills Lieutanent; Smyth Mills, Ensign; Robert Stevenson, Serjant; John Melton, Serjant; Solomon Webb, Serjant; Nathaniel Mills, Serjant
Jeremiah Cary; William Gillitt; Samuel Brittingham; Robert Lindale; James Burnett; Abraham Lambertson; Sam'll Lamberson; Hugh Mills; William Mills, son of John; Nathan Mills; William Ellis; John Webb; William Melvin; Moses Pilshard; Joseph Pane; Thomas Duberly; Robert Wattson; John Blades; Solomon Cary; William Veazy; Charles Wattson; John Brittingham; Nehemiah Dickerson; Moses Pane; John Pane; Joseph Stevenson; William Stevenson; Thomas Mulligan; Henry Lamberson; Wilburn Ramsey; Evander Cameren; Robert Pitts; John Whaley; Henderson Baker; Peter Redding; Daniel Ramsey; Jacob Hill; John Peacock; William Mills son of Sam'll; John Gillett; James Blades; James Phillips; Samuel Dorman; William Flord; George Duke; Charles Davis; Joshua Chapman; Henery Greer; George Greer; Samuel Blade; Lemuel Henderson; Barnaby Henderson; Levin Henderson; Jacob Pane; John Duberly; John Wattson; William Piper; Samuel Piper; William Agnifield; Simson Body; John Markel; Joseph Henderson; Israel Lane; Littleton Melton; James Davis - A True copy by me, E., T. Clk. (probably the initials of Elisha Tawes, since there is an earlier entry lined through, near the top of the page, which reads, Elisha Tawes, clerk)

A List of Capt Wm McClamy's Company March 24 1749
Box 1, Folder 17, Colonial Wars, (Somerset County), Capt William McClamy, John Turpin , Lieutenant; Sollomon Tull, Insine; James Furnis, Serjant; John Madux, Serjant; Jacob Airs, Serjant; Samuel Tull, Corporal; Isaac Hollond, Corporal; Randall Mitchall, Corporal
David McDaniell; Thomas More; Joshua Hall; John Ebet; Curtis Revell; Benjamin Grumble; Edward Culling; Samuel Miles; Stacy Miles; William Willis; Thoms Walston; William Mathis Senr; Benjamin Tilliman; Randol Fiddy; William Mathew(?) Junr; Richard Tull; James Dougherty; Martin Shepard; William

Collins; William Smith; Randol Revill Junr; John Rock; Ezekiel Gibbins; Henry Fisher; William Furnis; John Tillman; James Collins; Isaac Cullin; Denwood Turpin; William Culling; David Wood; Morgin Sanders; William Bolland; James Saylor; George Benston; William Outerbridge; William Macdormand; John Howard; William Young; John Davis; John Tindall; Isaac Mitchall; Charles Macnellford; John Holt; William Revill

March 28th 1749, A List of Troopers under Command of Capt Joseph Miller
Box 1, Folder 18, Colonial Wars (Somerset County?)
Perry Morgin, Leftenant; John Evans, Cornet; William Howard(?), Quarter Master; Hugh Tingle; George Howard; Thomas Collings; Ambrose White William Durkins; Hugh Tingle Junr; Abraham Linch; Alexander Linch; Daniel Cox (Cad?, Coe?); Samuel Hudson; John Tulle; John Howard(?); Calor(?) Godwin Junr; Thomas West Junr; George Wharton; William Tulle; Jonas Smith; Joshua Evans; Charles Smith; Samuel Hall; George Hudson; Joshua Wayat(?); William Hudson; William Wyat; John Bowden; Thomas Bowden; Mather Rogers; Joshua Rogers; William Woodcraft; William Coffing; Richard Tulle Junr; Absolom Hudson; Joseph Robinson; Solomon Evans; Edward Clark; Rades Clark(?); William Woods; Thomas Robinson Jr; Thomas Aydlot; Abil Collings; Joshua Burton; Rober(?) Smith; John Massey (Maessey?); Andrew Gray; Jacob Gray; Francis Beckam(?); Solomon Tingle; Samuel Aydlot; Nehemiah Howard Nathen Wiles, Clerk

A List of the Troop under the Command of Capt Joseph Mitchell
Box 1, Folder 19, Colonial Wars (Somerset County?)
Richard Blizard; Dennis Hudson; Ephram Heather; Sam'll Bratten; Charles Davis; Phillip Selby; John Schoolfield; Ratlif Poynter; John Hall; Natt'l Hopkins; Ezekiel Wise; John Purnal; Daniel Selby son of Park'n; Joshua Braten; Levin Hopkins; John Richardson; Matthew Selby; Nathan Brittingham; Sam'll Stevenson; Elias Poynter; Willson Bratten; Joseph Cord; Daniel Sturgis; Isaac Brittingham; Absolom Brittingham; Peter Lindal; Abraham Oughton; Littleton Brumly; Perker Selby Junr; William Sturgis; Sam'll Stevenson son of James; Natt'l Bratten; Parker Selby Senr; Stephen Waltom; George Jones; George Truit; John Bratten son of William; Joseph Morril; Littleton Boing; Poynter Brittingham; Job Waltom; Hinry Satchell; Parker Selby son of Phil; Hezckiah Purnal; Peter Johnson; Solomon Claywell; Jos'a Hill; James Bratten; Zadock Turner
John Selby Left Tennant; Peter Claywell, Cornet; William Waltom, Quarter Master; William Brittingham, John Richardson, John Johnson, John Teague, Corporals
A True List by me - Daniel Selby, Clerk

A List of Men Under the Command of Capt Day Scott, 1748
Box 1, Folder 20 Colonial Wars (Somerset County?)
Sam'll McCloster, Ensign; Daniel Walter, Sergent; Arthur Hickman, Sergent; Sidny Brown, Obediah Reed, Corporal; Robert Walter; John Wallace; David Hopkins; Daniel Wales; Abraham Bartlett; Isaac .Sirman; Benj'a Richardson; John Dean; John Hopkins Junr; Benjamin Messex; James Reed; James Laramore; John Anderson; Nicholas Dun; Thos. Dun; Joseph Husk; John Bartlett Junr; Teague Dickerson; John Nelson; Jonathan Hickman; Aaron Messex; Partrick Quaturmus; Bloyd Harriss; Elihu Messex; Wm Walter; Isaac Hopkins; Brion McCabe; Wm Phraiser; Richard Williams Junr; Wm Laramore; Daniel Jackson; Wm

More; Matthew Duncon; Covington Messex; Isaac Handy, Junr; Robert Farrenton; Levin Farenton; John Martin; Benjamin Bird; Pasque Bartlett; Wm Elensworth; George Dashiell; John Willing of Nanticoke; Aylward Barklett; Levin Goslin; Henry Richards; John Dyer; Isaac Jackson; Robert Low; Hugh Portor; Wm Roberson; Wm Eassom; John Dean Junr; Hane Browstrum; Thos. Jackson; John Bounds; James McMorrie; Winder Dashiell; James Nicholson - Wm Dashiell, Clerk

A List of Solders belonging to Capt. Joshua Sturges
Box 1, Folder 21, Colonial Wars (Somerset County?)
Officers Larzarus Dennis, Insign - Solomon Townsand, Daniel Dennis, Sam'll Tayler, Wm Tayler, sargents
Joshua Kelliam; Wm Ottwell; Jerimiah Townsand; Marshel Townsand; Na'tt Townsand; John Smith; Sam'll Cooper; Robt. Dukes; Wm White; Joshua White; Sam'll Beal (Boal?); Belitha Laws; Gabrel Powel; Roling Beavens; Vallentine Dennis; John Stephens; Randall Right; Jobe Tayler; James Tayler; Nicklus Crouch; Thos. Victer; John Ruark; Isaac Crouch; Wm. Scott; Andrew Brown; Charles Hammond; Ezekil Butler; Thos. Beavens; James Ottwell; Richard Ward; Gye Cook; John Melican; Joseph Townsand; Ezekiel Townsand; Wm Donaho; Wm. Gray; Benj'a Houston; Wm Bennett; Wm Hall; Travour Tayler; Thos Outten; Wm Willis; Richard Nickols; Joseph Godfree; Wm Beavens; Johnathun Noble; Robt Marin (Macin?); Thos. Butler Junr; Mical Vestry; David Lafeald; Peter Owen; James Noble   -   Cornelas Beavens Left Tanant & Elijah Laws Clk

A List of Soulgers Commanded by Captain Nath'll Waller - 1748/9
Box 1, Folder 22 Colonial Wars (Somerset county?)
John Polk, Leantetant; David Hale, Insine; Natt'll Waller Sergeant; Allen Gray, Sergent; Mathew Oliphan, Seargant; Jethro Vaughn, Corprill; Mathew Callaway, Corprill; Mathias Vinson, Corprill; John Tatom, drumer; William Callaway Senr; John Callaway Senr; Nath'll Waller Senr; John Godard; Robert Haistains; Alexander Maddux; William Maddux; John Roads; John LeCatt; Joseph Leanard; Thomas Hall; John Hitch, Junior; Nehemiah Hitch; Hill Coxk; Thomas Coxk; Daniel Coxk; John Coxk; John Chrouch; William Waller; William Kinning; Dutton Baker; James English; Thomas Waller Junior; John Callaway Son of Peter; Benjamin Parremore; Joseph Parremore; John Hastans; Robert Ring; Alexander Gibbins; Richard Waller; William Haistains; Ebenezer Callaway; Thomas Parremore; John Parremore; Ephrim Vaughn; John Speer; Job Sermond; John Cardery; Michael Linch; John Moor; John Callaway, Junior; Isaac Callaway

A List of a Troup under the Command of Capt John Waters
Box 1, Folder 23, Colonial Wars (Somerset county?)
Viz James Polk, Liut; Edward Waters, Quarter master; Wm Fleming, Aron Tilmon, Corporeals; Whittington King, Clark; Wm Polk; Tegue Riggin; George Benton; John Tull; Josep Riggin; James Haymon; Nathanell Smullin; John Harris; Wm Benston; James Bolen; John Pilcher; Wm Gray; Wm Smullin; John Benston; Wm Worrick; James Gray; Spencer Harress; Joseph Tilmon; Isiah Tilmon; Wm Hath; Edmond Smuling; Levien Conner; Mathias Costin; Stephen Costin; Edward Stephens; Ezekiel Costin; Stephen Ward; James Harriss; John Polk; Elijah Tilmon; Elisha Tilmon; Ezekiel Gibins; Sormon Donoho; Abraham Harriss; Zachariah Harriss

Somerset County Militia

A List of Souldiers under the command of Capt. John Williams Son Vizt -
William Turpin, Liutenant; Thos. Dixon, Cornat; Thos. Beauchamp,
Quartermaster; Corporals: Kirk Gunby; Whittey Turpin; Marcy Beauchamp -
March the 1st Day 1748-9
Box 1, Folder 24, Colonial Wars (Somerset County?)
Wm Walsson, Pistols; David Long, Pistols; Thos Tull, Condockway; Thos
Leon(?), Pistols; Ambrous Dixon, Pistols; John Long, Pistols; Jossephes
Bell, Pistols; James Gunby, Pistols; Isaac Dixon; John Davis, Pistols;
George Bozman, Pistols; Nehemiah Turpin, Pistols; Samuell Coulbourn; Isaac
Beaucham, Pistols; Stephen Horsy; Samuell Handy; Benjamin Lankford; Smith
Horsy; John Beaucham, Pistols; Thos Tull, Anomessick; Jacob Cullin; John
Scot Junr; Ezekiel Hall; Jessey Lister, Pistols; Jeffrey Long, Pistols;
Robert Carsey; Spencer Williams, Pistols; Joshua Tull, Pistols; Wm Conway;
Purnal Outen; Benjamin Coulbourn; Richard Tull; John Handy; Wm Beauchamp;
Thos Dixon son of Wm, Pistols; Outerbridg Horsey; Abraham Outen; Risdon
Dixon; Bell Maddix; Charles Hall, Pistols; Fountain Beaucham, Pistols; Isaac
Coulbourn; Southey Whittington; Michaell Holland; Elija Coulbourn; Killiam
Lankford

Talbot County Militia

A List of the Officers & men under Capt Robert Goldsborough, Talbot County -
1748
Box 1, Folder 25, Colonial Wars, Talbot County
Lieut: Woolman Gibson; Officers: Richard Bruff; Samuel Kininmont; David
Fitzpatrick; William Garey; Wm Brown Vickers; James Virgon; James Stainer;
Thomas Mason; Robert Hall; Ephraim Start
soldiers: William Fitzpatrick; David Prichard; John Jeffers; Thomas Scotts;
Thomas More; James Shield; James Sankston; Thomas Keets; William Beswick;
John Kininmont Junr; Christopher Plummer; Jonas Farrowfield; John Barwick
Junr; George Millington; William Lane; William Williams; Vincent Jonas;
Thomas Carslick; Lamb: Warner; Thomas Beswick; John Plummer Junr; John
Greenhawks; Cooley Jones; James Parsons; Edward Haughter; Anthony Gregory;
William Price; Lewis Jones; John Chapman; John Saunders; Abraham Sevire;
Thomas Lankston; William Cooper; William Hewo; Richard Barrow; John Garey;
Jonathan Gibson; Francis Armstrong; John Robinson; James Robinson; John
Gibson; Jonathan Willson; Thomas Willson; Richard Start; Richard Vinton;
William Roberts; James Roberts; Andrew Hennesey; Henry Male; Joseph
Kininmont; John Sutton; Daniel Maginney; Thomas Parr; John Smith; John
Nuttle; Moses Higgs; Benjamin Roberts; James Hawkins; Edward Shropshire;
Thomas Sherwood the Elder; Thomas Sherwood Second; Thomas Sherwood the
younger; Hugh Rice; Harwod Reame; Thomas Ozman; George Lemmon; William
Kelley; William Allen; William Whaley; Larkin Willson; William Hutton; James
Whaley; William Cole; William Nailor; James Saunders; Thomas Plummer; Isaac
Millington; John Morgan; Charles Morgan Junr; Daniel Martindale; David
Herrington; Isaac Herrington; Thomas Tharpe; James Kindrick; Sevil Morgan;
Oldern Williams; William Cullen; John Cullin Junr; David Cullen; George
Vickers; Joseph Nailor; William Shield; Joseph Vickers; Samuel Morgan; Jacob
Gore; Richard Sneed; Nicholas Brown; John Rage; William Hadden; Charles
Walker; Michael Kerby Junr; John Dobson; Thomas Hewett; William Grace;
Charles Kingston; John Cole Scott; Francis More; Thomas Thomas, William

Talbot County Militia

Price; Richard Kerby; Robert Kerby; Lamb: Kerby; John Kerby; William Kerby; David Kerby; Nathan Kerby; William Baley; Solomon Draper; John Benney; John Huston; James Millson; Robert Hunter; Sam'll Millson; Francis Stainer; Solomon Stainer; James Robinson; Stephen Huzzey; John Tucker; John Williams; Thomas Greenhawk; Joseph Eubanks; John Barrett; John Thomas; James Horney; John Standfast; Nathaniel Connor; William Horney; Moses Sneed; Thomas Benney; William Harris; John Benney; Joseph Faulkner; William Cockayne; Abraham Faulkner; Burton Francis Faulkner; Isaac Faulkner; Jacob Faulkner; William Oxenham; Richard Auston; James Perkin; Patrick Heart; Richard Dolvin – A True Coppy Taken of the Muster Roll by me – Wm. Lundergin, Clarke Jan'y 27f 1748/9

A List of the soldier's under Capt. Haddaway – Talbot County
(Same folder as above)
Arter Porter; John Porter; Frances Porter; Richard Camper; John Willson; Steven Stickbury; Daniel Nield; Thos Larremore; Thos Ashcraft; George Apelgath; Thos Cook; John Harrison son of Wm; Joseph Harrison son of Robt; Charles Nickells; John Harrinton; Thos Townson; Thos Love; Nathaniell Grase; Bennett Vallent; Thos Vallent; Wm Norrowd; James Marshell son of Richd; Wm Corsey; James Harris; Richard Ketley, Drummer; John Winter Bolton; Wm Dingell; Thos Camper; Henery Jefferson; James Harrison; John Harrison son of James; James Harrison Junr; Richard Bridges; Rowlen Haddaway; Thos Haddaway; John Cowley; Philimon Plowman; Robt Larremore; John Jones; Peter Hunt son of John; George Dawson; Robt Lamdin son of Daniell; James Lowe; Beni Jones; James Presley; John Briley; James Blades; Peter Haddaway; Charles Smith; Francis Korsey; Wm Korsey; Beni Cooper; George Haddaway son of Thos; Thos Commins; Patrick Roach; Elexdr Wilson; Thos Trott; Wm Collison; Edward Collison; Thos Adkock Junr; Wm Lamdin Junr; Robt Lamdin son of Wm; Robt Porter; James Calk; Philmon Spencer; Beni Spencer; Edward Hopkins; Wm Harrison Junr; Denis Connaway; Thos Cooper; John Wales; John Blades; Hugh Spencer; Abram Brumell; Wm Commins; Philip Sherwood; Ralph Dawson son of Robt; Robert Shaver; Jerey Maguay; Henery Manship; Nicholas Commins; Francis Hanning; Charles Macartey; Edward Haddaway; John Macartey; Noble Tucker; Davey White; Peter Hunt Junr; Elexd'r Larremore; James Jones; Robt Jones; John Brierwood; Gilbert Jackson; John Hopkins; Adam Corner; Lods(?) Mathews; James Spencer; Thos Sathells; Thos Higgins; James Kimmer; George Haddaway Junr; Robt Brumell; Charles Gossage; James Lee; Boni Stoker; John Nuttell; George Porter; James Harrison son of Wm; Perry Harrison; Francis Sherwood

A Roll of the Militia under the Command of Tho. Porter in Talbot County Viz.
(Same folder as above)
Joseph Turner; Thomas Loveday; James Farrell; George Parrott; Joseph Newman; Samuel Broadaway; John Farrell; Robert Greenwood; Jonathan Dobson; Peter Russum; Timothy Forth; Thomas Baynard; John Sylvester; John Nicherson; John Porter; William Purnell; John Slade; Robert Caide; John Templeman; Ambrose Broadaway; Alexander Codner; Thomas Matthews; William Frantom; Jeremiah Codner; Giles Hicks; Thomas Frantom junr; Caleb Greenwood; Anthony Booth; Thomas Frantom; Richard Whidby; William Arrington; Laurence James; Thomas Turner; Charles Manship; Stephen Burgiss; James Thomas; Aaron Bullen; Nehemiah Higgins; William Batchelor; Miles Fern; Edward Bandy; William Steuart; Abraham Camper; Charles Bandy; Ralph Kindrick; Edward Calsh (sic); Joshua Hurley; James Bell; Benjamin Sylvester; John Dyas junr; Thomas

Talbot County Militia

Russam; Uriah Matthews; Francis Duling; Absalom Turner; John Walker; Thomas Sard; Thomas Matthews; George Dobson; John Newman; John Arrington; John Turner; John Davis; Richard Glover; Moulton Eubanks; Joseph Merrick; John Catrop; John Brasscop; William Johns; William Oston; George Duling; Joseph Duling; Isaac Nit; Bazell Waring; Henry Waring; Thomas Harris; Lambert Ward; William Merrick; Shadrack Botfield; George Nix; Cornelius Shehorn; Michael Moloony; John Merchant; Darius Burn; Thomas Dudley junr; James Booth; Peter Russam junr; Bartholomew Greenwood; Joseph Barron

A List of Officers and others belonging to the troop of Horse of Lt. Tristrim Thomas
Box 1, folder 26, Colonial Wars (Talbot County?)
Lt. Tristrim Thomas, Lieutenant; Phillemon Hambleton, cornet; John Padison, Quarter Master; Corporals: William Allexander; Thomas Ray; Robert Spencer; David Robinson; Jacob Loockermon; Samuel Hopkins; Thos. Jenkins; William Harris; Impy Dawson; Rich: Goldsborough Junr; Peter Denny; Robert Newcom; Dennis Hopkins; Thos. Winchester; Abednego Botfield; Will'm Skinner; Arthur Rigby; Anthony Lecompt; James Denny; John Auld; Joseph Hopkins; Fedemon Rolle; Dan'l Sherwood; John Hambleton; Peter Calk; John Sherwood; Will'm Cooper; Will'm Dawson; John Robinson; Will'm Mills; Thos Martin; Thos Martin Junr; Henry Martin; Nich's Glen; Thos Whittinton; Abner Parrot; Will'm Mulikin; James Wolcot; Richd. Turbut; Thos. Skinner; John Lee; Will'm Sanders; John Barnet; Will'm White; John Sanders; Morris Giding; Walter Jenkins; James Chaplin; Polard Edmonson; Henry Delahay; Vincent Patison; Noah Cornish; Nathan'l Hull; John Kininmont; Will'm Trippe; Wolman Gibson; Mesheck Botfield; Phill'n Horney; John Blake; Robert(?) Willson; Thos. Roberts; Edw'd Carslake; Sam'll Cockayne; John Cooly; James Benson; Russel Armstrong; David Kirby; Vincent Finny; Edmond Ferril; Edw'd Griffeth; Job Keld; Charles Pickren; James Pickren; Andrew Skinner; Zadock Botfield; Nich's Low; Peter Blake; Ralph Elston; Nich's Goldsborough Tirpins; Edw'd Oldham; Will'm Delahay; Richd. Robinson; Willm. Finny; Danll. Manadear; Mathew Jenkins; Thos. Abbot; Loftis Bowdle; James Walker; Henry Dickinson; Danll. Dickinson; Powel Cox; John Bozman

Worcester County Militia

A List of men belonging to the company of Capt John Evans - 1748
Box 1, Folder 27, Colonial Wars (Worcester County?)
Thomas Midsly; Samuel Powell; Henry Hudson; Thomas Powell; Gamage Evens; Powell Paty; Calab Tingle; Kendel Collier; Walter Purnell; Isaac Coventon; Solomon Hudson; Thomas Gray; John Green (scratched through, died); John Bowen(?); Purnell Rackliffe (scratched thourgh, died); William Medsly; Elias Evens; Alexander Marey; John Cambell; John Lockwod; Vincin Crapper; Archabel Deall; William Bowing; William White; John Smith; Obed Gaught; Jacob Marshel; Joseph Gray; Solomon Baker; David Long; Solomon Crapper; Harison Ayrs; Alexander Mills; John Hudson; William Smith; William Richards; Brickhous Townson; John Turvill; Adam Breuard; Whitenton Bowing; John Frassit (Frassir?); Edmond Crapper; William Colings; Samuell Holland; Nehemyer Nock; Charles Rackliffe; Warring Hader; John Mumford; John Deal; Barthlewmy Bacum(?); Solomon Camell; Nathaniell Craper; Thomas Collino; Samewal Deal; Ebenezar Colings; Elisha Evens; Annanias Hudson; James Murry —

Worcester County Militia

Ebnzr Evens, Lieutentant; Wm Steven Hill, Quarter Master; Daniel Tingle, Insign

A List of Solders Commanded by Capt Adam Spence
Box 1, Folder 28, Colonial Wars (Worcester Conty?)
John Evens; John Outten; John Slinger; William Bishop; Roger Patrick; Daniel Patrick; John Houlston; John Blizard; Waller Mackhenry; John Walton; John Price; Giles Jones; Daniel Hencock; John Allan; Mickall Gar Junr; Thomas Brittingham; John Willet; John Jones Junr; William Priest; Adam ____; John Richardson; Joseph Puddrie; James Lensey; Walter Read; John Porter; John Gar; Elisha Gar; Eli Gar; Stephen Sturgis; Levi Beachbord; Watson Mackenry; Samuel Nilson; Joshua Guttrey; Elijah Guttrey; Philip Guttrey; Moses Guttrey; William Claywell; John Gar Junr; William Robenson; William Richardson; Isaac Pain
Sergants: William Willet; Joseph Bishop; Thomas Willit; Stephen Hall; Robert Nilson
John Scarborough, Clark; William Nilson Leiutanant

Lists from Parish Proceedings and Sessional Records

From the Sessional Record of Manokin Presbyterian Church, Somerset County, 1747-1750.
"Manokin Congregation, A Register of the Pews in their House as follows – Beginning at the West galary." (No date given, probably 1747)
Littleton Landon, Thomas Pollet, John Denwood, James Wilson Senr, Denwood Wilson, Wm. Strawbridge, Denwood Wilson, John Wilson, Wm. & Sam'l Pollit, Josiah Hobbs, Gillis Polk, George Waggaman, Henry Craig, John Irving, James Wilson Junr., George Irving, John Porter, Thomas Fitchet, Sam'l Wilson, Henry Jackson, Nehemiah King, William Jones, Thomas King, William Polk, Benjamin Polk, James Willin, Wm. Caimbridge, Wm. Stewart, Thomas Pollet, Wm. Dridden, John Law, James Polk, Revd. Wm. Ker, John Pollit, James Ewing, Josiah Heath, Wm. Heath, Jonathan Pollit, John & Jonathan Pollet (Pews 41 and 42 left vacant for strangers; also vacant was 28.)

St. Paul's Parish, Queen Anne's County, Vestry Proceedings

1723 – A register of the pews of St. Lukes Chapel at Wye: Jno. Emory, Robert Noble, Wm. Elbert, Charles Stevens, Wm. Clayton, pulpit, Thomas Emerson, Tristram Thomas Senr, Charles Neale, Wm. Finney, James Knowles, Joh. Emerson & John Downs, Roger Clayland & John Pursley, Joseph Earl, Henry Costin & Richard Costin, Edward Harris, Arthur Emory, Edmd. Thomas, William Turbutt, Wm. Hemsley & James Earl, Wm. Carnell, Jno. Fitzpatrick, Wm. Clayton, strangers, Wm. Cocklin, Wm. Brown, Thomas Yewell, Wm. Cole, Wm. Clayton, Senr, Wm. Ratclife, John Blackwell & Jas. Saunders, Jno. Morgan & James Morgan, John Miller & John Welch, Thos. Murphy & Wm. Durden

St. Stephens Parish, Cecil County

1703 – Gifts and subscriptions (rearranged in alphabetical order):
John Athey, James Barbott, Robt. Barker, Will'm. Bateman, John Bavington, Van Bebber, Jon. Beck, John Beedle, Mary Benson, Sam'll Bostick, Thos. Browning, Ham. Cahoune, Jacob Caulke, Cornelius Clements, Lusbert Cock, Benja. Cox, Thos. Cox, Gideon Cox, Thos. Crouch, Dr. Davis, Morris Davis, Charles Dermon, John Dowdalls, Nicholas Dowell, Richd. Foster, Mrs. Mary, Freeman, Willm. Freeman, Thomas Frisby, James Gray, John Hamin, James Harris, Matt. Hendrickson, Xpher Hendrickson, Willm. Hill, John Hinson, Phil. Holeadger, Wm. Husband, Thos. Jefferson, John Jones, John Keye, Thomas Killton, Edward Laddamore, Michll. LeNeve, Isaac Lovell, John Lowert, Thos. Mercer, John Moll, Robt. Money, James Morgan, Xpher Mounts, Otho Otterson, Thos. Parsley, Will'm. Parson, Gideon Pearce, Robt. Pennington, Richd. Powell, Sam'll Richardson, John Robinson, Charles Rumsey, John Ryland, Charles Sallyer, Nathl. Sappington, Walter Scott, Richard Sewell, Gyles Shute, John Stanley, John Stoope, Thos. Terry, John Umbers, Will'm Veazey, Edwd. Veazey, Matt's Vheyden, John Ward, Will'm Ward, Yock Yorkson

Abbo 7
Abigail 18
Abington 18
Abraham 18, 26
Abram 5
Adam 20, 24
Affey 19
Alce 26
Alice 17, 19, 28
Amy 9
Andrew 18, 26
Answer 30
Anthony 21
Attey 4
Augna 15
Bab 19
Ball 7
Bally 22
Barratt 26
Beck 19, 20, 25
Beleck 8
Belinda 21
Ben 10, 15, 16, 18, 20,
  21, 27
Benbo 26
Bendoe 4
Benjeman 6
Benn 27
Bes 6
Bess 4, 7, 8, 9, 10, 14,
  15, 18, 19, 21, 25,
  26, 27, 28
Bettey 16, 20
Betty 4, 14, 17, 18, 19,
  20, 21, 26
Billy 30
Binda 7
Black Nan 20
Blowes 20
Boa 22
Boatswain 26
Bob 19
Bobo 7
Bombro 26
Boson 14
Bridgett 8
Brissa 4
Bristo 4, 18
Bristoll 21, 25
Bubo 8
Burten 29
Bussey 4

Caesar 17, 18, 19, 20,
  22, 25, 26, 27, 28,
  29
Cambridge 28
Candace 27
Candlemas 26
Cate 6, 15, 18, 30
Cato 5
Catoe 4
Ceasar 7
Ceaser 4, 14
Charles 19, 21
Cherry 23
Cheshire 19
Chester 20, 26
Christian 22
Ciss 10
Cloe 17
Cobb 20
Coco 27
Coffee 6, 7, 8, 9
Coffey 15, 16, 20
Cook 4, 23, 25
Coop 7
Cornelius 43
Cox 5
Coy 5
Crambo 26
Crowtop 19
Cudgo 9
Cuffy 7, 25
Cummy 28
Dab 27
Daff 23, 24, 25, 26
Danby 17
Daniell 16
Daphney 18, 20
Daphny 21, 25, 26, 27,
  28, 29
Darkus 6
Darlphew 23
David 9, 22, 28
Davy 27, 28
Deborah 20
Dell 30
Denbigh 19
Denby 26
Diana 20, 26
Diana Hagar 18
Dick 5, 6, 7, 9, 10, 15,
  17, 18, 21, 22, 23,
  25, 26, 27, 28

Dide 5
Dido 17, 18, 19, 22
Dina/Dinah 16, 17, 20,
  22, 24
Diner 4
Dino 8
Dirna 4
Doctor 26
Dol/Doll 4, 7, 18, 19,
  20, 21, 26
Dominique 9
Donke 14
Dorcas 19
Dorithy 16
Doso 9
Dover 25
Draper 29
Dublin 7
Dugany 30
Durham 18, 23
Eby 22
Edinbergh 7
Edith 28
Ege 17
Elice 21
Elik 5
Elither 20
Enomony 7
Esau 19
Esop 18
Esther 20, 24, 26, 29
Eve 24, 27
Fanny 24
Fendo 4
Ffidolla 22
Ffrank 4
Finney 17
Fisher 15
Flora 19, 20, 21, 26, 27
Fong 6
Fortune 9, 19
Frances 13
Frank 19, 21, 22, 26
Frites 5
Gase 6
Geney/Genney 15
Georg/George 6, 16, 19,
  20, 21, 23
Gibbs 7
Gift 7
Goliah 8
Goodman 28

INDEX OF SLAVES

Grace 7, 8, 24
Grove 22
Guy 14, 18
Heger/Hagar 5, 9, 25, 26
Hago 4
Hana/Hanah/Hanna/Hannah
    4, 6, 7, 9, 16, 18,
    20, 22, 23, 25, 28, 29
Harey/Harry 6, 9, 10, 17,
    20, 22, 25, 26, 27
Harsy 5
Harvey 16
Hector 6, 7, 16, 17
Henny 4
Henry 21
Hercules 4, 10, 26
Herkulus 15
Hinman 13
Holiday 4
Hope 7
Hornens 21
Horsy 5
Huck 21
Husler William 22
Into 9
Isaac 19
Isabal 21
Ishmall 6
Jack 4, 5, 6, 7, 8, 9,
    16, 17, 18, 19, 20,
    21, 22, 23, 24, 25,
    26, 27, 29, 30
Jack Hannah 21
Jacob 4, 9, 10, 18, 22,
    26, 27
Jago /
James 9, 15, 19, 21, 24,
    25
James Pompey 15
Jamey 19, 25
Jan... 5
Jane 7, 9, 25
Janey 6
Jany 5
Jean 4
Jefery 14
Jeffrey 4
Jemey 20, 22
Jemimo 6
Jemmey 20, 21, 29
Jemo 29
Jemy 4

Jenney/Jenny 4, 17, 18,
    19, 20, 22, 26, 27,
    28, 29, 30
Jerry 5
Jessey 9
Jim 6
Joan 14, 17, 19, 23
Job 26
Joe 4, 15, 18, 20, 21,
    23, 24, 25, 26, 27,
    28
John 16, 20
John Proctor 25
Jone 6
Joney 21, 28
Joseph 8, 17, 26
Joy 9
Joyce 25
Jubey 25
Juday 4
Judith 17, 19, 20, 21,
    22, 27, 28
Julia 26
Julius 28
Jupiter 4, 25, 27
Kate (Also see Old Kate)
    23, 27, 28
King 22
Kitt 8, 19, 24, 26
Lambeth 26
Leander 19
Lemon 4
Lesley 14
Leverpool 19, 25
Lidia 22
Lilence 10
Lilly (Also see Old
    Lilly) 19, 24, 28, 29
Limas 23
Limbrick 29
Little Sarah 20
London 4, 25
Lopes 6
Luce 27
Lydia 18, 20, 27, 28
Lyla 19
Lyreo 5
Maffro 18
Major 7
Mall 14, 16, 19, 20, 21
Mansaul 18
Margaret 21

Margery 22
Maria 19, 25, 26, 27, 28
Mark 25
Mary 7, 9, 17
Matt 14
Matthew 18
Meareak 7
Megg 21
Merando 4
Mercer 7
Mercury 26
Mereah 19
Messenger 7
Min 9
Mingo 6, 7, 10, 16, 17,
    18, 19, 22, 25, 26,
    27, 28, 30
Mol/Moll 4, 5, 6, 7, 9,
    10, 17, 18, 19, 22,
    23, 24, 26
Molle 7
Monfurd 9
Monk 7
Moreah 23, 25, 28, 29
Morey 10
Moriah 16, 22
Morsar 6
Moses 10
Munday 4, 28
Murreas 4
Murry 7
Nabb 7
Nack... 9
Nan/Nann 6, 7, 16, 17,
    18, 19, 23, 25, 27, 29
Nancy 9, 19
Nanny 7
Ned 6, 9, 18, 19, 21, 26,
    27
Nell 19
Nero 22, 23, 26, 27, 29
Nick 19
Occoba 17
Occary 29
Old Kate 26
Old Lilly 24
Old Sarah 20
Oldfield Henry 30
Oliver 29
Otho 25
Oxford 19, 25

Pallina 4
Patience 8, 10, 15
Patt 29
Paul 22
Peacock 19
Peg/Pegg 9, 10, 13, 17, 23, 25, 26, 28
Pegr... 9
Penelopy 4
Peter 4, 6, 7, 10, 15, 16, 17, 18, 19, 21, 22, 25, 26, 28, 30
Phebe/Pheby 4, 27, 30
Phenix 23
Phill 19
Philis/Phillis 7, 9, 15, 17, 18, 19, 20, 21, 23, 26, 27, 28, 29
Pipgrin(?), Indian 16
Plaiser 28
Pleasant 7
Polidore 7
Pollipus 25
Polydore 17
Pomp 7
Pompey/Pompy 4, 7, 8, 9, 17, 18, 19, 20, 21, 22, 23, 24, 27, 30
Portsmouth 26
Preston 28
Price 25
Prince 4, 25
Prossey 22
Qua... 8
Quastus 26
Rachel/Rachell 21, 26
Robert Studd 20
Robin 4, 6, 7, 18, 19, 20, 21, 24, 25, 28
Roger 4, 10
Rosa 22
Rose 4, 7, 8, 10, 18, 19, 21, 22, 23, 25, 26, 27, 28, 29, 30
Sabina 4, 17, 28
Sall 24
Sam 7, 16, 18, 19, 21, 22, 26, 27, 28, 29
Sambo/Samboe 4, 5, 6, 8, 9, 10, 16, 22, 24, 25, 26, 28

Sampson 8, 17, 18, 20, 25, 26, 29
Samson 4
Santy 7
Sara/Sarah (Also see Old Sarah) 4, 7, 8, 15, 16, 17, 18, 19, 20, 21, 25, 26, 27, 29, 30
Sarry 10
Saunders 7
Scipio 7, 18, 20, 22, 25
Sebery 20
Sharper 27
She..y 5
Sherper 6
Shot wick 19
Sib 7
Silis 5
Simon/Simond 16, 17, 18, 28, 29, 30
Simus 7
Singo 23
Sinkels 24
Spindelo 20
Stephen 25
Steven 20
Strange 28
Sue 4, 9, 10, 18, 19, 21, 22, 26
Susan 25, 26
Susanna 27
Suslu..ker 5
Taby 7
Terry 22
Thamar 27
Theadore 4
Tice 25
Tite 7
Tites/Titus 6, 16, 21
Toalo 23
Tobby/Tobey/Tobie/Toby 4, 7, 8, 10, 14, 16, 17, 22, 26
Tom 6, 7, 8, 9, 10, 16, 17, 18, 19, 20, 21, 24, 25, 26, 28, 29
Tombo 23
Toney/Tony 9, 10, 14, 17, 18, 19, 24, 25, 26

Toping 19
Touse 15
Trummel 27
Ulysses 17, 19
Vago 21
Vio... 9
Wackra 26
Walle 19
Walley/Wally 19, 20
Wapping 7
Ward 25
Watt 6
Whitehaven 4, 19
Will 4, 5, 6, 8, 9, 10, 15, 16, 17, 18, 19, 20, 21, 22, 25, 26, 27, 28, 30
William 17, 20
Wye 27
Yam 26
Yocko 14
York 25
Young Kate 26

...GAN Edward 69
...LLETT Thomas 68
...MY..ON Michael 69
...RDUE ... 9
ABBAT Samuel 51
ABBITT John 41
ABBOT Thomas 83
ABBOTT John 15, 23, 25; Jonathan 24;
  Samuel 24; Silvester 24; William
  24
Abbotts Mill 47
ABRAHAMS John 25
ABRAMS Jacob 47
ACHAN John 27
ACKLAND William 33
ACKWORTH Richard 35, 40; Thomas 38
ACRES Widow 21
ACWORTH Charles 10; Henry 41; John
  10; Richard 10, 34, 53; Thomas 10
ADAMS Abraham 40; Alexander 8, 53;
  Anne 40; Colins 52; Collins 51;
  David 5, 39, 52; George 39, 52;
  Hope 52; Isaac 52; Jacob 3, 36,
  41, 52; James 42; Mary 40; Mr. 61;
  Philip 3, 36, 40; Phillip 36, 39,
  52; Samuel 51, 52; Thomas 3, 17,
  36, 52, 61; William 21, 51, 52, 62
ADCOCK Thomas 22
ADDAMS George 77; John 78; Stephen
  77; William 77
ADDISON William 23
ADKENSON John 61
ADKINS Robert 8
ADKINSON Thomas 47; Timothy 7
ADKOCK Thomas 82
ADLEY William 8, 78
ADOLLY Edward 64
AGNIFIELD William 78
AHERNE Philip 72
AILER Henry 64; James 51
AINSWORTH William 12, 61
AIRES George 64; William 59
AIREY Thomas 54
AIRS Jacob 78
AK... William 10
AL... Isaac 36
ALABY Peeter 31
ALCOCK Burtonwood 29
ALDERN Richard 27
ALDRIDGE Richard 37
ALEXANDER Andrew 40, 69, 70; Henry
  13; Jacob 71; James 68; Jedediah

68; John 26, 69; Joseph 69; Marten
  71; Moses 8, 69; Nathaniel 69;
  Samuel 8, 61; Theops. 69; Thomas 19,
  59; Widow 2; William 8, 20, 49
ALEY Michael 63
ALFORD Aron 56, 72
ALGUIRE Jacob 73
ALLABY Peter 31
ALLAN John 84
ALLCHURCH Mary 63, 67
ALLEGAND William 38
ALLEMBY Bridge 45
ALLEN Francis 2, 77; John 12, 18;
  Joseph 12, 77; Richard 34; Thomas
  19; William 81
ALLEXANDER Ffrancis 38; William 83
ALLFEE John 11
ALLFORD David 14; Edward 54
ALLIN William 52
ALLISS John 20
ALLISON Michael 17
ALLMAN Abraham 70
Allumby's bridge 46
ALLY John 31, 64
ALMAN Joseph 70
ALPEN James 32
AMBRAS Thomas 1
AMBROSE Abraham 57
AMES Joseph 5
ANDERSON Abraham 70; Archibald 28;
  James 70; John 7, 25, 35, 54, 79;
  Michael 29; Thomas 8; Urias 69;
  William 23, 24
ANDRA George 34
ANDREW George 25; Joseph 22
ANDREWS John 64; Moses 69; Samuel 33;
  Stephen 73
ANGE... James 3
ANGLE William 23
ANTERHAM Catherin 39; Richard 39
ANTHONY John 75
APELGARTH George 82
APPLEGARTH Robert 21
APPLESTONE Mary 41
APSLEY William 57
ARDELL George 23
ARDEREY William 25
ARES Thomas 33; William 46
AREY David 46; Davis 45
ARGO Elexander 5
ARINGTON William 24
ARMFIELD Philip 27

ARMINGTON Cornelius 43
ARMSTRONG Adam 68; Alexander 70;
   Archibald 70; Edward 71; Francis
   20, 59, 81; James 69; Russel 83;
   Thomas 25, 70; William 70
ARNETT William 22, 47
ARNOLD John 71
ARNOTT Francis 76
ARRINGTON John 83; Richard 64;
   William 82
ARTHER Mathew 69
ARTIGE John 71
ASGOOD George 74
ASH Mary 60
ASHCRAFT Thomas 82
ASHCROFT Thomas 22, 42, 59, 60
ASHFORD John 71
ASHLEY Richard 2
ASHLLE John 55
ASHLY Isaac 31, 56; John 56
ASKINE Phillip 35
ASKINS John 37; Martha 57
ASKUE Philip 39, 40
ASKWORTH Richard 34
ATHERLY Isaac 14
ATHEY John 85
ATKINS Stanton 16
ATKINSON James 52; Joseph 26, 42;
   Joshua 52; Thomas 26, 54
ATKONSON John 51
ATWELL Mary 26; Samuel 42
AULD John 22, 83
AUSITER Sarah 64
AUSTIN John 1, 25, 57; William 25,
   31, 64
AUSTON John 64; Richard 82
AVERY Elizabeth 36; John 34, 36; Mary
   36; Sarah 36
AYDLOT Samuel 79, Thomas 79
AYEDOLETT Benjamin 12; William 12
AYERS William 24
AYLER James 76
AYLEWARD John 37
AYRES Comfort 12; Henry 38; Marke 55;
   Thomas 57
AYRS Harison 83

B... James 70
BA...AN John 68
BACON Anthony 25
BACUM Barthlewmy 83
BADFIE John 26

BAGGS John 45, 64
BAIAN Cornelius 33
BAILEY David 1; William 53
BAILY George 8, 39; Jacob 64; Stephen
   8
BAINES George 40
BAIRN James 53
BAKER Charles 32, 76; Daniel 17, 44,
   76; Dutton 80; Henderson 52, 78;
   Henry 69; James 19, 75; John 15,
   75; Nathan 69; Solomon 83; Steven
   17; William 17, 37
BALDWIN John 50, 68
BALEY Henry 47, 73; Matthew 73; Peter
   73; Thomas 77; William 82
BALL Banjamin 45; Elle 34; Henry 71;
   John 23, 71, 76; Thomas 23, 29,
   34, 37
BALLADINE William 55
BALLARD Charles 7, 38, 40, 77; Henry
   61; Jarvis 9; John 77
BALLE Charles 34
BALLEY William 69
BALUNTINE William 58
BALY George 78; William 78
BANARD Thomas 76
BANCKS Charles 31
BANDY Charles 82; Edward 23, 82;
   William 27
BANE Patrick 75
BANING Andrew 51
BANISTER John 7; Thomas 10; William
   40
BANK John 29
BANKSON Andrew 26
BANNEN William 64
BANNIN Andrew 29; John 28; Richard 29
BANNING Phil. 17; William 75
BANNISTER Charles 53
BANSTON Benjamin 52; Edsua 52; Isaac
   53; Jacob 52; Lazrus 52; Thomas 52
BANUM George 37
BARBER James 53; John 38; Peter 27
BARBOTT James 85
BARD Thomas 68
BAREFOOT Nicholas 57
BARKER Arthur 1, 56; John 64; Richard
   25; Robert 85; William 25
BARKHUST James 64
BARKLETT Aylward 80
BARLETT John 20
BARMINGHAM John 64

INDEX

BARNABE Mary 34
BARNABY John 71
BARNES /BARNESS Francis 63; James 19;
   Stephen 35, Thomas 19, 74
BARNET John 83
BARNETT James 24; John 24; Richard
   24; Thomas 24, 73
BARNEY Francis 56; Joseph 57
BARNHILL David 9
BARNICKLOW John 76
BARNIT John 13
BARNS James 76; Thomas 52
BARNWELL James 25
BARON John 49
BARRATT Darby 26; Dennis 21
BARRE Elizabeth 34; Grissegon 34;
   Phillip 34
BARRETT Alexander 40; John 82
BARRON James 23; John 70; Joseph 83
BARROW Gilbert 17; Richard 59, 81
BARRY Andrew 69; John 69; William 68
BARSON Richard 24
BARTLET John 75
BARTLETT Abraham 79; James 28; John
   27, 60, 79; Joseph 27; Nicholas
   27, 29; Pasque 80; Richard 27;
   Samuel 28; Thomas 7, 28; William
   27
BARTOLLES Thomas 53
BARTON Ann 62
BARWELL Peter 76
BARWICK Edward 28; James 64, 75; John
   27, 28, 60, 81; William 28
BASENGAY Jospeh 56
BASHAW Andrew 8; Gerrard 8; Thomas 8
BASNETT Charles 75
BASSITT John 15
BATCHELDER John 51
BATCHELOR John 29; William 29, 82
BATEMAN Christopher 57; William 68,
   71, 85
BATEMEN Mary 57
BATH John 64
BATTHERSHELL Henry 32
BAVINGTON John 85
BAXTER Regere 31; William 74
BAY Henry 47
BAYARD James 70; Samuel 70
BAYLEY Elias 77; Henry 59; James 75
BAYLY Henry 21; Widow 20
BAYNARD Susanna 64; Thomas 64, 82
BAYNE August 50; James 53

BEA... Thomas 3
BEACH John 55
BEACHAMP Edward 3, 61; Fountain 52;
   John 52; Mercy 3, 52; Thomas 52
BEACHAMPS Edward 52
BEACHBORD Levi 84
BEACHOM Edmon 5; William 5
BEAKER William 3
BEAKSTON Thomas 48
BEAL Samuell 80
BEAN Thomas 71
BEANS George 3
BEAR William 25
BEARD John 78; Lewis 61; William 72
BEASLEY John 25
BEASLY Jeffery 70; Thomas 17
BEASTON Edward 50; Thomas 70; William
   49, 68
BEATHEARD Richard 16; William 15
BEAUCHAM Fountain 81; Isaac 81; John
   81
BEAUCHAMP ... 41; Alce 37; Dogel 41;
   Dogett 37; Edmund 35, 36, 37, 42;
   John 37, 42, 53; Marcy 81; Thomas
   39, 42, 81; William 42, 81
BEAVENS Cornelas 80; John 42; Roling
   80; Thomas 80; William 80
BEBBER Van 85
BECK Caleb 57; Edward 53, 56, 57;
   John 53; Joshua 57; Matthew 33,
   57; Samuel 50, 64; Vivian 57;
   William 33
BECKAM Francis 79
BECKETT Peter 15
BECKLY Thomas 32
BECKSBORNE William 12
BECKWITH Henry 43
BECK Jon. 85
BEDEEN 57
BEDLE William 71
BEECH Elizabeth 64, 67; John 1
BEEDLE John 49, 85
BEEN Thomas 49
BEESTONE Georg 48
BEETLE John 50
BECKWITH Henry 72
BELGRAVE Andrew 74
BELHOOK Jeremiah 19
BELIKIN Christopher 56
BELL Anthony 38; Anton 6; Antony 6;
   Edmond 22; George 34, 75; Jacob
   73; James 64, 66, 82; John 6;

91

Joseph 25, 51, 53; Jossephes 81;
  Thomas 6, 23, 53; William 64
BELLARMAN John 71
BELLICAN Chris 54; Christop 57
BELLIN Thomas 3
BENBRIDGE Edward 40
BENNET Edward 36, 77; George 77; John
  39, 50
BENNETT Edward 12, 38; Esqr. 18;
  Ishmell 33; Jane 38; John 37, 38,
  54; Mary 38; Richard 17, 19, 44,
  64; Thomas 45; William 27, 64, 73,
  80
BENNEY John 82; Thomas 82
BENNING Charles 25
BENNIT William 52
BENNY James 17, 42; John 17, 50;
  William 17
BENRRY James 50
BENSON Benjamin 71; George 61; James
  83; Joseph 39; Mary 85; Perry 18,
  59
BENSTON George 38, 61, 79; John 5,
  80; Tom: 7; William 5, 80
BENSTONE George 9
BENT Mathew 76
BENTLY Stephen 72
BENTON Edmond 74; George 80; Peter 2,
  61; Thomas 74; Vincent 77
BERCUM Roger 37
BERKE Edward 56
BERREY Patrick 23
BERRY Daniel 21; David 64; Edward 21;
  James 29, 64; Samuel 55, 57;
  William 72
BERSUM Roger 37
BERWICK James 51
BESSELL Robert 29
BEST Andrew 17; Henry 17; John 29
BESWICK Thomas 81; William 81
BESWICKS George 17; Richard 17;
  Robert 17
BETSWORTH James 4
BETTE John 68
BETTS Anne 38; Ffrancis 38; George
  38; John 68; Robert 27; Thomas 51;
  Thomas Pecock 77; William 72
BEVENS Rowland 37
BIGLANDS Robert 25
BIGNETT Robert 34
BILLTON Thomas 48

BIRCH Christopher 62, 66; Phillemon
  74; William 73
BIRCHEAD Christopher 24
BIRD Benjamin 80; David 52; John 75;
  Joseph 52; Thomas 52, 71, 78;
  William 64
BIRKHEAD Solomon 25
BISHOP Benjamin 14; David 35; Henry
  14, 35, 41; John 14, 15, 41;
  Joseph 84; Richard 31; Robert 18;
  Thomas 15; William 14, 64, 84
BIVAN William 1
BIVANS John 61
BIVENS John 2; Thomas 2
BLACK Alexander 71; George 1; Jack
  20; Jane 55
BLACKFORD Manuel 71
BLACKISTON John 55, 56; Predux 56
BLACKITT John 23
BLACKLEDGE Benjamin 56
BLACKSTON Benjamin 33, 57; John 57
BLACKWELL Charles 20; John 17, 85
BLADE Samuel 78
BLADEN Thomas 52
BLADES Benjamin 52; Edmund 22; James
  51, 64, 78, 82; John 4, 52, 78,
  82; Robert 4, 36
BLAKE John 18, 83; John Sayer 64;
  Peter 83; Philadelphia(?) 64;
  Phillch'r 64
BLAMAN Richard 26
BLANCH Thomas 26
BLANEY Widow 6
BLANGEY Jacob 49
BLAY William 32
BLESSETT William 27
BLEUET Jane 55
BLIZARD Benjamin 13; John 13, 84;
  Richard 14, 79
BLOWER Benjamin 73
BLOYCE Walter 52
BLOYS Thomas 34
BLUETS Jane 58
BLUETT Jane 58
BLUNT Benjamin 74; Richard 62, 64,
  74; Robert 49, 64, 74; Samuel 64
BLUSAR Thomas 23
BOAL Samuell 80
BOARDLEY Thomas 33
BOARDMAN Frenk 8; William 8
BOAST Daniel 34

BODFIELD Abednego 20; John 60;
Shadrach 20, 30
BODY John 57; Rachel 55, 57; Simson
78
BOGGER James 11
BOHANNON Nathaniel 71
BOIER William 32
BOING Littleton 79
BOLDING Alexander 71; Thomas 70
BOLEN James 80
BOLITHA Mary 62
BOLITHE Mary 62
BOLITHO Mary 6
BOLLAND William 79
BOLLERD Charles 39
BOLT John 63, 66
BOLTON John 64; John Winter 82
BOND James 33, 68; Robart 76; Samuel
69; Stephen 35
BONEAM William 2
BOOKER John 28, 45; Joseph 28;
Lambeth 28; Robert 28; Thomas 45
BOON J. 51; Jacob 51; Thomas 55;
William 64
BOOTH Anthony 30, 50, 82; George 34;
James 83; John 8, 60; Samuel 28;
Thomas 57; William 61, 78
BORDLEY Stephen 31
BORSMON Isaac 6
BORWING Thomas 21
BOSEMAN George 42
BOSH William 2
BOSMAN George 9; William 9
BOSMON John 6
BOSSMAN George 35; John 35; William
35
BOSTICK Samuell 85; Thomas 64
BOSTIN Anne 40
BOSTON Bette 40; Elizabeth 61; Esau
38, 40; Henry 34, 37; Isaac 41;
Isaac 3, 40, 61; Isaiah 37; Jacob
52; Richard 36, 41; William 5
BOSWELL Thomas 7
BOSWICK George 50; Robert 50
BOTFIELD Abednego 83; Mesheck 83;
Shadrack 83; Zadock 83
BOUCHER James 61
BOULTON Daniel 63, 64
BOUND Anne 37; Jacob 10; John 35;
William 39

BOUNDS George 62; Joh: 8; John 80;
Jonathan 77; Joseph Jones 77;
Richard Stpen 78
BOURMAN Graves 78
BOWDEN John 79; Thomas 79
BOWDETSH Robt. 37
BOWDIN Thomas 13
BOWDLE Henry 21; Joseph 24; Loftus
21, 60, 83; Mary 23; Thomas 21, 24
BOWE Humphry 17
BOWELL George 48
BOWEN John 83; Richard 70; William
35, 49, 70
BOWERS James 64
BOWES George 47
BOWIN David 15; John 15; Littleton
12; William 15
BOWING Whitenton 83; William 83
BOWKER Thomas 47
BOWLAND William 9
BOWMAN Thomas 72
BOWN Thomas 57
BOWND Edward 15
BOWWHANNAN John 10
BOWYER James 55
BOXE Ffrancis 32
BOYCE ALEXANDER 21; Augustine 33;
Joseph 40; William 33, 70
BOYD William 34
BOYER Augustin 56; Austin 57; Daniel
24, 59; James 57; Peter 69; Robert
3, 52; Thomas 55; William 57
BOYS Nathan 68
BOZMAN George 81; John 83; Risdon 22;
Thomas 19, 51, 59
BR... Richard 47
BRADBURY Jacob 29; Roger 30
BRADFORD James 21; John 15; Nathaniel
15
BRADLEY Charles 51; Henry 14, 72
BRADLY Charles 64
BRADSHAW Anne 36; Christopher 28;
John 28, 33, 59, 60; Thomas 20,
22; William 33, 36, 57
BRADSHAWE William 35
BRADY John 8; Phillip 64
BRAIMAUGH Amborse 40
BRANNOCK John 54
BRANOCK John 43
BRASIER Pet'r D. 7
BRASSCOP John 26, 83
BRATEN Joshua 79

BRATTEN James 79; John 79; Natthaniel
79; Samuell 79; William 12, 79;
Willson 79
BRATTON James 38; William 61
BRAUGHTON Bruff 52; William 52
BRAVARD John 70
BRAYNING Edward 23
BRAZER William 3
BREASTON John 52
BREDIL Isiah 14; William Gray 14
BREERLY Samuel 21
BRERETON Maror Thomas 36; Thomas 36,
61; William 36
BREUARD Adam 83
BREWAR William 56
BREWER John 76
BRIAN Dannelle 50
BRIANT John 74
BRICK Anthony 20
BRIDGES Richard 82
BRIDGEWATERS Emanuel 16
BRIEN William 4
BRIERWOOD John 82
BRIGES Charles 23; Daniel 23
BRIGHT Frances 74; Francis 64, 66
BRILEY John 82
BRILLEHANE John 2
BRIMFIELD Edward 68
BRIN Ann 25; John 47; William 25
BRINNINGUM Walter 52
BRINSFIELD George 24
BRISCO Alexander 32; John 56
BRISCOE Alexander 57
BRISTOW George 69; William 69
BRITTEN Richard 34
BRITTINGHAM ... 4; Absolom 79; Isaac
15, 79; John 4, 41, 78; Joseph 14;
Josiah 14; Nathan 79; Poynter 79;
Samuel 78; Thomas 84; William 14,
79
BRIUN John 59
BROAD... James 68
BROADAWAY Ambrose 82; James 29;
Samuel 29, 50, 82
BROCKETT William 58
BROKE Elinor 58
BROMLEY Thomas 40
BROOCKS Richard 19; Samuel 20
BROOKE John 33
BROOKS Francis 4; John 55, 72;
Margaret 57
BROOKSHAW James 39

BROOMS Samuel 22
BROTEN Samuell 14
BROTHER John 74
BROTON James 16; Quanton 16; Samuell
15
BROUGHTON John 2, 38, 52
BROWN Adam 21; Andrew 1, 21, 64, 80;
Bartholomew 33; Charles 18;
Christopher 20, 73; David 9;
Edward 17, 64, 74, 77; James 51,
62, 64, 72, 73; John 10, 56, 57,
63, 66, 69, 72, 77; Joseph 19;
Mary 28; Matthew 64; Morgan 77;
Nicholas 17, 81; Perrigrine 32;
Peter 69; Richard 64; Samuel 70;
Sarah 61; Sidny 79; Thomas 3, 9,
26, 61; William 10, 49, 59, 68,
85; Zacharias 58
BROWNBILL Henry 12; Nathaniell 12
BROWNE David 37; John 35, 38, 39, 49;
William 40
BROWNING Thomas 51, 55, 58, 85
BROWSTRUM Hane 80
BRUCHSHER James 4
BRUEING Henry 13
BRUERTON John 78; Samuel 78; Smith
78; Thomas 8; William 8
BRUFF Richard 18, 46, 59, 81; Thomas
18
BRULEY Timothy 15
BRUMELL Abram 82; Robert 82
BRUMEY Edward 20
BRUMLY Littleton 79
BRUMWELL Jacob 19
BRUSARD William 57
BRWARD Solomon 33
BRYAN Daniel 54; Isabealla 60; John
27; Mary 57; Patrick 32
BRYANT James 74; John 65
BRYLEY William 65
BU... John 36
BUCKINGHAM Catherine 30; Henry 29;
Howel 30; Isaac 30; Thomas 45, 46
BUCKLAND Richard 36
BUCKLEY James 20; Richard 65; Robert
24; William 20
BULEN Darby 22; Thomas 65
BULK John 36
BULKE John 36
BULLEN Aaron 82; Henry 59 ;
John 59; Thomas 51
BULLEY Mathew 69

BULLOCK Benjamin 24; James 24; John 24
BULLON Thomas 25
BUN John 34; Patrick 7
BUNDICKE Dorithy 36
BUNN James 8
BUNTON Joseph 25; Thomas 25
BURBAGE Edward 15; John 15
BURCK Thomas 65
BURDEN Richard 29
BURGESS Henry 26; John 21, 24, 29, 50; Stephen 29, 50, 51; William 71
BURGGER Isaac 31
BURGIN Daniel 9
BURGISS Stephen 82
BURK Edward 29; John 3, 73; Richard 26; Thomas 62; Tobias 7, 62; William 63, 64, 66, 67
BURKE Richard 32
BURLEIGH Pasque 38
BURMAN Robert 48
BURN Darius 83; Solomon 20
BURNET James 6
BURNETT James 78
BURNS James 70; John 70
BURRELL Alexander 50; Samuell 1
BURROUGHS William 65
BURSTUNS Roger 37
BURTON Benjamin 16; Joshua 79; Stratton 14; William 13, 50, 61
BUSE Joseph 34
BUSH Elizabeth 42; George 20; Joseph 20; Richard 20; Solomon 20; Stephen 29, 75; Thomas 20, 75; William 20
BUSHNALL John 65
BUSHSELL Peter 70
BUST Ann 55
BUTCHER Robert 38
BUTLER Benjamin 56; Ezekil 80; Joseph 10, 56, 65; Thomas 2, 18, 80
BYARD Peter 70
BYRD Thomas 53
BYRELL Jere. 29

C... Thomas 70
CAD Daniel 79
CADDENHEAD John 73
CADE Robert 49
CAHALL Edmund 65
CAHELL Edward 75; James 75; John 20, 75

CAHOON John 52; Samuel 52
CAHOUNE Ham. 85
CAID Robert 29
CAIDE Robert 82
CAIMBRIDGE William 85
CAINE William 2
CAIRE Thomas 34
CALACKHONE James 76
CALAWAY John 80
CALDER James 1, 63; St. Leger 55
CALDWELL James 53, 61; John 6, 11, 61; Margrett 6; Patrick 6; Thomas 6
CALK James 82; John 71; Peter 83
CALLAHAN James 17
CALLAHANE Ferdinando 17
CALLAWAY Ebenezer 80; Isaac 80; John 80; Mathew 80; Peter 80; William 80
CALLENHAUGH Rich. 72
CALLOWAY John 11; Peter 11; William 11
CALLWELL Edward 22; James 41; John 68; William 68
CALSH Edward 82
CALVART Charles 61
CALWELL Samuell 68
CAMBELL John 83
CAMELL Solomon 83
CAMEREN Evander 78
CAMILL John 13
CAMLEY Daniel M. 63
CAMMEL Charles 75
CAMMELL John 23
CAMMULL John 14
CAMPBELE John 69
CAMPBELL John 49; Walter 54; William 50, 62, 65, 77
CAMPBLE Archibald 68; James 68; Joshua 69; Peter 69
CAMPER Abraham 82; John 22; Richard 82; Robert 65; Thomas 82
CAMPERSON John 29, 65
CAMPISON Leonard 37
CAMPLIN Thomas 38
CAMRON James 76
CANADY Rogert 32
CANDRY John 41
CANE James 9, 20
CANHAR... Charles 6
CANN... Calip 70
CANNADY John 29

CANNEDY William 34
CANNING William 36
CANNON Charles 18; James 75
CARDERY John 80
CARE David 70; John 70
CARELO John 25
CAREY Dennis 25; Edmond 26; Florence 24; Francis 3; John 3; Philip 26; Richard 36; Sarah 3; Thomas 36; William 24, 26, 39
CARLILE Alexander 8; John 69; Robert 69
CARLYLE Alexander 61
CARMADY Daniel 23
CARMAN James 74; Mary 63; Thomas 73; William 66, 77
CARMICHALL Neall 68; Walter 63
CARNE James 34
CARNELL William 85
CARNES Thomas 23, 34
CARNEY Robert 40
CARNOWAY James 26
CARPENTER John 66; Nicholas 38
CARR John 23; Joseph 7
CARRADINE James 76; John 65; Thomas 76
CARRINGTON John 50
CARROKIN John 41
CARROL Denton 27
CARROLL Charles 22; Denis 1; Phillip 1; Thomas 34
CARROW Andrew 65
CARSEY Robert 81
CARSLAKE Edward 26, 83; John 26
CARSLICK Thomas 81
CARTER Arthur 23; Dennis 56; Henry 10, 74; Hercules 65; Jacob 74; James 69; John 10, 25, 36, 49, 62, 65; Madam 47; Phillip 10, 37, 40; Richard 62, 64, 65, 74; Vall 74; Vallentine 49; William 29, 76
Carters bridge 46
CARTEY Maurice 57; Timothy 24
CARTHEY Timothy 49
CARTIE James 28
CARTWRIGHT Charles 48
CARVELL John 33; Thomas 34
CARVILL John 57
CARY Edward 38; Jane 40; Jeremiah 78; John 40; Mary 41; Solomon 78; Thomas 4, 38, 41, 50; William 8
CASE Alce 59

CASEY John 21
CASSEY William 52
CASTEN Jos. 72
CASTRO James 70
CATCH William 71
CATHCART Robert 24
CATHE Edward 20
CATHELL James 3
CATING William 5
CATLIN Robert 36, 39, 40, 41; Sarah 39; William 39, 52
CATON Henry 6
CATROP John 83
CATROPE Lemon John 25; William 25
CATS Stephen 65
CATTLEN Robert 34
CATTLIN Joseph 35; Robert 35, 36
CATTON William 50
CAUGHTHRAN William 69
CAULK Isaac 48, 49; Jacob 33
CAULKE Jacob 85
CAUSEY John 72
CAVANAUGHT Bryan 18

CAVENOUGH John 15
CAWDERRY ... 7; Edward 7; Isaac 7; John 7
CAWDRY Daniell 2; Jacob 77
CAYTON John 6, 35
CAZIER Phillip 50, 68
CEARSY Joseph 39
CEDAR John 18
CEEF Hugh 23
CETCH James 69
CHA... John 71
CHACE John 75
CHADDOCKS Sarah 55
CHADDWICK James 8
CHADOCK Thomas 1
CHAIERS John 48
CHAIRES James 65, 76; John 31, 62; Joseph 65, 67; Thomas 62, 64
CHAIRS Joseph 77
CHAM... William 71
CHAMBERLAIN Samuel 19
CHAMBERLAINE John 9; Samuel 27; William 48, 62
CHAMBERLIN Jon 50
CHAMBERS Charles 74; George 29; James 29, 76; John 30, 50, 71; Mary 55; Richard 10, 37, 39, 61, 74; Robert 77; Thomas 74

CHANCE Douglass 21; John 20; Richard
  19, 59
CHANCELEER John 49
CHANDL... Richard 71
CHANDLER Thomas 26
CHANSELLOR George 14
CHAPLAIN Francis 24; James 24
CHAPLIN James 83
CHAPMAN Daniel 30, 50; Edward 3; John
  12, 81; Joshua 78; Silas 3;
  Umphery 12
CHAPNITE William 8
CHEASEMAN William 34
CHEEKE Edward 72
CHEESMAN William 72
CHEILLE Moses 50
CHELTON Matthew 65
CHERREX James 11
CHESELDICK Charles 24
CHESERIM Samuel 25
CHESMAN John 10
CHESSEY James 19
CHETHAM Edward 65, 67
CHEW Samuel 18
CHICK John 70; Joseph 71; William 70
CHICKEN Edward 31; Martha 31
CHICKIN Edward 31
CHILDS Benjamin 69; George 69; John
  69; Nathaniel 69
CHILTON Abel 75; Matthew 75
CHOCHUNE Matthew 24
CHRISTEFAR Clement 78
CHRISTIAN John 18, 29; Thomas 18, 56
CHRISTOPHER John 71
CHROUCH John 80
CHURCHELL John 76
CHURME Wilks 4
CIXER Mary 6; Samuel 6
CIYSER Mary 6; Samuel 6
CLARK Caleb 29; Charles 14; Edward
  13, 29, 70, 71, 79; Henry 26;
  James 75; John 2, 21, 28, 56, 68,
  69, 72, 76; Joshua 29, 50, 67;
  Mary 54; Mr. 43; Nathaniel 39;
  Race 13; Rades 79; Robert 44;
  Samuel 24; Thomas 42; William 9,
  19, 26
CLARKE Edward 41; George 54; John 33,
  41; Robert 44; Samuel 33; Thomas
  40
CLARKSON William 39, 42
CLARY Daniel 6

CLASH Edward 2; John 25; Nicholas 27
CLAYLAND Harris 17; James 27; John
  65; Lambert 50, 51; Roger 17, 85;
  William 18, 27, 59
CLAYTON Edward 76; John 33, 55, 56;
  Solomon 62, 67, 73; William 18,
  46, 59, 60, 85
CLAYWELL Peter 12, 79; Solomon 79;
  Thomas 12; William 84
CLEAVE Benjamin 65; Nathaniell 62, 73
CLEAVES John 55; Nathaniel 65
CLEMENS David 17
CLEMENTS Cornelius 85
CLEMMONS John 75
CLEMONS John 63, 65
CLIFF John 25, 76
CLIFT Joseph 65, 68
CLIFTON George 61; John 52
CLIMER Francis 75; Thomas 75
CLOAK Maurice 65
CLOSSY John 63
CLOUDS Benjamin 65; Nicholas 74
CLOUGH George 26
CLOUGHTANE Thomas 72
CLOVE John 56
Clovis Point 45
CLOW Nathaniel 30
CLUBEGE Gaven 69
CLUFF Edward 52; Michael 52
COADE John 48
COALK Peter 23
COBB John 13; William 12
COBOURN James 20
COBREATH John 62, 65
COCK Lusbert 85
COCKAYNE Samuel 17, 59, 83; Thomas
  26; William 82
COCKERILL Dennis 22
COCKETT Thomas 23
COCKEY Charles 74; Edward 62, 74, 75
COCKLIN Tiomothy 23; William 85
COCKY Edward 65
CODD St. Leger 48
CODNAR Alexander 29
CODNER Alexander 82; Jeremiah 82
COE Daniel 79
COFEN Thomas 13
COFFEY Daniel 21; Francis 14;
  Nicholus 14
COFFING William 79
COGGS Ralph 20

COHOONE Darley 72
COLE David 69; George 25; Jacob 19;
    John 17, 40, 57, 76; Peter 56;
    Richard 38; Thomas 57; William 17,
    60, 69, 81, 85
COLEBOURNE Anne 36; John 36; William
    36, 38
COLEHALÆ William 19
COLEMAN James 20; John 73; Surkick
    41; Thomas 65; William 73
COLENS John 75; Walter 75
COLESON Anne 40; John 40, 41;
    Margrett 40
COLGON Edward 74; John 73
COLHERNE John 39
COLHOUNE John 6
COLHOWNE John 6
COLINGS Abil 79; Ebenezar 83; William
    83
COLINS Ffrancis 59; John 51; John
    Offley 73
COLLBOORNE Sollomon 34; William 34
COLLEG... Hugh 2
COLLENS Thomas 72
COLLIENS Thomas 78
COLLIER Charles 74; Douty 77; Evans
    77; George 7, 77; James 42; Kendel
    83; Peeter 14; Robert 37, 42, 77;
    Thomas 8, 61, 62
COLLIERS Thomas 78; Timothy 78
COLLINGS Ebenezar 13; John 13, 73;
    Mary 13; Thomas 79; William 13
COLLINS Andrew 16; Charles 15; Edmund
    40; Elianor 62; Ffrancis 32; James
    79; John 41, 64, 65, 75; Price 14;
    Richard 6, 65; Samuell 37; Thomas
    15, 41, 61, 83; William 9, 50, 79
COLLISON Edward 22, 82; George 22,
    23; William 82
COLLVER Benjamin 68
COLSON James 60
COLTSTON John 49
COMEGYS Edward 33; Nathaniel 65;
    William 33, 56, 57
COMMEGYS John 77
COMMINS Nicholas 82; Thomas 82;
    William 82
COMPTON John 70
CONAWAY Thomas 26
CONDON Edward 70
CONER Nixon 12
CONGDON James 27

CONNAR Ann 59; Arthur 60
CONNAWAY Denis 82; James 58
CONNE... Owen 9
CONNEL John 23
CONNELLY Christopher 26; Terence 26;
    William 24
CONNER Anne 38; Arthur 20; Charles
    74; Daniel 20; Eliza. Mary 38;
    James 49; John 20; Levien 80;
    Nathaniel 74; Patrick 40; Philip
    48; Richard 12; Roger 26
CONNERS William 48
CONNOR Charles 49, 65; Lawrence 39;
    Mary 38; Nathaniel 49, 74, 82;
    Phillip 38, 49; Thomas 74
CONOR John 5; Philip 5; William 5
CONSTANTINE Robert 19
CONWAY William 81
COOK Francis 22; Gye 80; Hercules 64;
    Robert 3; Thomas 19, 43, 57, 82;
    William 70
COOKE Edward 43
COOKSON William 55
COOLY John 83
COOMBS William 19
COOPER Beni 82; Gabrell 11; George
    59; Isaac 11; James 11; John 18,
    25, 34, 50, 65, 71, 75; Jonathan
    38; Peter 50; Richard 75; Samuell
    11, 38, 52, 80; Sharpless 75;
    Thomas 82; Widow 18; William 18,
    65, 75, 81, 83
COPE John 8
COPEDGE John 31
COPLAND Laurence 51
COPLEN Lawrance 75
COPPAGE Phillip 74
COPPER George 32
COPPIN John 71
CORD Joseph 79; William 12
CORDERY Daniel 61
CORK Laurence 18
CORKEN John J. 49; Richard 6
CORKER Daniel 73; John 22
CORKERILL John 18
CORKERIN Peter 23
CORKRIN William 25
CORKRINE Daniel 24; James 24, 26;
    John 26
CORN William 20
CORNELIUES Peter 74
CORNELIUS William 33

CORNER Adam 82
CORNISH Neah 19; Noah 83; Solomon 19
CORNWELL Nicholas 38, 49
CORSE Edward 18
CORSEY William 82
CORSINE John 70
CORSON George 48
COSDEN Alphonso 69
COSTEN Ahab 77; Isaac 2; Stephen 2
COSTER Ahab 77
COSTIN Ezekiel 80; Henry 65, 85;
   Mathias 80; Richard 65, 76, 85;
   Stephen 36, 61, 80
COTINGHAM Jonathan 5, 42
COTINGIM Charles 6
COTMAN Henery 15; John 6
COTTER John 19
COTTINGHAM Charles 41, 61; John 41;
   Jonathan 42; Thomas 37
COTTMAN Benjamin 8, 77; Ebenezer 10;
   Joseph 8; William 8, 77
COTTON Jeremiah 27
COULBOOURN Solomon 52; William 53
COULBORN William 40
COULBOURN Ann 5; Benjamin 53, 81;
   Elija 81; Isaac 53, 81; John 2;
   Samuel 52, 81; Solomon 52, 53;
   William 52
COULBOURNE Solomon 5; William 6, 40,
   49
COULMAN Henery 15
COULTER James 68
COUNCILL Henry 65
COUNTESS William 51
COUNTIS James 62, 65
COURSE James 56
COURSEY Henry 48, 65; James 53; John
   65; Samuel 52; William 44, 48, 62,
   65, 73, 76
COVENTON Isaac 83
COVENTUN John 75; Nathaniel 75
COVINGTON Henry 65; John 37, 38;
   Nehemiah 34, 37, 77; Philip 4, 38;
   Rebecca 38; Thomas 6, 34
COVINTON Jeremiah 57
COWADON James 71
COWARD John 19, 33
COWIN John 40
COWLEY John 82; Joseph 19
COX Benjamin 85; Christopher 76;
   Daniel 79; Gideon 85; Henry 69,
   71; Isaac 28; Israel 21; Jeffery

21; John 21, 50, 76; Joseph 21;
   Nathaniel 21; Powel 83; Thomas 9,
   36, 69, 75, 85; William 3
COXILL John 71
COXK Daniel 80; Hill 80; John 80;
   Thomas 80
COYNE Daniell 59; William 73
COZENS Edward 57
COZINE George 71
CRABURN John 22
CRADOCK Bryan 71; George 25
CRADUCK John 17
CRAIG Henry 85
CRAIGE Edward 39; James 71; William
   71
CRANER Thomas 76
CRANOR Thomas 27
CRAPER Nathaniell 83
CRAPPER Ebenezar 15; Edmond 14, 83;
   Nathanal 14; Sollomon 14, 83;
   Vincin 83
CRASSON James 41
CRAWFORD Samuel 68; William 68
CRAZY James 4
CREAGH Patrick 31, 32
CREW John 34
CRISP Thomas 69
CRISTOPHER Ephraim 8; John 8
CRITTEL John 33
Crock's bridge 45
CROCKETT John 7; Richard 7, 36, 61;
   Robert 7, 42
CROKER Robert 50, 71
CROKET Samson 5
CROMMY James 68
CRONEAN Edward 19
CRONEY John 76
CROOK Robert 48
CROOKE Zebbs 44
CROOUCH Wedge 56
CROPPER Edmond 50; John 37; Nathaniel
   50; Nehemiah 14
CROSS James 65
CROSSWELL John 68; Joseph 68; Samuell
   68
CROUCH Ann 8; Isaac 8, 80; Jacob 8,
   78; John 8, 77; Joseph 20; Josiah
   58; Nicklus 80; Rachell 4; Richard
   56; Robert 35, 41; Thomas 70, 77,
   85
CROUSE Robert 37

CROW Edward 56; Isaac 33; William 56, 71
CROWDER Francis 10; Joseph 37
CROWLEY John 36
CROXALL Richard 22
CRSLEY Cornelius 32
CRUCKSHANKS James 56
CRUICKSHANKS James 1
CRUMP Michael 26; Robert 65
CRUPPER John 37; William 64, 65
CUCKOW John 29
CULLEN David 81; Edmond 10; Jacob 53; William 81
CULLIN Isaac 79; Jacob 52, 81; John 28, 40, 81
CULLINDER William 20
CULLING Edward 78; Mary 41; William 79
CUMINGS Nicholas 65
CUMMBERFORD George 64
CUMMINS Nicholas 21; Thomas 22; William 22
CUNINGHAM Arthur 4
CURRE william 39
CURRER William 69
CURRIER John 68
CURTICE John 72
CURTIES Nathaniel 75
CURTIS Daniel 34; Daniell 35; Elizabeth 34; James 35; John 65; Martin 49; Thomas 64
CUSHINGTON Robert 27

D... James 9
D...te John 5
DA...GE John 68
DA...N Nathaniel 69
DAINTY William 74
DALANAWAY Thomas 75
DALANY Danaell 78
DALEY Henry 46; James 75; John 75
DALTON James 72
DANCASTER John 5
DANE Thomas 68
DANIEL Richard 31; William 69
DANIELL John 42; William 12
DANNIEL William 69
DARBY John 11, 48
DARRINGTON John 76
DARSON Ralph 48
DASEY Thomas 13
DASHELL Jane 60

DASHIALL James 77
DASHIEL George 61; Henry 77; Thomas 40
DASHIELD James 41
DASHIELE Robert 41
DASHIELL Charles 4; Clement 77; George 7, 80; Harb: 7; Isaac 77; James 34; Jesse 77; Louther 77; Mitchell 77; Robert 7; Sarah 7; Thomas 4, 7, 62, 77; William 80; Winder 80
DASHILL Elizabeth 34
DAUGHERTY John 53; Nathaniel 53; Peter 53; Stephen 53
DAVICE John 33
DAVID John 19
DAVIE Richard 68; Samuel 68
DAVIES Daniel 9; James 39; John 9, 52; Richard 55
DAVIS Absolem 74; Adria 61; Benjamin 76; Capt 44; Catharine 67; Charles 12, 78, 79; Cornelius 59; Daniel 14, 27; David 1, 59; Dr. 85; Edward 14, 24, 35, 37, 40; Elizabeth 27, 35, 61; George 18, 57; Henry 56, 57; James 1, 6, 34, 40, 78; John 5, 25, 27, 35, 37, 41, 42, 55, 72, 77, 78, 79, 81, 83; Johyn 77; Jonas 34; Joseph 2; Katherine 65; Lazarus 2; Morris 85; Nathaniel 2, 40; Peter 74; Philip 1, 56; Richard 1, 33, 34, 40; Robert 16; Samuel 9, 13, 15, 36, 41, 61; Sarah 5, 41; Simon 63, 64; Tamerlane 17, 27; Tamerlin 59; Thomas 5, 26, 34, 35, 39, 41, 54, 62, 64; William 14, 16, 19, 29, 34, 40, 61, 71, 77
DAVISON James 18, 75; John 18, 20, 24; William 14
DAWES James 34
DAWLEY John 21; Thomas 21
DAWSEY John 19, 72
DAWSON Anthony 72; George 82; Impy 83; James 22; John 45, 46; Joseph 22, 25; Ralph 22, 27, 48, 82; Richard 22, 56; Robert 22, 82; William 22, 64, 65, 76, 83
Dawsons 47
Dawsons Creek 46
Dawsons Rich land 47

DAY Edward 37; George 34; Mathias 33, 56
DAYE Mathias 50
DAYLEY Joseph 74
DAYSONE William 72
de BRULAGH John 38
De HART James 50
DEAL Archbald 13; John 13, 83; Samewal 83
DEALE John 49
DEALL Archabel 83
DEALY Patrick 2
DEAN Henry 19; John 79, 80; William 57
DEANE John 2; William 33
DEANS Thomas 73; William 33
DEAR Stephen 40
DEARDS Ffrances 41
DEARE Stephen 9
DEATH Edward 68; James 68; John 68; Randell 68
DEAVEN Emanuel 73
DEBRULAR George 33
DEBRULER George 56
DEDULPHUS William 37
DEE James 29
DEEN David 76
DEFORD John 75; Lewis 65; William 75
DEHORTY Morgan 18; William 18
DELAHAY Henry 83; James 25; Thomas 24; William 83
DELANAWAY Thomas 65, 75
DEMONSON Polard 83
DEMPSTER John 51, 65
DENAIRE John 72
DENCUM William 38
DENEY Peter 49
DENGHBY William 23
DENIS Doneck 15; John 15; William 15
DENISON Daniell 14
DENNING John 50
DENNIS Daniel 37, 80; Dannarka 35; John 3, 51, 52, 61; Larzarus 80; Littleton 52; Vallentine 80
DENNY James 83; John Earle 62; Joseph 28; Peter 28, 42, 83
DENSON William 8, 40
DENSTON William 2, 61
DENT Barbiry 39; Peter 41
DENTSON John 2
DENWOOD Esther 9; John 9, 85; Levin 4, 34; Thomas 34

DEPARNER John 1
DEREXSON Joseph 13; Samuel 13
DERICKSON Anderend 42
DERMON Charles 85
DEROACHBRUNE Joseph 65; Lewis 65
DERRAGIN Darby 60
DERRUM Daniel 61
DEVALL William 68
DEVERIX John 14; Nicholas 18; Samuel 14; Thomas 65
DEVRIX Thomas 73
DEWLAND John 19
DEWLIN David 1
DIAS Thomas 36; William 36
DICAS Edward 32; John 29; William 32, 33, 56
DICKENSON Charles 54; William 46
DICKERSON Nehemiah 78; Teague 79
DICKES Thomas 27; Abram: 3; Cornelius 2; Edmund 2, 38; Edward 2; James 3; Peter 3; Som.set 3; Teague 3
DICKINSON Charles 73; Daniell 83; Henry 83; James 25, 41; John 24; Richard 18; Samuel 26
DICKMAN Ffrancis 59
DICKSON ... 8; Ambros 34; Anthony 68; Benjamin 68; Edward 34; Mary 34; Robert 68; Sarah 34
DICUS William 1
DIDIS Thomas 19
DIEGAS Devoraux 49
DIES Daniel 53
DIGSON Charles 68
DIKES Edward 52; George 6
DILL James 1,33
DILLAHA John 12
DINGELL William 82
DIRKENSON Edward 34; John Peter Edward 34
DISHAROON John 8, 9; Lewis 9, 61; Michael 8
DISHAROONE John 42
DISHARUN Luoss 49
DISHROON John 77; Michael 37, 77, 78; William 77
DIX Robert 6
DIXON Alce 36; Ambrose 36, 52; Ambrous 81; Elizabeth 35; Grace 36; Isaac 27, 81; John 13; Jonathan 13; Mary 36; Risdon 81; Sturgis 13; Thomas 6, 35, 81; William 6, 45, 69, 81

DIXSON Thomas 4
DO... Robert 9
DOARE Stephen 9
DOBERLY William 19
DOBSON Anne 30; George 73, 83; Isaac
   29, 30, 50, 51; John 81; Jonathan
   82
DOCKERY Matthew 77
DODD George 76
DODS Thomas 65
DODSON Robert 23
DOE Ralph 41
DOIRNIN William 35
DOLAP Ninian 39
DOLTON James 65
DOLVIN John 17; Richard 82
DONAHO William 80
DONELSON John 61
DONES Thomas 31
DONILEY John 24
DONNAHOE Daniel 34
DONNELL Nicholas 71
DONNISON Patrick 10
DONOHO Sormon 80; William 52
DONOHOW William 2
DONOWHO Thomas 75
DOPMAHOY Alexander 19
DORMAN Ezekiel 77; Henry 4, 42; John
   77; Mathew 35, 61; Mathewe 36;
   Richard 59; Samuel 3,61, 78
DORON Daniel 2
DORRINGTON Jospeh 32; William 72
DOUDE Edward Spencer 42
DOUGHERTIE Nathaniel 37
DOUGHERTY James 78
DOUGLAS Reynolld 36
DOUGLASS Samuel 19; Thomas 26
DOUGLIS Archibald 17
DOVE Richard 20
DOWDALL John 32
DOWDALLS John 85
DOWDELL Cristopher 8
DOWDEN James 76
DOWELL Alexander 72; Nicholas 85
DOWIN Widow 14
DOWNES Charles 65, 76; George 4, 36;
   Henry 19, 76; Hynson 76; James 76;
   John 62, 63, 65, 67, 76; Robert 11
DOWNEY Elexander 75; Vallentine 74;
   Valln. 74; William 74
DOWNS John 85; Robert 41, 53
DRAPER Allexander 34; Solomon 82;
   William 75

DREADEN John 12
DREADON David 52; John 14; Robert 14
DREDDON David 40
DREDEN Jane 38; John 41
DREW William 76
DRIDDEN William 85
DRIGAS Deverix 16
DRISKELL Moses 53
DRISKILL Denis 41; William 65
DRUMLEY Timothy 15
DRURA Matthias 66, 67
DUAS John 29
DUBERLY John 78; Thomas 78
DUDLEY James 29; Richard 46, 51;
   Samuel 29, 50, 51; Thomas 29, 50,
   51, 83; William 29
DUDSON Rich. 72
DUELL James 72
DUER William 12
DUERLY William 32
DUETT William 51, 52
DUHURST Jane 59
DUKE George 78
DUKES Robert 80; Thomas 2
DUKS William 52
DULANAWAY Phill 76
DULAP Charles 10
DULEN John 24
DULIENTE Daniel 1
DULIN George 50
DULING Francis 83; George 83; Joseph
   83
DULLIENT Daniel 1
DUN John 29, 71; Nicholas 79; Thomas
   79
DUNAHO Nathaniel 9
DUNAHOE mathias 71
DUNBAR Allan 14
DUNCAN John 33
DUNCON Matthew 80
DUNING Samuel 29
DUNKIN John 4
DUNN Robert 54, 56; William 22, 55,
   56
DUNNAHAW John 58
DUNNAHAWS John 55
DUNNOVAN Darby 19
DURDEN Joseph 1; Rebecca 30; William
   85
DURKINS William 79
DUSKEY Dennis 9
DUSKY James 9; Moses 9; Richard 9

DUSSE William 34
DWIER Darby 25
DWIGGENS 28
DWIGINS Robart 75
DYALL Catn 62
DYAS John 82
DYCAS William 32
DYER Daniel 55; John 80; William 17
DYRE Samuel 64

E... Richard 70
EACHELSMITH ... 63
EAGLE Henry 75; Solomon 75; William 65
EAGLEY Samuell 49
EAMES Joseph 39
EARECKSON Charles 31, 74; Dorothy 31; John 74; Matthew 31, 49, 64
EARIKSON Benjamin 74
EARL James 85; Joseph 85
EARLE Carpender 63; Carpenter 63; James 51, 62, 65, 66, 73; John 58, 65; Joseph 65; Mary 67
EARRICKSON Mathew 75
EASON Joseph 21
EASSOM William 80
EASTON Francis 21
EATON Richard 27; Thomas 27
EAVENS John 5, 11
EBET John 78
EBTHORP Thomas 70
ECCLES John 23
ECCLESTON John 72; Richard 26
EDDGS Joshua 11
EDGAR Robert 22
EDGE Thomas 30; William 30
EDMON Noll 49
EDMONDS Isaac 36; John 41
EDMONDSON Holland 42; John 20, 24; Robert 70; Solomon 54; William 17, 21
EDRINGTON Barth'w 69
EDWARD Dr. W. 65
EDWARDS Elizabeth 42; George 65; Richard 67; Thomas 25, 69; Walter 75; William 18, 55, 58, 67
EGG James 72
EGLE William 76
EHLENAS Andrew 31
ELBERRY Federick 70
ELBERT William 18, 59, 76, 85
ELDEST Henry 48

ELDRACK James 24; John 24
ELENSWORTH William 80
ELEY Benjamin 56
ELGEY William 53
ELGITT William 7
ELIASON Cornelias 70; Elias 71
ELIPHANT William 10
ELIS John 53
ELLEMES William 35
ELLET John 53
ELLGATE William 36
ELLICKSON John 65
ELLIJOTT William 34
ELLINGSWORTH Richard 11; Robert 11
ELLIOT Edward 22, 23; Elianor 61; George 51, 65; John 65; Joseph 65; William 65
ELLIOTT Edward 59, 60; John 75, 76; Joseph 74, 77; Steven 34; Thomas 74; William 49, 73
ELLIS John 3,34, 41; Joseph 76, 78; Mary 38; Merrick 7, 60, 61; Thomas 3, 41; William 41, 50, 68, 78
ELLISON John 13
ELLISS Thomas 23
ELLIT John 53
ELSTON Ralph 20, 83; William 60
ELSTONE Roger 65
ELSTONS Ralph 44
ELWOOD Patrick 23; Philip 70; Richard 71
ELZERY Peter 49
ELZEY Arnold 40, 61; Elizabeth 42; Ffrances 42; John 10; Peter 34, 42
EMBERT Thomas 76
EMERSON Joh. 85; John 76; Joseph 67; Philip 18; Richard 76; Thomas 44, 46, 47, 85
EMERY James 76
EMMETT Abraham 39; John 35, 39; Josias 39
EMMORY Arthur 44
EMORY Arthur 51, 62, 76, 85; John 62, 64, 65, 67, 76, 85; Thomas 76; William 56, 75
EMPEOU(?) Ellis 35
ENDLESS Abraham 13
ENGLAND Isaac 33
ENGLISH James 11, 80; Thomas 11; William 11
ENNALLS Bartholomew 72; Henry 72; J. 54; Thomas 54

ENNIS Cornelius 14; William 16
ENOCK John Wilson 57
ENOUCHSON Enoch 68
ERICKSON John 31
ERNSHIRE Isaac 41
ERRECKSON Matthew 66
ESGATE Stephen 60
ESKRIDGE William 10, 60
ESOME Benjamin 61
ETHERINGTON Thomas 69
EUBANKS John 75; Joseph 82; Moulton
83; William 47
EUSTACE John 29
EVANS David 4; Edward 36, 49; Evan
18; Griffith 46; Henry 33, 57;
James 49, 65; John 7, 35, 40, 41,
53, 77, 79, 83; Jonathan 75;
Joseph 74; Joshua 79; Nathaniell
3; Nicholas 7, 77; Rachell 7;
Richard 53; Robert 69, 72; Solomon
79; Thomas 3, 48, 53; William 8,
53, 72
EVENES John 10; William 10
EVENS Ebenzer 84; Elias 83; Elisha
83; Gamage 83; James 64; John 84;
Jon 14; Thomas 41; Widow 14;
William 13
EVERITT Thomas 65
EVERSON Elias 70
EVERTON John 7; Thomas 39
EVERTSON Evert 68, 71; Jacob 68
EVETT John 39
EVETTS Nathaniel 31
EVINS James 75; John 65; Thomas 76
EWBANKS George 27; John 27; Martha
26; Morton 26; Thomas 20, 26, 44
EWING James 85; Nathaniel 68; William
68
EXLEY John 42

FAERHURST Thomas 21
FAHAY John 24
FAIRBANK Benjamin 23; James 23; John
23; Thomas 23; William 23
FALASPY Alexander 71
FALCONAR Abraham 26; Barton Francis
76; Benjamin 76; Francis 65, 76;
Gilbert 57; Jacob 26; John 65, 76
FALKNER Thomas 64, 65
FANING Robert 74
FANNEN John 55; Jon'n. 32
FANNING James 1; John 1, 59

FAREWELL Richard 38
FARMAR William 65
FARMER Daniel 57
FARNALL Thomas 41
FARRELL James 51, 82; John 82;
William 46
FARRENTON Robert 80
FARROWFIELD James 76; John 65; Jonas
81
FASSIT Franklyn 13; John 13; William
14
FASSITT John 50
FAULKNER Abraham 82; Burton Francis
82; Ffrancis 59; Isaac 17, 82;
Jacob 82; Joseph 82
FAUSITT John 16; William 16
FAWL John 14; Widow 14
FEASTON John 24, 60
FEDDEMAN Philip 28; Phillip 59;
Richard 44, 46, 48
Feddeman's bridge 47
FEDEMAN Phill 65
FEDEMON Henry 76
FEDEN Randell 5
FEILDING James 72
FELLOWS John 26; Mathias 71
FENTON Moses 3, 61; William 65
FERENTON Levin 80
FERGERSON John 9
FERILL Edmund 50; Thomas 14
FERN Miles 82
FERREL John 69
FERRELL Edmond 26; James 20, 21, 23,
59; John 12, 20, 37; William 59
FERRIL Edmond 83
FERRILL Daniel 56
FIDDIS John 1
FIDDY Randol 78
FILLINGHAM Richard 32, 31
FILLIPS Samuell 1
FINCH Samuel 72
FINDLEY james 73
FINDLY James 75
FINLEY Andrew 65; Coll 47; James 68
FINNEY Widow 17; William 46, 85
FINNY Vincent 83; William 83
FISH Edmond 20; John 72
FISHER ... 9; Alexander 72; Henry 10,
79; John 41, 76; Jonathan 1;
Richard 62; Samuel 17; Simon 23;
Thomas 17, 62, 76; William 75
FITCHET Thomas 85

FITTEMAN Joseph 12
FITZGERALD Garrot 21
FITZPATRICK Charles 32; David 65, 81;
    John 65, 85; William 81
FLA... Edward 8
FLEETWOOD John 11
FLEMAN Lodowick 15
FLEMING John 2, 17, 52, 61; Joshua
    52; William 52, 80
FLEMMING William 10
FLEMON John 75
FLEMOND John 24; Pearce 26; Thomas 23
FLETCHER John 39; Michael 20, 27;
    Thomas 15, 50
FLIN Daniel 58; Laughlan 58
FLINN Daniel 55, 56; Laughlan 57
FLINT James 76; John 76
FLOOD Patrick 20
FLORD William 78
FLOWERS Thomas 72
FLOYD Charles 18, 32; Francis 72;
    Jeremiah 30, 75; John 28, 34;
    Robert 65, 75
FLY Thomas 22
FOLEY Denis 4
FONTON Moses 39
FOOKS William 25
FOORD Absalom 53; John 72; Richard 70
FORAD Absolom 52; Ambros 45
FORBUSH John 73; Mary 54
FORCUM John 65; Peter 65
FORD Ablosom 6; Charles 71; Daniel
    73; James 71; John 70; Robert 32;
    Thomas 20; William 32, 65
FOREMAN Arthur 57; Aurthur 1; Frances
    73; Francis 1, 65; Robert 1, 33;
    Widow 1; William 1, 21
FORMILLER Francis 21
FORREST'R John Cooper 57
FORTH Timothy 82
FORTUNE David 72
FOSQUE Benjamin 10; Luke 78; Thomas
    10
FOSSETT John 39
FOSTER Andrew 65; Isaac 70; James 71;
    John 7, 76; Richard 69, 70, 85;
    Rigby 19; Thomas 17, 22
FOTTRELL Edward 19, 28; Mr. 24
FOUNTAIN ... 10; John 10; Marcy 40;
    Marsy 40; Mercy 10; Merry 35;
    Nicholas 10; Samuell 10; William
    10

FOUNTAINE Dennis 35; Marsy 40; Mercy
    38
FOUNTAYNE Nicolas 34
FOURACRES John 73
FOVEY Samuel 32
FOWLER Edward 7, 37; Henry 69; John
    77; Thomas 78
FOX Nathaniel 20
FRAHIL Phillip 1
FRAISHER John 21
FRAME Arthur 35
FRAMPTON Robert 50; Thomas 50;
    William 50
FRANCES ... 9
FRANCIS Arnold 37; Tench 26
FRANKLIN Ebynezar 15; John 15;
    Richard 70
FRANKLYN Edward 50
FRANTOM William 28; Robert 30;
    Thomas 29, 82; William 82
FRASSIR John 83
FRASSIT John 83
FRAY Philip 20
FRAYSHER Hen 78
FRAZER Peter 5, 61
FREEKES Henry 41
FREEMAN Isaac 57; John 27, 35; Joseph
    37; Mary 37, 85; Minikin 27;
    William 13, 85
FREENE Peter 11
FRENCH Nathaniel 22
FRIEND George 76
FRIGGS Henry 11; Robert 11
FRISBY James 33; Peregrine 50; Thomas
    85; William 31, 48, 56, 58
FRITH Henry 46, 48; John 20
FRITZ Henry 46
FRIZELL John 39
FROGETT John 32
FROST John 25
FRYE Thomas 65
FULLERTON Alexander 78
FULSTON John 32; Richard 32, 33
FURBUS Peter 7
FURLONG Edward 34
FURNER William 59
FURNIS Comfort 35; James 78; Samuel
    37; Sarah 35; William 34, 35, 79
FURRON Edward 50

G... Archibald 70
GAD Thomas 76; William 17

GAFFORD Charles 56
GALE Betty 4, 7; George 4; John 57;
    Levin 4, 50, 61; Thomas 65
GALES Gabriel 19; Levin 7
GALL... George 68
GALLAHER Farril 20
GANNON Charles 29, 50; William 30
GANT Robert 61
GAR Eli 84; Elisha 84; John 84
    Mickall 84
GARATT Edward 19
GARDNER Francis 69; John 70
GARES John 29
GAREY George 18; John 81; William 81
GARNETT Thomas 57
GARRATT Thomas 18
GARRETT Thomas 36
GARSONS John 41
GARVIS Samuell 11
GARY Stephen 72
GASKIN John 59
GASKING John 24
GATES Henry 26
GAUGHT Obed 83
GAULT Robert 13
GAYLE George 42
GEDDES Robert 52
GEFFERYSON Richard 11
GEORGE Daniel 71; Joshua 59; Nicholas
    70; Robert 56, 57; William 7
GIBBINS Alexander 80; Ezekiel 79
GIBIN Ezekiel 80
GIBS John 65; Robert 4
GIBSON Bartholomew 18; Jacob 18, 44,
    46; John 19, 81; Jonathan 42, 81;
    Richard 18; Woolman 18, 81, 83
GIDDINS Maurice 28; Thomas 40
GIDING Morris 83
GILBURT John 74; Soloman 74
GILES Clement 49; William 3, 20, 36,
    38, 40, 77
GILLETSON William 70
GILGO william 65
GILL James 67; John 31; Robert 20;
    Roger 31; Sarah 31
GILLAGHUES Widow 1
GILLELAND John 14
GILLES Thomas 9
GILLET John 3; Samuell 3
GILLETT John 78
GILLIAGAN Bryan 10
GILLIS John 10, 34, 40; Thomas 34

GILLISS Levin 77; Thomas 77
GILLITT William 78
GINKINES Jarvis 78
GINKINES John 78
GINKINS David 78
GIRRARD Mary 8
GISLIN John 37
GIVAN Robert 38, 61
GIVEN James 39; Thomas 35
GLADEN Thomas 51
GLADSTONE John 37
GLANDENNING George 38
GLANDIN Thomas 65
GLANVILL William 31
GLASCOCK James 1
GLASS Christopher 12; John 36
GLASSCOCK John 23
GLEAVE Joseph 54
GLEAVES George 56, 57; Joseph 54
GLEN Nicholas 83; William 47
GLENDEN Thomas 12
GLENN Jacob 33; Robert 71; William 46
GLOVER Daniel 48; John 25; Richard
    83; William 17
GODARD George 3; John 80; Longland 3;
    Thomas 3
GODDARD George 8; John 8; Landgen 37;
    William 42
GODWIN Edward 75
GODFREE Joseph 80
GODFREY Charles 14; Joseph 14
GODGIN Benjamin 15
GODMAN George 60; Thomas 49, 65, 73
GODWIN ... 13; Calor 79; Cezar 13;
    Edward 51; Mary 13; Michael 13,
    50; Thomas 65; William 65, 77
GOGGIN David 3; Edward 3
GOGIN David 53
GOLD James 77
GOLDSBOROUGH J. 50; John 26; Nicholas
    20, 26, 28, 59; Richard 83; Robert
    26, 30, 59, 81; William 20
GOLDSMITH Anthony 42; John 10, 34,
    36; Mary 36; William 34
GOLET John 69
GOODHAND Joner 74; Marmaduke 49, 62,
    65, 74
GOODIN Jacob 1; Samuel 56
GOODING Samuel 33, 57
GOODMAN Elizabeth 57; Richard 74
GOORDON John 76; Thomas 76
GORDAN Thomas 61

GORDEN Thomas 11
GORDIN John 5
GORDON John 76; John 18; Peter 8;
    Robert 70; Thomas 53
GORDY Thomas 78
GORE Jacob 30, 81; Thomas 33
GORS James 76
GORSUCH Charles 21; Richard 21
GOSLIE John 77
GOSLIN John 7; Levin 80; Mathew 78;
    Richard 7
GOSSAGE Charles 82
GOSSLING James 11; Thomas 11
GOUGH John 26; William 64
GOULD Edward 39; James 65, 73;
    Richard 73; Thomas 59
GOULDEN John 9
GOULDESBOROUGH Robert 65
GOULDING James 64
GOULDSBROUGH Ro. 48
GOWS James 75
GRACE Abel 29; Nathaniel 23, 27;
    William 29, 81
GRADEN Ffrancis 4
GRAHAM John 54; Joseph 19; William 39
GRAHAMS Terence 26
GRAINGER Lazerus 70
GRANGER H'm (Hiram?) 62; John 65, 74;
    William 33
GRANTHAM William 54, 72
GRASE Nathaniell 82
GRASHAM Joshua 20
GRAVENER Thomas 11
GRAVERNER Phillip 41; Thomas 41;
    William 41
GRAY ... 9; Allen 80; Andrew 79; Dent
    41; Elie 62; Isaac 71; Jacob 79;
    James 75, 80, 85; John 11, 70;
    Joseph 2, 13, 37, 71, 83; Oliver
    72; Sollomon 52; Thomas 83;
    William 10, 80
GREAR William 41
GREAVES Matthew 73; Thomas 73
GREEN Bowles 57; Elizabeth 36; Henry
    32, 65; James 68; John 44, 56, 57,
    65, 76, 83; Joseph 48; Lucy 32;
    Margret 42; Peter 57; Phill 76;
    Robert 55; Vellentine 76; William
    36; Zeakell 11
GREENDIZE Charles 33
GREENE William 34
GREENFIELD John 23

GREENHAWK Thomas 82; William 75
GREENHAWKS John 81
GREENHOCK Thomas 27
GREENWOOD Bartholomew 83; Caleb 82;
    John 56; Jonathan 65; Robert 82;
    William 76
GREER George 10, 78; Hencry 78; John
    15; Mark 10
GREGORY Anthony 26, 50, 81; Edward
    73; Joseph 45; William 73
GRESHAM Andrew 18; George 18; Richard
    18
GREWER William 33
GRIAN Robert 53
GRIDLEY Jeremiah 50, 71
GRIEVES Matthew 65
GRIFFETH Edward 83
GRIFFIN Benjamin 58; Charles 25;
    Edward 19; Enoch 42; George 57;
    Lewis 72; Mathew 76; Thomas 25;
    William 15
GRIFFITH Benjamin 56; Charles 56;
    George 54, 56; John 34; Matthew
    49; Thomas 74
GRIMES Jeremiah 74
GRINDAGE Charles 55
GROOM William 13, 61
GROOME Elizabeth 35
GROSIER John 29
GROVER Thomas 15
GROVES Robert 26
GRUMBLE Benjamin 53, 78
GRUNDY Robert 44, 45, 47
Grundy's Mill 45
GULET William 6
GULLERY Hugh 71
GULLET William 37
GULLICK John 71
GULLY Thomas 26
GUNBY James 52, 81; John 6, 41, 52;
    Kirk 52, 81; Kurk 6
GUNDRY Gideon 48
GUNING Thomas 19
GUNN William 54
GUNTER Philip 72
GURRLY John 10
GUTTREY Elijah 84; Joshua 84; Moses
    84; Philip 84
GUY Ben 20; James Williams 18

H... Andrew 69
H... John 10
HA... John 9
HACKET Michael 1
HACKETT John 27, 31, 32, 65, 73;
  Michael 1, 56; Thomas 51, 65, 77
HACKIT William 48
HADDAWAY Capt 82; Edward 82;
  Elizabeth 22; George 23, 82; Peter
  22, 82; Rowlen 82; Thomas 22, 82;
  William Web 22
HADDEN William 44, 81
HADDER Antony 15; Warrin 15
HADER Warring 83
HADLEY Thomas 65
HAFE... James 69
HAFFURT George 35, 39
HAGE John 17
HAGGATHY William 57
HAILE James 72
HAILS John 78
HAINES John 6
HAIRNE Thomas 6; William 6
HAISTAINS Robert 80; William 80
HALE David 80
HALES Roger 57
HALEY Honour 55; John 73
HALL Alexander 10; Anne 36; Charles
  6, 36, 37, 53, 81; Edward 22, 76;
  Ezekiel 53, 81; Fenix 2; Francis
  55, 58; Henry 36; Isaac 22; Jacob
  62; James 12; John 6, 22, 35, 42,
  65, 76, 77, 79; Jos'a 53; Joseph
  57; Joshua 78; Lawrance 77; Mary
  36; Pheanix 38; Richard 5, 28, 53;
  Robert 14, 18, 37, 81; Samuel 79;
  Stephen 8, 84; Steven 23; Thomas
  30, 80; William 5, 15, 57, 70, 76,
  80
HALLCEY John 20
HALLER William 37
HALLON John 34
HALLS Edward 31
HALOS Martha 6
HALTHAM Charles 71
HALY John 57
HAMBLETON James 73; John 1, 23, 48,
  70, 83; John Hawkins 63, 67;
  Philemon 23, 83; Samuel 25; W. 48;
  William 23
HAMBLIN George 35
HAMELTON John 75

HAMER Anne 32; Collins 74; John 62,
  64, 77; Sarah 32; William 32
HAMILTON Andrew 48; James 51, 77
HAMIN John 85
HAMLIN Elizabeth 37; Francis 13;
  George 37; John 13
HAMM Jacob 70; John 70
HAMMET John 74
HAMMON John 14
HAMMOND Charles 80; Edward 15; John
  15, 62
HAMOND Edward 15; Thomas 62
HAMONE Rose 63
HAMOR William 65
HAMOUR John 65
HAMPTON Andrew 56; David 69; George
  71; Mary 3, 15; Thoams 65
HAMTON Thomas 74; William 74
HANDCOK Daniell 15; William 15
HANDS Bedingfield 63
HANDSWORTH John 24
HANDY ... 7; Ebenezar 9, 61, 62;
  Isaac 80; John 7, 53, 77, 81;
  Samuell 6, 36, 38, 39, 52, 53, 81;
  Stephen 5, 53; Thomas 39; William
  2, 38, 61, 62
HANE Robert 1
HANECEY William 73
HANGE John 27
HANNAH Michaell 38
HANNING Francis 82
HANSON Fredrick 55, 59; George 32;
  Hance 31; Haunce 32; Hense 57;
  William 32
HANSONE Margret 31
HARBERT William 65
HARBET Michael 48
HARDASSOL Robert 75
HARDE Robert 34
HARDEN Benjamin 76; John 21, 76;
  Joseph 24; Robert 24; William 24
HARDGRAVES John 25
HARDIN Edward 47
HARDING Edward 26, 28
HARDY Henry 38; James 7; John 7; Mary
  38; Rebecca 38
HARES William 72
HARGADINE John 76; Mark 67, 76
HARGISSONE George 72
HARIM Jane 58
HARIS Jeremiah 42

HARMAN Edward 28; Manuell 12; Mark
76; Richard 20
HARNEY Elizabeth 39; Thomas 13, 61;
Timothy 39; Tymothy 38
HARNY Thomas 50
HARPE... John 71
HARPER Edward 2, 40; Jacob 70; John
2, 61; Michael 27; Richard 2;
William 17, 70
HARRESS Spencer 80
HARRETT John 41
HARRIN Jane 55, 58
HARRINGTON Anthony 76; Joohn 23
HARRINTON John 82; Richard 59
HARRIS Caleb 2; David 38; Edward 85;
George 37; Henry 24; Isaac 31, 49;
James 2, 54, 62, 75, 82, 85; John
2, 65, 80; Moses 44; Patrick 70;
Philip 8; Richard 7; Robert 2, 62;
Robon 41; Thomas 19, 83; William
7, 31, 38, 60, 77, 82, 83
HARRISON Erasmus 14; James 22, 68,
82; Jeremiah 40; John 23, 27, 35,
59, 82; Joseph 22, 23, 82; Moses
46; Perry 82; Richard 68; Robert
23, 48, 82; William 21, 23, 24,
25, 27, 59, 82
HARRISS Abraham 80; Amos 24; Bloyd
79; James 80; Jane 55; Moses 47;
Zachariah 80
HART Henry 20; John 73
HARTNESS John 70; Robert 70
HARTSHORN Benjamin 68; Jonathon 68;
Thomas 68
HARTSHORNE George 32
HARVEY Henry 72; James 26; Kemperson
74; Robbert 74; Thomas 74; William
38
HARVY William 11
HARWOOD Patrick 72; Peter 28, 45, 47;
Robert 28; Samuel 28
HASBU... George 36
HASELWOOD William 72
HASS Daniel 35
HASTANS John 80
HASTING Robert 6
HATCH Adam 40
HATCHISON Vincent 55, 56
HATFIELD William 44
HATH William 80
HATTERSON Jane 60
HATTERY James 70

HAUGHTER Edward 81
HAUGHTON Thomas 50
HAULTS William 57
HAWK John 22
HAWKINS Emant 73; Ernault 65, 77;
James 81; John 48; Matthew 77;
Robert 77
HAXTER Henry 74
HAYLOR Henry 39
HAYLY John 26
HAYMAN Arthur 9, 39; Charles 39;
Henry 36; James 39, 41; William 8,
9, 36, 39
HAYMON James 80
HAYNES William 32
HAYS James 22; John 65
HAYWARD Francis 72; John 62; Thomas
61
HAZARD Cord 13; David 13; Edward 34,
35
HAZELDINE Richard 36; Francis 18
HAZZARD Edward 35
HEADING John 32
HEALTH Jacob 10
HEARN Edward 6
HEARNE Darby 31
HEART Patrick 82
HEARTSHORN William 75
HEATCH Adam 7, 38; William 6
HEATH Abraham 10, 36, 61; James 31;
Jarrat 17; John 37; Josiah 85;
William 85
HEATHER Ephraim 15, 79
HEATHERLEY 53
HEATICK John 6
HEBRON Thomas 56
HEELIS John 28
HELSBY Thomas 23
HEMSLEY Mr. 17; Phi. 47; Philemon 48;
Vincent 45; William 65, 73, 85
HENCOCK Daniel 84
HENDERSON Barnaby 78; Bishop 12;
Charles 4, 16; Daniell 77; Francis
3; James 3, 14; John 3, 37, 52;
Joseph 10, 78; Lemuel 78; Levin 78
HENDRICK John 71
HENDRICKSON Christopher 85; Florence
65; John 56; Matt. 85
HENDRIXON Henry 69
HENERY Gabriell 39
HENESEY Andrew 18; William 17
HENLEY Lawrence 34

HENLY Lawrence 37
HENNESEY Andrew 81; John 13
HENNEY Thomas 68
HENRICKS Henry 25; John 25
HENRIX John 45, 47
HENRY John 19; Robert 50; William 69
HENS George 6
HERBERT Charles 23; Edward 24; James 23
HERD Edward 17
HERIS Jeramiah 5
HERMAN Casp'r Agust. 48
HERRING William 19, 20
HERRINGTON Anth. 29; David 81; Isaac 81; John 29; Joseph 23; Richard 23; William 23
HESKETH John 17
HEWETT Joshua 27; Thomas 81
HEWS William 81
HEWY Widow 18
HEY George 39
HEYDON Samuell 38
HEYMORE Henry 34
HEYSOM Mary 7
HIATE Edward 25
HICKEDY James 21
HICKENBOTTOM Oliver 56
HICKES Giles 82
HICKMAN Arthur 79; Benjamin 7; Jonathan 79; Richard 50
HICKS James 75; Joseph 27; Levin 72; Thomas 54
HICKSON John 25, 51
HIEBUS George 9
HIELLEY Edward 9
HIGGENBOTTOM Oliver 57
HIGGINS James 19; John 18, 23, 73; Nehemiah 29, 82; Nicholas 24; Otho 75; Thomas 17, 21, 82; William 24
HIGGINSON John 62, 66; Joseph 63
HIGGS Aaron 18; Moses 81
HIGHWAY Abraham 14
HIGNETT James 35; John 35; Robert 35, 40; William 35
HIGNITT James 35; John 35; Robert 35; William 35
HILL ... 9; Abraham 12; Alce 39Charles 8; Edward 76; Francis 33, 56, 59; Henry 21; Hutten 12; Jacob 78; James 42; John 4, 10; Johnson 12; Jos'a 79; Richard 49; Robert 12, 15; Thomas 42, 61;

Walter 71; William 43, 85; William Steven 84
HILLARD John 34
HILLIARD Isaack 35
HILLMAN Edward 8
HILLS Hasaida 31
HILLSON Thomas 38
HILLYARD Isaack 36
HILMAN Ezekiel 78; John 78
HINDERSON James 35
HINDRIXON John 54
HINDSLEY Thomas 73
HINE John 39
HINES Ben. 74; James 65; Natthaniel 75; Vincent 75
HINESLY Nathaniel 65; Peter 64, 65; Solomon 51
HINESON Richard 75
HINGE John 34
HINSLY Thomas 75
HINSON Elizabeth 57; John 85
HIRTSON Nicholas 35
HITCH ... 53; Adam 53; John 53, 80; Nehemiah 80; Solomon 10, 41
HITCHCOCK John 70; Thomas 70
HIX Roger 58
HOBBS Benjamin 77; James 67; Josiah 85; Joy 4, 37; Marsilleous 4; Meridlin 77; Noble 4; Stephen 77; Thomas 4, 37, 38
HOBSON William 27, 70
HODDGE William 70
HODERT William 52
HODGE Robert 15, 36
HODGES Robert 56
HODGGEN Richard 8
HODGIN John 42
HODGSON Mathew 69; Phemi 70
HODSON John 72; Peter Taylor 54
HOG James 13
HOGG Daniel 53; John 12; Roland 12
HOLBEADGER PHILLip 50
HOLBROOK Thomas 60
HOLBROOKE Thomas 36
HOLD Arthur 51
HOLDER John 42
HOLDING John 73
HOLEADGER Phil. 85
HOLEBROOK Thomas 7
HOLEY Robert 68
HOLINGS Abraham 71

HOLLAND John 15, 37, 49, 70; Michael 5, 6, 39, 62, 81; Nehemiah 12, 41; Richard 14, 50, 72; Samuell 83; William 3
HOLLIDAY Edward 58; James 65
HOLLINGSWORTH Charles 32; John 65, 73; Thomas 65; Zebulon 69
HOLLINS Joseph 17
HOLLINSWORTH Charles 48
HOLLON John 29
HOLLOND Isaac 78; Michal 52
HOLLONDY Michel 52
HOLLOWAY ... 14
HOLLY William 68
HOLLYDAY George 65; James 19
HOLLYFIELD William 27
HOLMES Archibald 38; Mary 26; Richard 26; William 59
HOLMS Ralph 28; Robert 28
HOLSTEINE William 37
HOLSTON John 12
HOLSTONE Charles 14
HOLT Anne 60; John 79
HOLTON George 71
HOMES Abraham 69
HONEY Thomas 65
HOOD Matthew 72
HOOK Jeremiah 37; Roger 15; William 15
HOOKES Benjamin 53
HOOPER Henry 72; John 54; Roger 72
HOOPES Jeremiah 35
HOP... Thomas 46
HOPKINGS Jerge 5
HOPKINS Benjamin 28; David 79; Dennis 20, 28, 46, 83; Edward 21, 82; George 36, 53, 76; Isaac 79; James 28, 59; John 21, 27, 53, 79, 82; Jonathan 28; Joohn 50; Joseph 20, 23, 83; Josiah 12, 50; Levin 79; Mathew 69; Nat 61; Nathaniell 12, 79; Phillip 31; Richard 26, 28; Robert 20, 36; Sa. 12; Samuel 12, 20, 27, 50, 83; Thomas 17, 27, 46, 47, 48, 59; William 12, 20, 53, 55, 58
HOPPER William 64, 65, 77
HOPWOOD Sarah 57
HORDELL Edward 40
HORNER Benjamin 5; George 10; John 5; Joseph 50

HORNEY James 18, 59, 82; Jeffery 26, 59; Phillmon 83; Solomon 22; Thomas 75; William 26, 82
HORSEMAN Henry 53; Thomas 41
HORSEY Isaac 6; John 10, 53; Nathaniel 6; Outerbridg 81; Revell 61; Revil 10; Samuel 5, 37; Smith 53; Stephen 5; William 10
HORSI Steven 34
HORSLEY James 73; Ralph 36
HORSTMAN Thomas 37
HORSY Smith 81; Stephen 52, 81
HOSIER Samuell 12
HOSKINS Edward 55, 58
HOSSER Henry 58
HOSSEY Mathew 11
HOSTON John 40
HOUGH Edmand 15; Edmond 62
HOUGHTON Richard 68
HOULSTON John 39, 84; Sarah 40
HOULT John 24
HOULTON James 24
HOUSTON Benjamin 2, 80; Ja. 3; Joseph 2, 3, 62; Robert 35
HOWARD Edmund 41; Edward 37; George 13, 50, 79; John 7, 13, 52, 79; Joseph 13; Michael 20, 59, 64; Michall 56; Nehemiah 50, 79; Samuell 13; Thomas 4, 22, 25, 34; William 25, 34, 79
HOWELL Cove 44; Joseph 65; Thomas 54
HOWES Joseph 35
HOWESTLARKE John 34
HOWGIN Sarah 8
HOZIER Jacob 68
HUBANKS Edward 26
HUCHESON John 75
HUCHONS George 53
HUCKLEY Hannah 41; John 41
HUDDEN William 45
HUDSON Absolom 79; Andrew 24; Annanias 83; David 13; Dennis 79; George 79; Henry 83; John 72, 83; Richard 13; Samuell 12, 79; Solomon 83; William 62, 79
HUDSONE John 72
HUER John 31
HUETT John 38, 39, 49
HUFF John 33, 55, 56, 57; Margret 33
HUFFINGTON John 11; Jonathan 11; Richard 11; Thomas 11
HUC... Abraham 70

HUGG John 33; Thomas 9, 61; William
  17
HUGGINS Charles 11; Edmon 11; John
  11; Nehamiah 11
HUGH Robert 59
HUGHES Christopher 17; James 68;
  Martha 39; Samuel 71
HUGHS David 23; Richard 18
HUGS John 23
HUKILL Richard 70
HULBROOK Thomas 77
HULL Daniel 5; David 33; Edward 5;
  Leonard 29; Nathaniel 29, 83
HUMPHREY Ellis 31
HUMPHREYS Thomas 7, 39
HUMPHRIS Ezekiel 77; Joshua 78
HUMPHRY John 27; Thomas 36, 53
HUMPHRYS Thomas 7, 25
HUNT John 23, 44, 45, 82; Molbrough
  74; Peter 22, 82
HUNTER Anne 31; J... 68; John 70, 71;
  Mary 31; Robert 30, 82; Roger 60
HURD John 75; Peter 75
HURDY Robert 78
HURLEY Joshua 82; Timothy 31
HURLOCK George 28; James 28, 29
HURSEY Micheal 76
HURST Emanuel 56; John 60
HURT John 31, 58; Morgan 58
HUSBAND John 70; William 85
HUSE Joseph 35, 79
HUSK Joseph 79
HUSSEY Michaell 51, 65; Thomas 51
HUST John 4, 36; Joseph 9
HUSTON Charles 69; John 82
HUTCH Robert 67
HUTCHENS John 20, 29
HUTCHESON John 51
HUTCHINGS James 74
HUTCHINS George 7, 61; Henry 7; James
  73; Samuel 21; Solomon 26; Thomas
  30; Thomas Elliott 77
HUTCHINSON James 26
HUTCHISON George 63
HUTCHYSON Charles 72
HUTSON Denis 14; Elis 14; John 14,
  16; Robert 14; William 14
HUTTER Thomas 20; Widow 20
HUTTON Henry 34; John 21; William 28,
  81
HUZZEY Stephen 82
HYDE Edward 72

HYE Ann 42
HYLAND Nicholas 68
HYNSON John 32, 48; Nathaniel 32, 56;
  Richard 51; Thomas 50, 56, 58
HYWAY Isaac 8

IDELETT Benjamine 40; John 40
IDOLETT John 50
INDIANS: Alexander 49; Asick 49;
  Basteby 49; Chinramack 49; Gorge
  49; Mianita 49; Mr. Bearatt 49;
  Mr. Nanoy 49; Mr. Rango 49;
  Panquash 49; Peetor 49; Pettor 49;
  Powinixus 49; Robin 49; Sawamack
  49; Will 49; Winomatoakem 49;
  Witaricon 49; Wittangebott 49
INGHAM Robert 31
INGLE William 37
INGLISH James 38
INGRAM Abraham 11, 61; Ann 34; Isaac
  11; Jacob 11; James 37, 40; John
  33, 58; Mary 40; Robert 11, 31, 34
INNES Robert 35
INNIS Ann 37; Kersey 37; Samuel 37
INSLEY James 72
IRINS Charles 75
IRONSHIRE Isaac 41; John 15
IRVIN John 69; Mathew 70; William 69
IRVING George 85; John 85
ISENOTT Edward 41
IVERY Margaret 34; Mary 34

JACKSON Archibald 65, 70; Daniel 79;
  Edward 68; Enock 27; George 64,
  65; Gilbert 22, 82; Henry 68, 85;
  Isaac 61, 80; John 74; Joseph 8,
  64; Joshua 77; Mary 65; Samuel 8,
  35, 37, 69; Thomas 49, 76, 80
JACOB Samuel 36
JACOBS Henry 76; William 27
JADWIN Jeremiah 51; Robert 44, 45
JAGGERMAN John 17
JAGGERS James 4; Mendum 5; Thomas 5
JAME... William 71
JAMES Anthony 39; Edward 29; Gil...
  37; John 19, 25, 27; Joseph 24;
  Laurence 82; Richard 50; William
  19, 20
JANE John 71
JARMAN ...e 15; Amos 76; Henerey 15;
  Jobe 16; John 15; Robert 15;
  Stephen 76

JARMON Joseph 76
JARRETT John 36
JARVIS William 9
JEFERSON Richard 39
JEFFERS George 76; John 81; William 74
JEFFERSON George 23; Henry (Henery) 22, 82; Richard 38; Thomas 85
JEFFORDS Simon 24
JEMISON Allexander 34
JEMSON William 70
JENCKINS David D. 40; Ffrancis 42
JENCKINSON John 40
JENKINGS Enock 70
JENKINS Enoch 70; Jane 67; Jarvis 8; John 70; Mathew 24, 83; Philip 20; Samuel 20; Thomas 83; Walter 24, 83
JENKSON Charles 23
JENNINGS Bartholomwe 65
JENSON John 6
JERMAN Robert 62, 65
JEROM Thomas 56
JERVICE Margarett 60
JERVIS Elizabeth 61
JEWEL Ann 67
JINGLE Hugh 49
JO... Ephraim 68
JO... Francis 71
JOBSON Philip 50
JOCE Nicholas 55; Thomas 55
JOCY Nicholas 56
JODGEHEAD John 69
JOHNES Joseph 15
JOHNINCS Thomas 65
JOHNS Thomas 19; William 83
JOHNSON ... 14; Abbot 73; Afria Doze 14; Anthony 34, 35; Charles 71; Cornelius 34; David 7; David 50; Edward 68; Elizabeth 2; Gabriel 56; George 14, 34, 36; Henry 7, 65, 72; Jacob 68, 70; John 6, 12, 13, 14, 31, 34, 35, 39, 48, 50, 57, 58, 61, 64, 68, 73, 75, 79; Katharine 34; Leonard 13, 50; Mary 35, 39; Oliver 69; Peter 12, 61, 65, 69, 79; Powel 70; Purnell 7; Robert 12, 35, 49; Samuel 40; Sarah 7; Simon 69; Thomas 11, 39, 68; Whittington 52; Willliam 7, 17
JOLLEY Thomas 19
JOLLY Jonathan 64; Thomas 3

JON... Matthew 9
JONASA Vincent 81
JONE John 71
JONES Anne 36; Beni 82; Charles 1, 37; Christmas 23; Cooley 81; Daniel 41, 42, 72, 78; David 1, 24, 43, 60, 71; Edward 3, 35, 54; Elizabeth 36; Francis 18; George 37, 78, 79; Giles 84; Griffin 56; Griffith 48; Hancock 76; Henry 65; Howel 74; James 4, 11, 34, 71, 82; John 4, 20, 23, 32, 35, 49, 51, 55, 57, 58, 69, 70 71, 82, 84, 85; Joseph 20, 23; Leonard 38; Lewis 4, 18, 42, 81; Lowe 42; Margaret 36; Mary 35, 38; Mathew 49; Peter 55, 56; Phillip 33; Pool 19; Rice 1; Richard 44, 45, 48, 65; Robert 4, 40, 64, 66, 67, 82; Roger 24; Rue 55; Samuel 35, 42, 69; Thomas 1, 18, 36, 42, 49, 56, 78; Vincent 18; William 4, 9, 11, 17, 18, 19, 24, 25, 34, 35, 36, 37, 38, 50, 60, 68, 70, 78, 85
JONNES Ebenezer 13
JONS Solloman 75
JORDAN James 65
JORDINE Aron 2
JORDON James 76
JORENSINE Porter 50
JORMAN John 35; Mathewe 35
JOSE Nicholas 58
JOSEPH Frederick 11
JOYCE Henry 24
JOYNER Absolam 74; Dobs 74; Willliam 31, 74
JUDRELL John 40
JULIEN Steven 70
JULION Stephen 71
JUMP Abraham 75; Peter 75; Solomon 76; Thomas 64, 65, 76; Vaughn 75; William 51, 65, 73
JURDIN Alexander 22; William 22
JUSTICE Mounts 68; Peter 68

KABBLE James 42
KABBLES Daniell 42
KAINDALL William 33
KALLEN George 35
KAN... Donnan 36
KANE James 1
KANKEY John 68

KAREY Richard 37
KARVY Richard 37
KAW James 1
KEAR James 58
KEARSEY Elizabeth 31
KEENE Sarah 39; William 35, 36, 39
KEENES William 37
KEES James 70; Thomas 50
KEETS Thomas 17, 81
KEIGHLY Richard 22
KEIZER Benjamin 38
KELD Job 83; John 29, 44, 45, 46, 51;
    Simon 29, 76; Thomas 29
KELLAM John 52
KELLD John 50; Simon 50; Thomas 50
KELLEGAN Byan 40
KELLEY James 74; Tobias 31; William
    73, 81
KELLIAM Joshua 80
KELLY Benjamin 56; Edmond 19; Edward
    19; Elizabeth 61; James 33, 53;
    Martha 66; Patrick 68
KEMINDLY Richard 23
KEMP Baldwin 51, 75; Bolen 65; Henry
    51; John 22; Matthew 78; Richard
    65, 75; Thomas 75; William 51
KEMPER Thomas 76
KEMS James 22
KENDERDINE John 51, 75; Thomas 21
KENDRICK Ralph 28
KENETSON William 12
KENNARD Nathaniel 56; Richard 57, 58
KENNEDY James 68; John 30; Timothy 9
KENNERLY William 54
KENNETT Elizabeth 38; Martin 61; Mary
    38; Susanna 38; William 38, 61
KENNIT William 13
KENNY Joseph 13; Lazerus 13
KENSEY James 65; Robert 53
KENSLAIGH Dominick 33
KENT John 76; Robert 48
KENTING James 75
KER William 85
KERBY Benjamin 76; David 82; John 82;
    Lamb: 82; Michael 81; Nathan 82;
    Richard 82; Robert 82; William 82
KERNEY Morriss 74
KERRON Richard 65
KERSEY James 77; Patrick 9; William
    22
KERY Matthew 26
KETCH William 58

KETLEY Richard 82
KEYE John 85
KEYS John 64, 65, 77; Richard 62, 65,
    66
KEYSER Edmund 35
KIBBLE John 8, 35; William 8, 41, 77
KICKLEY Richard 18
KIETLEY John 70
KILLGORE Thomas 69
KILLMAN Thomas 43
KILLPATRICK John 71
KILLTON Thomas 85
KILLUM Edward 11; Richard 11
KILOM John 6
KIMBER John 69
KIMBLE John 27; Richard 27
KIMMER James 82
KINARD Thomas 57
KINDERDINE John 22
KINDRED James 29
KINDRICK James 81; Ralph 82
KINEY Morriss 74
KING ... 10; Benjamin 10, 42; Capell
    62; Charles 73; Hugh 38; James 6;
    John 10, 32, 35, 38, 39, 43, 44,
    45; Nehemiah 85; Phillop 11;
    Robert 38, 40, 52; Thomas 85;
    Whittington 80; William 7, 10, 20,
    22
KINGE Alexander 34
King's Creake bridge 46
KINGS John 47
KINGSTON Charles 17, 81
KININMONT Andrew 18; John 81, 83;
    Joseph 81; Samuel 81
KINNAMONT Andrew 46; Samuel 18
KINNERAN John 60
KINNIDY Hen 78
KINNIMMONT Ambrose 17
KINNIMON Ambrous 76
KINNING William 80
KINNINMENT Andrew 18; John 18
KINNINMONT Joseph 18
KINSAY Ffrancis 58
KINSEY Cahrles 39
KIRBE John 35
KIRBY David 50, 83; James 26; Matthew
    26; Michael 29, 50; Richard 50
KIRCKHAM James 75
KIRK John 36
KIRKBY David 29; Richard 29; William
    29
KIRKE John 72

KIRKHAM Africa 65
KIRVEN Dominick 20, 25
KITELY Philip 70
KITTS Michael 24
KNARESBROUGH William 49
KNATS John 75
KNEE Naomi 42
KNIGHT Christopher 55, 58; Lewis 39;
  Richard 2; William 70
KNOCK Henry 33, 55, 56
KNOTS Nethanel 75; William 75
KNOTTS James 51, 63, 65, 75;
  Nathaniel 51, 65, 75; Robart 75
KNOWLES James 85; John 32, 76
KNOX Alexander 49; James 40, 49; John
  49; Robert 8; Simon 64
KOLLY William 68
KORSEY Francis 82; William 82
KURK William 75

L... John 69
LACKEY Henry 10
LADDAMORE Edward 85
LAFEALD Daid 80
LAHEY William 28
LAHN Josep 5
LAIN John 62; Richard 74
LAINE John 29
LAIRD (?) Cols. hous(?) 60
LAKE Henry 38
LAKEY Andrew 8
LAKINS Benjamin 23
LAMB Francis 56; John 48
LAMBDEN Daniel 22; John 22; Thomas
  52; William 22
LAMBERSON Abram 3; Henry 78; Robert
  52; Samuel 52, 78
LAMBERSTON Sarah 3
LAMBERT Joseph 48
LAMBERTSON Abraham 78
LAMDIN Daniell 82; Robert 82; William
  82
LAMERSON Elias 52
LAMPIN Thomas 36
LANAGAR George 56
LANCASTER Philip 70
LANCASTOR Benjmain 71
LAND Henry 53; Potter 53; Randolph
  53; Thomas 53
LANDCAKE Francis 7; George 7
LANDEN Henry 53
LANDER Thomas 19

LANDERS Isabell 55
LANDING Henry 52
LANDON James 75; Littleton 85
LANDOW James 62
LANDSBERRY John 23
LANE Abraham 3; Catherane 40; Dennis
  40; George 2, 6, 40; Israel 78;
  James 65, 75; Jasper 34; John 2,
  37, 38, 62, 65; Timothy 26, 65,
  73; Walter 37, 41; William 3, 28,
  62, 78, 81
LANELY Nathann1 11
LANES Richard 36
LANGDELL George 40
LANGFORD Anne 39; Benjamin 52; John
  39; Joseph 53; Pussy 53; William
  62
LANGLEY Charles 22; Thomas 65;
  William 66
LANGREENE James 38
LANHAM Josiah 57, 58; Josias 48
LANKE Ffrancis 62
LANKFORD Benjamin 81; Joseph 6;
  Killiam 81; William 6, 24
LANKSTONE John 11; Thomas 81
LARAMOR Thomas 37
LARAMORE James 79; William 79
LARCUM Thomas 1
LAREMORE Richard 23; Robert 23;
  Thomas 21
LAREY Denis 51; Dennis 29; Solomon
  29, 42
LARKINS Jeremiah 70; William 26
LARRAMORE John 41
LARRAMUR Levin 77
LARRANCE Samuel 56
LARREMORE Elexander 82; Robert 82;
  Thomas 82
LARRIMORE James 10
LARWOOD John 65
LASHLEY George 68; Robert 68
LASLEY Eliza. 59
LATHAM Aron 71; Edward 45, 47; George
  20; John 24; Moses 69
LATHBERY John 13
LATHEM John 70
LAURENCE Richard 32
LAVIN William 50
LAW John 85; William 39, 72
LAWES James 10; John 35
LAWLY Nathann1 11
LAWRENCE Henry 53; John 72; Joseph 29

LAWRENCESON Lawrence 70
LAWS Belitha 80; Elijah 80; Even 2;
John 4; Robert 4; Thomas 4
LAWSON Hugh 69; Peter 70
LAYFEILD Thomas 3
LAYFIELD Elizabeth 41; Robert 52
LAYTON John 5, 8, 65; William 40
LEA... Thomas 4
LEABON Henry 38
LEACH John 24; Margaret 61; Richard
65
LEAKE James 70
LEANARD Joseph 80
LEATH Jane 63
LEATHERBURY Charles 77; John 8, 77,
78; Robert 77
LeCATT John 80
LECKEY Alexander 9
LECOMPT Anthony 24, 83; John 43;
Peter 24
LEE Alexander 73; Edward 20, 24;
James 82; John 25, 32, 83; Oliver
25, 51; Thomas 51, 73; William 27,
65, 73
LEECH David 70
Leeds Creeke 46, 47; John 22
LEG Edward 21
LEGG John 65, 74; Thomas 74; William
74
LEHAY Joseph 20; William 20
LEIGHTON William 36
LEISTER Thomas 37
LEITH Alexander 28; Jane 63, 67
LEMAR Charles 51, 65
LEMBERT Henry 73
LEMMON George 81
LENARD Patrick 25
LENEGAR William 17
LENEVE Michaell 85
LENHAM Josia 56
LENNY George 27
LENOX Thomas 17
LENSEY James 84
LEON Thomas 81
LEONARD John 27, 65
LERED John 20
LESTER Thomas 11, 37
LEVERTON John 29
LEWIS Christopher 19; Corporal 72;
Edward 35; Francis 1, 33, 56, 58;
George 71; James 32; Joseph 13,

61; Richard 69; Thomas 44; William
29, 38; Zapher 32
LEWOC John 41
LIBBEY John 26
LIGERIUS John 37
LILLISTON Thomas 12
LIN... James 10
LINCH Abraham 12, 79; Alexander 12,
79; James 65, 76; John 12, 13;
Michael 80
LINDAL Peter 79
LINDALE Robert 78
LINDALL Peter 16; Thomas 6
LINDOW James 62; Robert 52
LINEGAR George 33
LINEGER George 58
LING Robert 17
LINGLY John 11
LINNE George 34
LINSEY David 42; Thomas 5
LINZEY David 42
LISHER Will 5
LISTER Jessey 81
Lister Will 5
LISTON Morris 34
LITTLE Christopher 37; Thomas 24;
William 24
LITTLES John 70
LIZENBE Henry 73
LLOYD Coll. 44; Edward 17; Elizabeth
63, 67; Esq. 64; James 19; John
28; Majr Genrll 47; Margaret 24;
Philemon 64; Robert 19
LOBINS William 4
LOCK Elizabeth 57; Henry 67
LOCKWELL Thomas 46
LOCKWOD John 83
LOCKWOOD William 7
LODGE Ann 63
LODGWOOD Richard 13
LOE Charles 39, 42; Robert 38
LOFTUS John 71
LOING Jeffery 61
LOKEAR John 42
LOLLES Jacob 78
LONDON Ambros 34, 37, 40; Mary 37
LONG Daniel 6, 40, 41; David 41, 81,
83; Jeffery 5, 41, 81; John 45,
46, 69, 81; Randolph 6; Samuel 5,
34, 52; Solomon 6; Thomas 72;
Tobias 68; William 5; William
Samuel 61

LONGFELLOW Joseph 75; Thomas 76
LONGLAKE Franis 53
LONGODON John 42
LOOCKERMAN Jacob 27, 54; John 27; Mrs. 20
Loockermon Jacob 83
LOOMAN Joseph 70
LORD Francis 5; James 60; Mary 60; Randall 5
LOVE Anguish 73; Thomas 82; William 24
LOVEDAY John 29; Thomas 51, 82
LOVEGROVE John 33
LOVELL Isaac 85
LOVERING John 50
LOW John 22; Nicholas 83; Robert 80
LOW... George 9
LOWD Charles 26; Robert 26
LOWDAR James 29; Robert 29
LOWDER Bridgett 62; Margrett 60
LOWE Charles 7; James 82; John 42; Nicholas 20; Thomas 22; Vincent 19
LOWERT John 85
LOWES Henry 42, 77
LOWNS Charles 19
LOWREY Robert 19
LOWS William 34
LOYD James 47; John 51, 65; Thomas 4
LOYDS Coll. 46
LUCAS Thomas 41
LUKEY Alexander 9
LUMBARD James 26
LUNDERGIN William 82
LUNDERKING Luke 24
LUNDEY Nicholas 19
LUNN John 72; Michael 69
LURDEN Cornelius 72
LURTY John 19, 22; Thomas 22
LUSBY John 68
LUSSE Stephen 38
LYMAN John 1
LYNCH Anthony 68, 69; Cornel: 7; Henry 40; Hugh 24
LYON James 70

M'CLEAN James 54
M'Clean William 54
M... James 9
M... William 9
MA... Richard 9
MACARTEY Charles 82; John 82
MacCLANAHORN Nathaniel 54
MacCLASTER John 39; Noah 40

MacDANEIL Zachariah 32
MacDORMAND William 79
MACE James 19
MacFALL John 19
MacGEORGE Hugh 23
MACHEND Marty 68
MACIN Robert 80
MACKAY 36
MackDANNELL Edmond 32
MackDOWELL John 8
MacKEELE John 72
MacKENRY Watson 84
MacKENY William 61
MacKEW Cesiah 61
MACKEY William 24, 32
MackHENRY Waller 84
MackHUGH Bryan 26
MACKLIN Richard 48
MACKLIN Robert 48
MackMERRY John 27
MackMULLEN William 41
MackNEAL John 75
MackNEMAR John 33
MackNEMARA Thoams 59
MackNESH Gilbert 1
MackNITT John 38
MackOFFAIRK John 34
MackONAKIN Daniel 56
MackWAY patrick 27
MACLEAN Daniel 71; John 71
MACLENY William 61
MacMURRY James 7; John 7
MacNEAL John 22; Patrick 57
MacNELLFORD Charles 79
MacNEMARA John 58
MACON John 26
MACOY Neal 40
MADAX Thomas 52
MADDEN John 23, 65
MADDIN Timothy 21, 55
MADDIX Bell 81
MADDOX ... 9
MADDUX Alexander 10, 36, 80; Daniel 10; Larzarus 60; Thomas 10; William 80
MADING Martin 75
MADOX Alexander 5; Thomas 5
MADUX Alexander 52, 53; Bell 53; John 78
MAESSEY John 79
MAFFAT William 69
MAGEE George 40; Peter 8

MAGGEE George 8; John 8
MAGINNEY Daniel 81
MAGLAGHLIN Daniell 6
MAGLAMARY George 7
MAGLOGHLIN John 8
MAGRAW Richard 9
MAGUAY Jerey 82
MAHANE Rose 67
MAHAUN John 38
MAHERN Robert 65
MAHON Thomas 56
MAHONY Charles 71
MAID Thomas 60
MAINLY John 70
MAITLAND James 4
MAKEELE John 43
MAKLOND Rowland 11
MALAVELL(?) Edmond(?) 10
MALE Henry 81; John 28
MALIN JOhn 26
MALLATTO Manuel 3
MALONE Robert 78
MALOONY Michael 28
MAN Pollard 43
MANADEAR Daniell 83
MANERY John 68
MANGOR John 8; Mary 8
MANGUDGE Timothy 73
MANKLIN Richard 14
MANLEY Thomas 34
MANLOE John 34
MANLOVE Elizabeth 34, 35; John 35;
   Marke 34
MANLOW Elyzabeth 34; Marke 34
MANNERING Elisha 76
MANSFIELD Edward 73; Jacob 19; John
   75; Robert 54; Samuel 54; William
   18, 65
MANSHIP Charles 29, 51, 82; Henry 29,
   82
MANSON James 65; William 69
MARADETH William 51
MARCH John 55, 56
MARCHENT William 72
MARCHMENT Samuell 4, 38; William 4
MARDEREY William 21
MAREEN John 49; Robert 50
MARETIN Robert 62
MAREY Alexander 83; John 11
MARGLAMARY Edward 6
MARIN Robert 80
MARK Jankin 36

MARKEL John 78
MARKLAND Charles 19
MARLETT John 34
MARLIP Richard 19
MARLRA Boven 34
MARR John 24, 60
MARRETT Sarah 36
MARRISS William 14
MARSEY Alexander 13; John 13; William
   13
MARSH Edmund 23, 59; George 36, 37;
   John 23; John Paull 35; Sarah 23;
   Thomas 49, 74
MARSHAL Isaac 14, 50
MARSHALL George 3; James 27, 82;
   Randall 68; Richard 27
MARSHEL Jacob 83
MARSHELL John 74; Richard 82
MARSUM John 34
MARTEN William 71
MARTIN Ffrancis 37; George 4; Henry
   26, 83; John 80; Mary 61; Philip
   21; Robert 14; Samuel 26; Thomas
   20, 21, 51, 83; William 17, 21
MARTINDALE Daniel 81; Thomas 28;
   Daniell 30
MARTINDIL Thomas 75
MARVELL Thomas 11
MASHALL William 26
MASHELL Samuel 6
MASLIN Thomas 54
MASON Abraham 12; Henry 29; Henry 51;
   Joseph 33, 65; Margaret 31;
   Matthew 65; Richard 31, 51, 65;
   Thomas 81; William 39, 63
MASSAY John 57
MASSEY John 50, 79; Nicholas 56;
   Samuel 54; Thomas 55, 56, 57;
   William 58
MASSY Jac. 65
MATHES David 60; John 5
MATHEW Cesiah 61; William 78
MATHEWS Ezeke. 53; Isaac 53; John 3,
   53; Lods 82; Maurice 72; Samuel 3,
   52; Teague 3, 52; Thomas 50;
   Whilly 53; Whitty 53; William 37,
   52, 53, 62
MATHIS William 78
MATTHEWS David 27; Lewis 27;
   Nottingham 4; Patrick 9; Thomas
   25, 30, 82, 83; Uriah 29, 83;
   William 63

MAUDIN Benjamin 70
MAUHAWN James 9
MAUNY John 55
MAURLING Isaac 27
MAXWELL Robert 32
MAYCOME John 4; Robert 4
MAYNADIER Daniel 25, 51
MAYNER Edward 65; Timothy 65
MAYO Samuell 2
McALASTER Hugh 68
MCALESTER Joseph 53
McCABE Brion 79
McCALEY John 15
McCAMLEY Daniel 67
McCARLORE John 42
McCARTER John 69
McCARTY Owen 27; Philemon 23
McCARY Richard 71
McCLAMERY William 14
McCLAMY William 78
McCLEAN John 53
McCLEARY Robert 68
McCLELEN John 68
McCLEMEY Elisabeth 15
McCLERY Samuel 70
McCLESTER Jo'n 14; Joseph 62; Matha 41
McCLOSTER John 41; Samuell 79
McCLVER William 70
McCO... Thomas 71
McCOLLOON Hugh 42
McCONEL Alexander 69
McCOY Henry 70
McCOYE James 73
McCRA... David 68
McCREADY Alexander 3
McCREDEY Soloman 53
McCREDY Isaac 53
McCRERY John 70
McCULLETH Alexander 40
McCULLOCK John 40
McCUNE John 70
McCURREL Elizabeth 54
McCURREY James 71
McDANEL Allen 3
McDANIEL Angus 26; Daniel 22, 23
McDANIELL David 78
McDERMENT Hugh 20
McDONALD David 53; Eneas 17
McDONNALD C. 60
McDORMAN William 10
McDOWALL William 68

McDULL Patrick 8
McFADDEN John 68
McFARREL James 69
McGLAMRY Edward 39
McGLAUGHLIN John 68
McGRIGORY Alexander 13
McH... John 71
McHAFFEY Martin 70
McHENDERICK Charles 3
McINTIER Daniell 77
McKAN Daniel 29
McKEEL Thomas 73
McKENDLEY David 69
McKENNEY John 68
McKEWN William 68
McKEY James 70; Robert 70
McKITTERICK James 71
McLAUGHAN Jane 40
McLELAND Alexander 25
McMAHAWN John 28; Thomas 28
McMASTER John 70
McMORRIE James 80
McMURRIE James 41
McNISH Henry 17
McQUEAD Henry 18
McQUILLIN Robert 41
McTEAR John 68
McWILLIAMS John 14
ME... Joshua 3
MEAD William 39
MEADS William 77
MEAKINS Joshua 69
MEALY John 78
MEARS John 8
MECATTER John 23
MECLASTER John 40
MECONEKIN John 74
MECONIKIN Elias 74; Emanuel 74
MECONNICKIN John 65
MECORS William 65
MECOTTOR Hezekiah 23
MEDAIN James 25
MEDCALF John 6
MEDCALFE John 60
MEDSLY William 83
MEEDS John 65, 75; Meths. H. 74; Thomas 65, 75; William 65, 76
MEEK Robert 55
MEEKS Elizabeth 55, 58 Francis 57
MEGINNY Daniel 28; Eliza. 28; John 28; Michael 18
MEGRAH Francis 20

MEGRAW James 23
MEGRAY Arthur 24
MEGROLY John 41; Mary 41
MEHANNEY Dennis 69
MELEAYED Thomas 75
MELICAN John 80
MELLALEY Patrick 60
MELLSON Samuel 11
MELONE Joonathan 71
MELTON James 24; John 78; Littleton 78
MELVEN Robert 3
MELVIN William 78
MERADAY John 32
MERADITH John 77; Thomas 77
MERAY George 33
MERCER Thomas 69, 85; William 50, 71
MERCHAMANT William 61
MERCHANT Ann 67; Benjamin 28; James 25; John 25, 83; Joseph 51
MEREDITH Sophia 65; W. 73; William 64, 65
MEREY Thomas 58
MERICK Alexander 25; Isaac 65
MERIDETH John 74; Nathaniel 74
MERRICK James 27; John 21; Joseph 27, 83; William 83
MERRIDAY John 65
MERRIDETH James 74
MERRILL John 3
MESSETER Abraham 31
MESSEX Aaron 79; Benjamin 79; Covington 80; Elihu 79
MESSHIER William 72
METCALFE Thomas 51
MIDDLETON Martha 33
MIDGLEY Thomas 49
MIDLETON John 70; Luckenor 58
MIDSLEY Thomas 15
MIDSLY Thomas 83
MIERICK David 71
MILBORN Ralph 52; William 52
MILBOURNE Ralph 41; William 32
MILBURN Mary 3; Robert 70
MILES Henery 53; Henry 5, 34, 53; Robert 62; Samuel 6, 10, 78; William 10, 53, 60, 62
MILFORNE Thomas 12
MILLAR John 23; Jonathan 23
MILLER Andrew 39; Arthur 55, 56; David 39; Henry 71; James 18, 24; John 4, 12, 17, 49, 51, 75, 85;

Joseph 14, 79; Martha 33; Michael 31, 32, 33, 56; Peter 7; Robert 8, 70; Samuell 2; Thomas 35, 68
Miller's quarter 19
MILLINGTON Eliza. 28; George 81; Isaac 81; Oliver 28, 45
MILLION Edward 12
MILLIS James 50, 65
MILLNOR Robert 36
MILLS Alexander 83; David 21, 65; Hugh 78; Jennet 3; John 1, 3, 69, 78; Jonathan 53; Moses 78; Nathan 78; Nathaniel 78; Robert 3, 62; Samuell 3, 78; Smyth 78; William 3, 21, 53, 72, 78, 83
MILLSON James 82; Samuell 82
MILMAN Thomas 38
MILNER james 20
MILS David 78; Stacy 78
MILTON Patrick 70
MINSHALL Jeffery 34; Randall 35, 38
MIRREDEATH William 75
MISHELL Teage 35; Thomas 50
MISTER William 5
MITCHALL Isaac 79; Randall 78
MITCHEL John 70; Walter 25
MITCHELL Allexander 34; Benjamin 78; Edward 50; George 34; Isaac 52; John 24, 68; Joseph 79; Mark 72; 32; Randoll 5; Robert 2, 52, 61, 62; Thomas 10, 76; William 29
MOCK Henery 15
MOHANEY John 22; Patrick 73
MOKE John 69
MOLIN Isaac 60
MOLISON Thomas 26
MOLL David 1; John 1, 85
MOLOONY Michael 83
MONEY John 69; Robert 85
MONT William 70
MONTAGUE William 51
MONTROSSE Elizabeth 31
MONTSOUIR Tymothy 31
MOO.DEY Andrew 9
MOODE Peter 8
MOODY James 76; Robert 28
MOOLSON Thomas 35
MOONI Martin 34
MOONING Charles 19
MOOR Edward 13; James 27; John 32, 73, 80; Mary 32; Thomas 53; William 56

INDEX

MOORE Aron 70; Christopher 60; Daniel
  35; Isaac 52; Israel 59; James 54;
  John 32, 37, 58; Martin 34, 35;
  Nathaniel 69; Rose 8; Samuell 34;
  Stephen 52; Thomas 52, 70; William
  37, 71
MOORES Eleanor 66
MOOTH Thomas 77
MORDICK Ezekiel 76
MORE Charles 50; Elizabeth 36;
  Ffrancis 6, 81; John 11, 41, 53,
  65; Joseph 30, 70; NJicholas 32;
  Richard 31; Thoams 78, 81; William
  30, 80; William Rider Wilson 77
MORES John 9
MORGAN Charles 22, 28, 50, 72, 81;
  Edward 69; Henry 35; Hugh 17, 69;
  James 17, 69, 85; John 29, 47, 75,
  81, 85; Joseph 2; Level 42; Mary
  17; Richard 21; Robert 17, 68;
  Rowland 72; Samuel 28, 50, 81;
  Sevil 81; William 69
MORGIN Perry 79
MORISS Charles 13
MORRANE Thomsa 71
MORRIL Joseph 79
MORRIS ... 15; Bebbins 50; Bivens 2;
  Cornelius 34, 35; Dennis 25;
  George 29; Jacob 78; Jinkin 35;
  John 28, 78; Joseph 15, 78; Manns
  39; Manns Cox Daniel 37; Peter 3;
  Thomas 38; William 15, 56
MORRISON John 14; Robert 70
MORRISS John 13; Sarah 13
MORSE Jeremiah 65
MORSEY William 23
MORTON John 76; Thomas 76
MOSE Jeremiah 74
MOSER John 68
MOSES Philip 21
MOSLEY James 72
MOSS William 28
MOTT John 6
MOUNTECUE William 65
MOUNTS Christopher 85
MOUNTSEIR Thomas 73
MUIR Adam 54
MULCAH Jane 40
MULIKIN William 83
MULKA Cornelius 38
MULLAN Christopher 14
MULLETT William 74

MULLIGAN Thomas 78
MULLIGIN Daniel 31
MULLIKIN John 24; Patrick 21; Samuel
  21; William 24, 51
MULLNOR William 36
MULPHEY John 7
MULREE Cornelius 25
MUMFORD ... 13; Anne 38; George 15;
  James 15, 62; John 14, 65, 83;
  Thomas 13
MUNLAVELL Edmund 41
MUNROOKE Daniel 10
MUNT Elizabeth 34
MUNTY Ricahrd 34
MURDICK Ezekiel 28
MURDUGH Robert 35
MUREY Jenken 50
MURFE... Jean 41
MURFEY Edward 69
MURMURENOUGH Gregory 40
MURPHEY James 19, 20; John 31
MURPHIE JOhn 38; Thomas 38
MURPHY Charles 75; George 55; James
  48, 56; Roger 1, 56; Thomas 85
MURRAH James 41
MURRAY John 8, 15, 61; Robert 58
MURROW James 13; Richard 13
MURRY James 83; John 9
MYERS John 56; Stphen 56

NAB John 76
NABB Charles 73; John 45, 48
NAEAREN Robert 3
NAILOR Joseph 81; William 81
NANNIN William 21
NANSWYN JOhn 58
NASH John 71; Samuel 71
NAVELL James 68
NAYLOR John 17; Joseph 17
NEAL Edward 25; Francis 25; Mary 57
NEALE Charles 32, 85; John 11
NEALEY John 70
NEALL Thomas 68
NEAREN James 3; Robert 3
NEDELS Edward 29, 51
NEEDLES Edward 59; Thomas 65
NEIGHBOURS John 28
NELLSON John 34
NELSON Bridgett 35; John 7, 25, 35,
  79; Thomas 65; William 7, 38, 41,
  69, 77
NESHAM Ben. 37

NEVETT Thomas 54
NEVIL William 22
NEVILL David 73; John 65, 73; Walter
  64, 65
NEVILLE Walton 62
NEWBELL Henry 72
NEWBOLD Francis 3; John 3, 50; Thomas
  3
NEWCOM Robert 27, 83
NEWELL John 33
NEWGONS Chrisipher 35
NEWMAN Charles 1, 55, 56; Comfort 61;
  George 38; John 19, 27, 48, 83;
  Joseph 82; Richard 16; William 61
NEWNAM Benjamin 67, 73; Charles 63;
  Daniel 65; Joseph 67; William 77
NEWTON Charles 11; Edward 72; Johen
  11; John 72; Thomas 12, 52, 75
NICHERSON John 82
NICHOLAS John 72
NICHOLS Edward 8; Henry 21
NICHOLSON James 10, 80; John 65, 77;
  Joseph 54, 77; Richard 10, 53;
  Roger 61, 77
NICKASON John 28
NICKELLS Charles 82
NICKOLS Richard 80
NICKOLSON Daniel 74
NICOLAS Charles 2; James 2; John 2;
  Samuell 2
NICOLLS Isaac 54
NICOLLSON James 34, 37
NICOLS Henry 26, 28; James 7;
  Jeremiah 25; Richard 7
NIELD Daniel 82
NILSON Robert 84; Samuel 84; William
  84
NIT Isaac 83
NIX George 83
NO... Henry 9
NOARRIS Phillip 35
NOBLE George 39; Isaac 8, 42, 78;
  James 2, 80; John 23, 42;
  Johnathun 80; Mark 4, 23, 33;
  Robert 17, 45, 85; Widow 17;
  William 10, 38, 40
NOCK Nehemyer 83
NODIKE Maurice 58
NOONER Thomas 43
NOOTH Thomas 73
NORCOTT Richard 32
NOREMAN James 56

NOREST Robert 48
NORGATE Honor 62
NORMAN Thomas 71
NORRIS Samuel 56
NORRISS John 21
NORROD Edward 27
NORROWD William 82
NORTH Henry 74; William 32
NORTON John 13
NOWDELL James 72
NOWELL William 48
NOWELLS Edward 11
NOWLAND James 69; John 22; Richard 69
NOX James 69
NULL John 69; Robert 69
NUMBERS Peter 69
NUNAM Joseph 25
NUSAN John 1
NUTON Thomas 65
NUTS Thomas 58
NUTT Jane 62; Thomas 55
NUTTELL John 82
NUTTEN Christopher 34
NUTTER Christopher 35, 36; John 18,
  75; Nathaniel 18
NUTTERWILL Richard 23
NUTTLE John 81
NUTWELL John 27

O CASSADY Owen 14
O FLANAGON ... 14
O SHONHANAS William 16
OAGLE Margraret 57
OBRYAN Patrick 65
OBRYON Thomas 77
OBURN Samuel 74
ODAW Owen 8
ODCOCKE Henry 48
ODEAR John 41
ODOUGHERTY Hederak 40; James 42
ODUE Thomas 11
OENS Francis 70
OFFLEY Robert 65, 73
OGELBY Robert 12
OGLE James 19, 50, 51
OGLESBY George 71; John 70; William
  70
OGLSBY John 70
OLDFIELD George 48; Herey 51; William
  29
OLDHAM Edward 19, 51, 83; Mary 19
OLDSON John 75
OLIPHAN Mathew 80

OLIVER John 56
OLSEN William 53
ONEAL Arthur 17; Charles 62, 65; Hugh 54
ONEIL Ann 54
ONIONS John 12
OOR Michael 5
OREM Andrew 42; Maurice 27
ORGIN Joseph 6; Richerd 6; William 6
ORN Aron 6
OROM Andrew 22
ORRE William 68
ORREAL Mary 33
ORREL Francis 75
ORSBURNE William 74
ORTON James 70
OSBURK William 62
OSBURN John 1, 68; William 65
OSEY Daniel 19
OSMENT John 18
OSTON William 83
OTHERSON Otho 69
OTON John 5
OTTERSON Otho 85
OTTWELL Francis 52; James 80; William 80
OTWELL Charles 2; Francis 2
OUGHTON Abraham 79
OUTEN Abraham 81; Obediah 53; Purnal 81
OUTERBRIDGE William 79
OUTON Thomas 14
OUTTEN John 84; Thomas 80
OVERSTOCK Peter 50
OWEN Moyses 35; Peter 80; Richard 72; Thomas 35, 71
OWENS George 9; Robert 11, 41; Samuel 11, 41; Thomas 18; William 39, 65
OXENHAM William 82
OXFORD Thomas 11
OXINGHAM William 18
OZIER Francis 70; Jacob 50
OZMAN Thomas 81
OZWELL Edward 29

P... James 69, 71; Mathew 71
PA... John 4
PABY Joseph 9
PADISON John 19, 83
PAGE James 27; Ralph 58; Stephen 39
PAGEMAN John 41
PAIN David 69; Isaac 84; Jacob 74

PAINE Robert 36
PAINES Joseph 32
PAINTER John 13; William 61
PALMER Benjamin 58; George 50
PAMPHILION Thomas 19
PANDER Edward 72
PANE Jacob 78; James 75; John 78; Joseph 78; Moses 78
PANTER John 34
PARAMOR John 35
PARDUE Mary 62; Stephen 72
PARIS John 9
PARKER Charles 39; George 16, 37; John 16, 17, 36, 39, 61, 69, 75; Joseph 18; Philip 2, 39; T. 51; William 65
Parker's Bridge 47
PARKERSON Thomas 70
PARKS Arthur 53; Artor 5; Job 53; John 5; William 66
PARLAND Walter 74
PARLETT Sarah (Senah ?) 29; Thomas 29
PARNES James 65; Richard 48
PARR John 17; Richard 42; Thomas 81
PARRADICE Christopher 12
PARRAMORE Thomas 40
PARRAROW Thomas 73
PARRATT Francis 24
PARREMORE Benjamin 80; John 80; Joseph 80; Thomas 80
PARRIMORE Thomas 11
PARROT Abner 83
PARROTT Aaron 29; Abner 25; George 82; Henry 20; Isaiah 20; Joseph 21, 50; William 20
PARSANS Benjeman 50
PARSLEY Barthol... 69; Richard 70; Thomas 85
PARSON William 85
PARSONS James 81; John 8, 37, 39, 49, 73; Joseph 33; Landing 46; Peter 8, 37; Thomas 65
PARTRIDGE Richard 36
PASSONS Thomas 74
PATERSON Thomas 10; William 38
PATISON Vincent 83
PATON Thomas 15
PATRICK Daniel 84; John 15; Mathew 14; Rodi 35; Roger 14, 84
PATRIE Robert 40; Sarah 40
PATTERSON David 69; Edward 70; Irvin 70; Robert 69

PATTEY John 13
PATTON Hance 71; Robert 15, 68, 70
PATY Powell 83
PAUL William 4, 53
PAYNE Thmas 75
PEACOCK Edward 3; John 78; Richard 58
PEAKS Daniel 18
PEALE Rob... 2; Thomas 62
PEARCE Daniel 56; Gideon 50, 54, 56, 57, 58, 85; James 70; John 75; Thomas 50, 75; William 50, 68
PEARS Thomas 23
PEARSE John 36
PEARSON Ralph 27
PECK Daniel 27; John 27, 59, 60
PECO Peter 70
PEDINGTON Henry 34
PEDRY John 65
PEEKE William 48
PEEMER William 42
PELTY John 39
PEMBERTON John 76; Joseph 7, 53, 62
PEN... Jacob 71
PENFILD George 28
PENINGTON Henry 50; J. 50; John 49; Robert 50
PENKIND Michael 18
PENNELL Charles 16; John 16; Richard 16; Thomas 16
PENNINGTON Henry 68, 71; John 68, 69, 71; Richard 68, 71; Robert 71, 85; Thomas 71; William 50, 71
PENNY William 75
PENNYMORE William 24
PEOPLE John 72
PEPERDINE John 76
PEPPER Arnold 13; Christopher 14; Elizabeth 37; John 14; Richard 37; Tobias 12, 36, 37; William 12, 13
PERAMAN Henry 33
PERESON John 3
PERKINS Daniel 54; Edward 26, 39; Isaac 56, 58; James 82; John 53; Mich'l 53; Thomas 60
PERLE James 72
PERMAR James 75; William 75
PERRY Hugh 32; James 13; Samuel 32
PERRYMAN Roger 68
PERSON William 4
PERSONS Thomas 6
PETERKIN James 54, 72
PETERS William 1

PETHER Lazarus 31
PETTIS Thomas 7
PETTY Francis 29
PEW Rowland 55, 58
PHEBINS George 36
PHEBUS George 42; Mary 42
PHILBETT James 3
PHILIP Henry 2
PHILIPS Henry 4, 49; Jacob 3; John 9; Richard 8; Samuel 70
PHILLIPS Elizabeth 42; James 78; John 42, 69, 76; Richard 65, 77; Robert 65; Roger 36, 39; Rubin 69; Samuel 73; Thomas 69, 72; William 11, 69
PHILLIPSON William 41
PHILLOPS John 11
PHIPPEN Mathias 69
PHRAISER William 79
PICKARD William 69
PICKELS Nathan 70
PICKERING Francis 18, 26, 59; John 26; Robert 26; William 18
PICKERSON John 77
PICKETT John 55, 58
PICKREN Charles 83; James 83
PICKRINE William 28
PIERSON John 72
PILCHER John 80
PILKINTON Abraham 23
PILSHARD Moses 78
PINAR Thomas 55, 56
PINDER William 65, 73
PINER James 1; Mathew 32; Rebeckah 1; Thomas 1
PIPER Christopher 62; Isaac 3, 61, 62; Joseph 77; Samuel 78; William 62, 78
PIRKINS Daniel 33; Thomas 17
PIRRIE Robert 39
PITCH William 71
PITCHER John 53
PITCHFORK Thomas 19
Pitts bridge 45, 46, 47
PITTS John 4, 17, 41; Robert 78
PLANER William 6
PLANNER Capt 61; Maj. 61
PLANNOR William 34
PLATT Samuel 26
PLOUGHMAN Thomas Davis 36; James 76; John 76; Philemon 22; Philimon 82
PLUMB Nathaniell 10
PLUNKETT James 28

PLUMMER Christopher 81; Henry 72;
John 72, 81; Thomas 81
PLUNKETT Richard 40
POALKE William 42
POINTER Edward 16; Elias 15; Ffrancis
62; Nathaniell 16; Thomas 15, 62;
William 15, 16, 61, 62
POLIT ... 13
POLK Benjamin 85; Charles 4; David 4,
77; Gillis 85; James 4, 80, 85;
John 37, 80; Joseph 4; Robert 9;
Thomas 37; William 80, 85
POLKE Ephraim 42; William 40
POLLE Thomas 35
POLLET John 85; Jonathan 85; Thomas
77, 85
POLLETT William 4
POLLINGTON John 72
POLLIT John 85; Jonathan 85; Samuel
85; William 85
POLLOCK JOhn 52
POLOCK Hery 76
POLOVEY William 72
POLYK John 39; Robert 39
PONDER Daniel 73; Ephraim 73; James
64, 65, 73; Richard 73; William 73
PONTON Robert 16
POOLE Elizabeth 35, 37; John 35;
Rachell 35; Thomas 34, 35, 37
POOLLET Jonathan 77; William 77
POOR Catharin 57, 58; Henry 65;
Jeremiah 65; John 22
POPE Elisabeth 14; George 12; John
12, 62, 72; Mary 12; Mathew 53;
Richard 8; Rob... 36
PORTER ... 4; Arter 82; Frances 82;
Francis 3, 22; George 82; Hugh 2,
39; James 52, 71; John 2, 16, 18,
22, 82, 84, 85; Joseph 6, 14, 18,
42, 50; Laurence 22; McClintuck
14; Phil. 22; Philip 20; Richard
20; Robert 49, 68, 82; Samuel 50;
Sarah 22; Thomas 20, 76, 82;
William 14
PORTOR Hugh 80
POTER Henery 5; Thomas 5
POTTER Elizabeth 38; Henry 38, 52;
John 21; Marvin 54; Thomas 38
POTTS John 26
POUCH Mark Anthony 65
POULSON Jacobas 69; Peter 70
POUND Andrew 2

POURTER John 52; Joseph 52; William
52
POWDER William 13
POWEL Gabrel 80; Howel 25; James 26;
Nehemiah 1; Thomas 65; William 77
POWELL Daniel 26; Daniell 47;
Elizabeth 35; Gabriel 13; Howel
26, 45, 47; James 30, 65; John 3,
25; Joseph 25; Mary 35; Richard
32, 85; Samuel 13, 83; Susannah
25; Thomas 26, 32, 41, 83; Walter
35; William 58
POYNTER Elias 79; Ratlif 79; William
40
PRAT Elizabeth 65; John 77; Thomas 75
PRATT Edward 17; Henry 76; James 75;
Samuel 76, 77; Thomas 28; William
17, 77
PREESLY James 22
PRENTICE Robert 7, 40; William 35
PRESLEY James 82; Richard 69
PREWET Andrew 32
PREWIT Andrew 63, 67
PRICE Allexander 38; Andrew 56, 58,
62, 65, 69, 73, 75; Charles 62,
64, 65, 76; Cris 53; David 12;
Henry 48, 65; James 69; John 11,
20, 32, 35, 38, 59, 71, 84; Joseph
69; Richard 56; Robert 69; Samuel
20; Thomas 11, 20, 34, 40, 46, 65,
70, 74, 77; Vincent 75; William
63, 69, 70, 74, 81, 82
PRICES Franis 10
PRICHARD David 17, 81; Edward 21;
John 19, 21; Peter 21; Samuel 20;
Widow 21
PRIER John 33; Thomas 33; Webb(?) 15;
Wieb 15
PRIEREEL John 25
PRIEST William 84
PRIMROSE George 65, 73, 77; John 73;
Vilet 73; william 65
PRING Robert 74
PRIOR Thomas 5
PRISE Allexander 39; Chis... 39;
James 40; Jinkin 34, 35; John 35;
Margaritt 35; Martha 35; Mary 39,
40; Rebecca 39; Robert 40
PROCTER Alexander 49
PROSSER William 10
PROUSE George 29, 51
PROUT Joseph 27

PRUETT Andrew 72; James 24; John 24
PRYER Thomas 3, 40
PRYOR Edmund 65; John 33, 56; Thomas 32; William 77
PUCK Meredith 21
PUCKAM Richard 8
PUCKER Nathaniel 48
PUCKUM Abraham 8
PUDDRIE Joseph 84
PULLETT Thomas 8
PULLING John 75
PULLIT George 78
PURKINS John 3; Samuel 3; Thomas 3
PURNAL Hezekiah 79; John 79; Thomas 28
PURNALL James 54; John 16; Katharine 16; Mathew 16; Thomas 16; William 54, 65
PURNEL John 50
PURNELL John 11; Thomas 35, 37, 50; Walter 83; William 82
PURNERL Thomas 75; William 75
PURNIL John 14
PURSLEY John 85
PUSKELL John 17
PUTT Edward 17
PYLE Thomas 38
PYNE Francis 31

QUATURMUS Partrick 79
QUEALL William 69
QUEATT William 69
QUELLIN Samuell 38
QUILLANE Daniell 34
QUILLEN Thomas 13
QUIN John 26
QUINTON Philip 3; Walter 44, 46, 47

R... John 71
RACKLIF Charles 14; Nathanael 12
RACKLIFFE Charles 62, 83; Purnell 83
RADISH Haraen 78
RAGE John 81
RAILEY Thomas 15
RAINE Mathew 15
RAKES John 76; Nicholus 76; William 22, 27
RALEY Charles 77; John 73
RALPH Thomas 41
RALY Edward 60
RAM... William 69

RAMSEY Barnet 3; Charles 3; Daniel 78; Wilburn 78
RANDALL Robert 56; Theophilus 54
RANDALLS Mill 46
RANDOLL Robert 48
RANGER John 1
RANSTEAD John 18
RANZER John 71
RAPOON Isac 13
RASHFIELD Joseph 18
RASIN Thomas 56
RASSEY Alexander 20
RATCLIFE William 85; James 26; John 27; William 60
RATCLIFE William 62
RATHBER Andrew 6
RATHEL John 29
RATHELL Thomas 21
RATHER David 51
RATLIEF Robart 75; William 75
RAWLEY George 41
Rawley James 38
RAY Alexander 18, 60; John 18, 76; Thomas 83
RAYMOND Jonathan 8; Judith 65
READ Francis 55; George 34; James 71; John 11, 68; Joseph 56; Robert 27; Walter 84
READING John 63; Ppeter 52
READY Nicolas 9
REAME Harwod 81
REAVES James 76
RECORDS Phillip 53
REDDING Peter 78; William 32
REDEN William 20
REDFORD Thomas 62
REDGISTER Robert 45
REDGRAVE Abraham 33, 55, 58; Isaack 33
REDISH Joseph 22
REED Gilbert 74; James 79; Obediah 79; William 12, 74
REES David 69; George 71
REEVES Joseph 72
REGISTER David 29; Francis 29
REILY James 58
RELPH John 11; Thomas 11, 37; William 11
RENCHER ...wood 9; Underwood 62, 77; William 77
RENNALDS Andrew 19; John 18
RENSHAW John 49

RENSHAWE John 35
RENSHER Thomas 7
REVELL Charles 10; Curtis 78; Randall
    34, 38, 62; Randell 40; Randolph
    49; Sarah 40
REVILL Randol 79; William 79
REVULL William 5
REYLEY James 55, 56; Nicholas 55, 56
REYNARDS Henry 75; John 75; Richard
    75
REYNER Ebenezer 54
REYNOLDS John 7; Richard 70; Thomas
    70
RICCAR Benjamin 56
RICCORDS John 7; Philip 7
RICE Cornelius 32; Hugh 81; John 23;
    Nicolas 34; William 23
RICH Peter 76; Stephen 65
RICHARDS Henry 80; John 34, 53;
    William 15, 31, 41, 42, 83
RICHARDSON Anthony 25, 50; Benjamin
    79; Charles 14; Daniel 29; David
    37; John 22, 72, 79, 84; Peter 23;
    Robert 14; Samuell 85; Thomas .
    22,25; William 12, 24, 42, 61, 71,
    84
RICHINSON Samuel 39
RICKARDS John 37
RICKETS John 13, 50; Jones 13;
    Nathaniel 1; Tobies 50; William 13
RICKETTS David 71; John 40, 60, 69;
    Jones 41; Nathaniel 55, 56, 58;
    Phillip 56; Thomas 70; William 71,
    75, 77
RICKINS John 38
RICORDS John 9; Samuel 7
RIDDLE Benjamin 65
RIDER Andrew 71
RIDGE Benjamin 71; James 71; William
    71
RIDGER Benjamin 65
RIDGWAY William 27
RIDSON John 58
RIGBY Arthur 27, 46, 47, 83; John 74
RIGEN Ambrose 2; Elizabeth 3; John 3,
    6; Joseph 2; Samuell 3; Thomas 3
RIGGBY ... 9
RIGGEIN Teage 34
RIGGEN Ambrose 36, 40; Darby 52; John
    53; Jonathan 53; Peirce 52; Teage
    36; Teague 39; Teague 52

RIGGIN Charles 53; Cornealus 53;
    Darby 41; John 53; Joseph 80;
    Teague 2; Tegue 80
RIGHT John 22; Randall 80; Solomon 53
RIGING Ambros 78; John 6
RINE John 40
RING Robert 80
RINGGOLD Elias 56; James 54, 65;
    Josias 33; Thomas 48, 55, 56, 76;
    William 56, 57
RINGOLD Thomas 77
RIPLEY John Johnson 66
RIPP John 55, 58
RIPPER James 74
RITCHE James 69; Robert 69
RITCHINS John 39
RITE Thomas 69
RITHE John 69
RITHERFORD Joseph 68
RO... Allen 69
ROACH Catherine 42; Charles 8, 52;
    Elizabeth 41; John 8, 34, 41, 42,
    53; Michael 6; Nathaniell 53;
    Patrick 82; Richard 70; Samuel 6;
    Sarah 6; William 8
ROAD Humphry 39
ROADS John 34, 80; Ruben 70
ROAH John 41
ROBBINS Ellin 34; Mary 34
ROBBINSON William 34
ROBENSON William 84
ROBERSON Thomas 70; William 6, 78, 80
ROBERTS Alice 28; Andrew 28;
    Bartholomew 22; Benjamin 77, 81;
    Edward 4; Else 2; George 28; James
    29, 66, 81; John 4, 18, 42, 66;
    Margaret 17; Mary 58, 60; Nicholas
    22; Robert 69; Thomas 13, 17, 19,
    83; William 4, 22, 28, 29, 32, 81
ROBERTSON George 69; James 58; John
    69; Sarah 63, 67; William 11, 62
ROBERTSONE Robert 72
ROBESON John 37; Thomas 37
ROBIN Sockrockett 49
ROBINS Boden 12; Bowd'n 50; George
    20, 24, 59; Joh. 50; John 28;
    Stanley 20; Thomas 12, 50; William
    25, 50
ROBINSON Alexander 24; Alsip 33;
    Charles 48; David 19, 83; Henry
    27; James 81, 82; John 13, 19, 21,
    27, 39, 46, 81, 83, 85; Joseph 79;

Joshuah 50; Mary 13; Michael 13;
Patrick 35; Peter 13; Rachel 33;
Richard 83; Small Samuel 28;
Solomon 21; Thomas 13, 23, 27, 50,
79; W. 76; William 7, 13, 19, 23,
77
ROBISON William 16
ROBSON James 20; John 54, 59, 73;
William 72
ROBSONE William 72
ROCHESTER Francis 66, 77; Henry 77
ROCK John 38, 79
ROD James 76
ROE ... 62; Abner 51; Anthony 77;
Edward 66; John 45, 66; Joseph 5;
Nicholas 4; Thomas 4, 36, 66, 75;
William 75
ROFF John 57
ROGER Edward 33
ROGERES Nathaniel 32
ROGERS Claudius 58, 59; Edward 32,
55, 58; Eliza. 32; Iris 37; Jns(?)
37; John 32, 33, 34, 37; Joshua
79; Mary 32; Mather 79; Rachell
32; Richard 66; Roger 21
ROLES Francis 21; Robert 21
ROLLE Fedemon 83
ROLLISON John 56
ROLPH John 58, 74; Thomas 74
ROOK Edward 53
ROOKS John 19
ROSE Samuel 76; Thomas 36
ROSS Anthony 70; Edward 39; Glanvill
56; Hugh 69; John 18, 45, 46, 50,
51, 72
ROTHEL John 29
ROTHELL David 29
ROUCH Garrat 20
ROUND James 37
ROUSE Thomas 49
ROUTH Christopher 77
ROWE Thomas 73
ROWLAND Thomas 18
ROWLES John 66; Edward 62; James 16,
62
ROWNDS Mary 7
ROYALL John 38; Thomas 38, 42
RUARK John 9, 80
RUE John 45, 74
RULY Michael 69
RUMSEY Edward 70; William 70
RUMSEY Charles 85

RUSH John 38; Thomas 33
RUSSAM Edward 29; Katherine 29; Peter
19, 83; Samuel 29; Thomas 19, 75,
83
RUSSELL Godfrey 41; Thomas 18, 78;
William 11, 18
RUSSOM John 75
RUSSUM Edward 50; John 66; Peter 50,
82; Thomas 50
RUTH Mable 66; Thomas 31, 66
RUTTER John 39, 40, 70; Richard 40
RUXE Isaac 28; Nathaniell 29
RWEE Naomi 42
RYAL Edward 22; James 23; Michael 25
RYALY Patrick 23
RYDER Richard 53
RYE Joseph 56
RYLAND John 49, 50, 68, 85; Thomas 71
RYLEY John 67; Joseph 69
RYMOUR Edward 22
RYNE Catherine 61
RYON William 17

SADLER Micayah 49
SAILES Gabriel 59; George 59
SAINTEE Nathaniel 18
SAIR George 70
SALES Clement 44, 45, 46; Leonard 19;
Mary 24
SALISBURY John 62; Thomas 24
SALLYER Charles 85
SALTER John 41
SAMAN Rowland 17
SAMCSTONE James 28
SAMMON Edward 33
SAMMONS William 13
SAMON Thomas 26
SAMPSON William 17
SAMSON Benjamin 37; John 71
SAMUELL Richard 36
SAMUELLS Abel 7
SAMWELLS Peter 11
SANCSTONE John 28
SAND Robert 60
SANDER William 83
SANDERS Ann 57; Aron 75; John 23, 83;
Morgin 79; Thomas 69; William 21,
71
SANDS Robert 23
SANGSTEN James 37
SANKSTON James 81

SANSETON William 17
SAPP John 58; William 58
SAPPING Hartly 71; Nathaniel 71
SAPPINGTON Nathaniel 85
SARD Thomas 83
SASER Benjamin 4; Thomas 4; William 4
SASNETT Henry 39
SATCHELL Hinry 79
SATERFIELD Edward 75; William 75
SATHELLS Thomas 82
SATTERFIELD Edward 51, 66; William 51
SATTERFOOT Edward 45
SAUNDERS Andrew 66; James 17, 81, 85;
    John 21, 40, 66, 81; Richard 10;
    William 21
SAVAGE John 72
SAVIN Samuel 69; Thomas 68; William
    68
SAVORY William 58
SAWELL Thomas 36
SAWER John 42
SAWSER Benjamin 36
SAYLOR James 79
SCAGG Richard 56
SCANDRET William 64, 66
SCANDRETT William 64
SCANLON Edward 53
SCARBOROUGH John 50, 62, 84
SCARBROUGH John 12, 61; Mathew 12, 38
SCHOLDFIELD Henry 52
SCHONE Thomas 52
SCHOOFIELD Jospeh 52
SCHOOLFIELD John 79; Joseph 3
SCISE Richard 50
SCOFFILD Margaret.t. 38
SCOOLFALD Henry 52
SCOORFIELD Henry 52
SCOT George 11; John 9, 53, 81;
    Nathaniel 51; Robert 53; Thomas 17
SCOTT Alexander 71; Charles 68; Day
    7, 79; Edward 1, 24, 32, 55, 56,
    58; Elisabeth 5; George 7, 24, 62;
    Henry 14; Isac 6; John 2, 27, 62,
    66, 75; John Cole 81; Mark 14;
    Mary 24; Nathaniel 51, 66, 75;
    Robert 6, 12, 61, 62; Solomon 28,
    51, 75; Susanna 27; Thomas 14, 17,
    81; Walter 68, 85; William 6, 12,
    26, 28, 35, 42, 77, 80
SCOTTON James 66; John 66; Richard 66
SCRIVENER Richard 66
SCULLY William 76

SCURRY Robert 69; Thomas 69
SEAET Charles 69
SEAGAR Samuel 71
SEAL Mathias 70
SEAWARD Josias 37; Thomas 66
SEBY John 52
SEDDEMAN Ricahrd 48
SEE James 69
SEENY Bryan 24; William 24
SEGAR John 70
SELBE Daniell 36, 37; Thomas 35
SELBEY William 16
SELBY Daniel 15, 79; George 50; John
    50, 79; Mathew 12, 79; Park'n 79;
    Parker 12, 15, 79; Phil 79; Philip
    12, 41, 50, 62, 79; Thomas 14;
    William 62
SELLWOOD Sarah 57
SELVESTER Benjamin 75; David 76;
    James 75; William 75
SELVESTOR Thomas 75
SENTON Patrick 66
SERIL Thomas 23
SERMAN Peter 78
SERMON Alexander 9
SERMOND Job 80
SERNAM Thomas 40
SEROSBERRY William 75
SERTAIN John 74
SETH Charles 66
SEVERSON Thomas 69
SEVERY Abraham 18
SEVILL John 18
SEVIRE Abraham 81
SEWELL John 75; Richard 58, 85
SEXTON Patrick 66
SEYMOR George 75
SEYMOUR John 27
SHAHAWN Daniel 25
SHANE George 78
SHANNAHAN William 24
SHANNAHANE George 20, 59; Jonathan
    27; Peter 25
SHARD John 5
SHARP Benjamin 10; Isaac 21; James
    27; John 11; Samuel 42; Solomon
    21, 24; Walter 69; William 21
SHARPE Benjamin 52; William 44
SHAVER Robert 82
SHAW Eliza. 60; John 24, 32; Joshua
    10; Thomas 41
SHEAPARD James 21; John 31

SHEARES Jonathan 42
SHEELD Lambert 50
SHEHANE Maurice 66
SHEHAWN Cornelius 25; Daniel 21;
    David 20, 25; Patrick 25
SHEHE David 40
SHEHORN Cornelius 83
SHEIN Robert 9
SHELDON John 52
SHELLEY John 71
SHELTENHAM Jacob 35
SHEPARD Frances 74; Martin 78;
    William 75
SHEPERD William 1
SHEPHARD Francis 48
SHEPHERD William 66
SHEPPARD William 66
SHEREDINE Francis 24
SHERIN Abraham 51
SHERLEY Anne 38
SHERLOCK Nicholas 51, 66
SHERMAN Edward 8; Jon 8; Joseph 36;
    Peter 8; Thomas 8; William 36
SHERWIN Abraham 29
SHERWOOD Daniel 22, 44, 46, 47, 59,
    83; Edward Man 21; Francis 21, 82;
    Hugh 22, 48; John 19, 21, 46, 47,
    51, 59, 60, 83; Josh. 21; Philip
    21, 46, 82; Thomas 23, 81
Sherwood's Bridge 46, 47
SHIALL Thomas 34
SHIELD Elizabeth 33; James 81; Rachel
    33; Widow 17; William 30, 58, 59,
    81
SHIELS Ann 61; John 7; Patrick 7;
    Thomas 7
SHILD Thomas 49
SHILES James 77; John 36, 37, 77;
    Thomas 37
SHILLETO Thomas 36
SHILS Naomi 7
SHIPHAM Edward 38
SHIPPAM Edward 40
SHIPWAY John 34
SHOCKLEY David 2; John 9; Richard 36,
    38
SHOEBROOKS Thomas 66
SHOLLITTO William 38
SHORS John 42
SHORT Adam 69; John 50
SHORTE Edward 6
SHORTER William 63, 67

SHOWERS Alice 67
SHROPSHELL Edward 18
SHROPSHIRE Edward 81
SHURDIN John 21
SHUTE Gyles 85
SHUTTLEWORTH Vincent 36
SIDBURY Edward 37
SILCOH Volentine 69
SILLIVANE Dennis 69
SILLSON Joseph 21; Sarah 21
SILVER Christopher 25
SILVESTER James 66, 75; Thomas 29,
    62, 63, 66
SIMCOCK William 55
SIMKINS John 74
SIMMONS Henry 71; Thomas 18
SIMONDS Richard 32
SIMPSON Richard 15; Samuel 18;
    William 55
SIMSON Robert 49; Thomas 19; William
    15
SINCLAIR Alexander 22; Charles 27;
    Thomas 17
SINCLAR Lawrence 66
SINNET Solloman 75
SINNETT Nicholas 32; Thomas 50
SIRMAN Edward 78; Isaac 79; Isaak 78;
    Joshua 78
SISFEILD Henry 62
SISK David 23
SITH John 70
SKIDMORE Edward 56
SKILLETT Mathew 60
SKILLINGTON Elijah 21; Kenelm 21;
    Thomas 21
SKINNER Andrew 45, 83; Charles 32;
    Edward 63, 66; Philemon 23;
    Richard 18; Thomas 27, 83; William
    19, 23, 24, 27, 44, 59, 76, 83
SKIRVEN George 33
SKIRVIN Esther 2
SKYN William 38
SLADE John 82
SLANEY James 66; Maurice 66
SLATER John 19
SLAUGHTER Edward 28; Susannah 29;
    William 26
SLEBEWS Edward 40
SLEVENS Richard 40
SLINGER John 84; Thomas 14
SLIPPER William 58
SLONE David 69

SLUBY William 70
SLYTER Benjamin 70
SMALL Christopher 29; John 25;
  Richard 37, 74; Robert 66
SMALLCORN Margery 26
SMALLWOOD Thomas 36
SMILE... William 69
SMITH Abraham 14; Andrew 15, 41;
  Archibald 40; Bartholomew 68;
  Casparus 66; Charles 55, 79, 82;
  Daniel 48, 74, 77; Edward 22, 35,
  38; Francis 23; George 18, 34, 66,
  77; Henry 5, 22, 36, 50; James 1,
  6, 7, 9, 32, 39, 48, 49, 56, 58,
  59, 70, 71; Jeremiah 29, 52; John
  2, 10, 13, 15, 23, 28, 29, 50, 66,
  74, 80, 81, 83; Jonas 13, 79;
  Joseph 28, 29; Mathew 32, 44;
  Nicholas 33; Peter 27; Ralph 3;
  Richard 50, 71; Robert 8, 9, 27,
  37, 75, 77, 79; Stephen 42; Thomas
  11, 22, 31, 49, 67; William 12,
  15, 17, 51, 57, 71, 76, 79, 83
SMITHE James 54
SMITHERS James 55; John 58; Mary 56;
  William 33, 57, 58
SMITHIES Sergt. 50
SMITHSON Coll 45; Thomas 46, 48
Smithsons 47
SMOCHE John 49
SMULING Edmond 80
SMULLENS Randall 2
SMULLIN Nathanell 80; William 80
SMYTH Charles 54; John 74; Thomas 48
SNAGNETT Ralph 25
SNEE Bryan 7, 42; Naomi 42
SNEED Moses 82; Richard 28, 81
SNELLING Thomas 26
SNOOKE John 72
SNOWLING John 21
SOANES John 67
SOANS John 66
SOLOWAY Josias 74
SOMMERS Samuel 53; Thomas 53
SOMURS Isac 5; Marget 5
SONGO Solomon 19
SOTT John 77
Southbeys Mill 46
SOUTHEY William 12
SOUTHRIN Edward 35
SOUTZERINE Edward 34
SOVEREIGNE John Barnet 32

SOWARD Daniel 74; Isaac 74; John 74;
  Thomas 74; William 73
SP... Philip 9
SPARKE Joseph 74
SPARKES Benn. 74; Edward 74; James
  74; John 74; Joseph 66; William 66
SPARKS Absolom 77; Caleb 77; John 66,
  77; Milington 77; William 21
SPAULINS Andrew 1
SPEAR Henry 61
SPEARE Andrew 38; Henry 11
SPEARMAN Phillip 56
SPEDDAN Edward 21; Hugh 21; John 21
SPEER Andrew 11; John 80; Robert 33
SPENCE Adam 16, 49, 62, 84;
  Allexander 37; Andrew 20; Anne 37;
  David 34, 37; James 41; Patrick 20
SPENCER Beni 82; Charles 23; Hugh 82;
  Humphry 29; James 22, 23, 82;
  Jarvis 33, 56; John 26, 27;
  Philmon 82; Robert 83; Thomas 50;
  William 19
SPHEAR Andrew 7
SPRIGNAL JOhn 28
SPRINGER Hannah 17; Thomas 17
SPROUCE George 72
SPRY Christopher 28; Francis 64, 66;
  Thomas 28, 59
SPURIWAY William 72
SQUIRE John 36
STADK William 45
STAFFORD Ann 60
STAINER Francis 82; James 81; Solomon
  82
STAINES John 22
STAMWARD John 72
STANBRIDGE Thomas 35
STANDFAST John 82
STANDFORD Augustine 37; Jonathan 78
STANDLEY John 24; William 33
STANDRIDGE Thomas 37
STANFIELD John 23
STANFORD Thomas 78
STANFURD Joseph 8
STANLEY John 85; William 1
STANTON Francis 26; John 28; Jonathan
  8; Stephen 7; Thomas 76; William
  75
STAPLEFORD Barnbas 24; Daniel 25;
  John 24; Raymond 72; Robert 25
STAPLES James 9

STARKEY John 75
STARKY William 64, 66
STARLING Armstrong 52; Henry 52; John 5, 52; Joseph 52
STARRES Bennett 31
STARRETT John 38
STARROT John 69
START Ephraim 18, 81; Richard 28, 81
STATIN Joseph 38
STEAL William 29
STEALE James 15
STEEL John 39; Mathew 71
STEPHEN Julia 25
STEPHENS Edward 80; John 80; William 72
STERLING John 35; William 71
STEUART Francis 53; William 82
STEVANS John 74
STEVENS Abigal 8; Charles 49, 85; Elisha 21; Elizabeth 21; Ellenor 2; Georg. 48; John 8, 25, 47, 54; Joseph 75; Mary 60; Peter 1; Richard 8, 34, 38, 40, 70; Samuell 2; Thomas 8, 25, 66; William 2, 8, 12, 34, 36, 38, 45, 53; Willis 47
STEVENSON James 15, 79; Joseph 78; Robert 78; Samuell 79; William 12, 15, 78
STEVINSON Hugh 38
STEWARD James 19; John 72; Thomas 75
STEWART Alexander 14; Charles 55, 70; John 54; Thomas 70; William 17, 85
STICKBERRY Stephen 24
STICKBURY Steven 82
STIFF Joseph 26
STILL George 33
STINSON John 13, 69; Robert 15
STIVENSON Thomas 49
STOCKLEY Richard 42
STOCKWELL Alce 41; Edwart 6; Thomas 5, 41
STOKER Boni 82; Eliza. 60; James 27; Michael 27
STOKES Francis 18
STONESTREET Robert 28
STOOPE John 85
STOOPES Phillip 68
STOREY Charles 51; Francis 17; Joseph 17; Marmaduke 17; Richard 17
STORY Robert 68; William 4, 62
STOTT Robert 40
STOUGHTON William 4

STOUKLEY John 39
STRAWBRIDGE James 9, 39, 62; John 39; William 85
STRAWHAN Richard 17
STREAKS Mary 40
STREET Robert 33; Samuel 74
STRINGER George 4
STRONG Thomas 58
STUARD Benjamin 19; John 11
STUART Benjamin 26; Duncan 27; James 21, 70
STUCKLEY William 12
STUDHAM John 21; Thomas 22
STUDSON Thomas 20
STURGES Daniel 50; Jonathan 52; Joshua 80
STURGIS Daniel 79; John 12; Jonathan 12; Joshua 12; Stephen 84; William 12, 79
STURGISS Richard 12
STURTEM George 48
STUTON Francis 24
SUDLER George 31; James 49, 66, 74; Joseph 31, 64, 66, 74, 77; Rachell 31; Rebecca 31
SUILIVAN William 78
SULEVAN Owen 25
SULLEVAN Owen 24
SULLEVANT Thomas 19
SULLIVAN William 8
SULLIVANE Dennis 33
SUMERS David 52; John 6; Jonathen 5; Thomas 5
SUMMERS Benjamin 52; George 52; John 52, 75; Jonathan 52; Lazrus 52; Richard 52; Robert 18; Thomas 52; William 66
SUMMERSON John 26
SUMNER Benianion 34
SUMPTER Robert 51
SUPLE Anthony 22
SURCOM Thomas 74
SURGEN John 70
SURNAM Anne 35; Edward 35; Peter 36, 41
SURNAN Edward 34
SUTHERIN Vallentine 31
SUTTON Ashbury 58; John 28, 31, 49, 62, 81; Philip 72; William 24
SWAINE John 48
SWAN ...tt; 7; John 14; Thomas 66, 75

SWEAT Edward 76; John 17; Vaule 17
SWEATNAM Stephen 66
SWEATT John 76
SWEELS Richard 30
SWEET Sarah 63, 67
SWETMANS Mill 47
SWIFT Absalom 51; John 66; Richard
    51; William 66
SWILLIVANE John 42; Timothy 42
SWILLIVIN William 78
SWON James 75
SWOON Evin 75; John 75
SWORDIN Henry 23
SWYMOUR John 66
SYLVESTER Benjamin 29, 51, 82; John
    82
SYMMONDS Thomas 72
SYNORS Joseph 20

TAEGUE John 79
TAGAN Owen 20
TALBOT Walter 39
TALBOTT Rodi 39
TANNARD Thomas 62
TANNER Benjamin 74; Thomas 74
TAPTICO William 72
TAR Michael 11; Samuell 12
TARBUTTON Edward 75; William 75
TARCELL Frances 72; Francis 72
TARR Daniel 18; John 19; Thomas 19;
    William 18
TATMAN John 11
TATOM John 80
TAWES Elisha 78
TAYLER ... 4; Cornelius 15;
    Coulbourne 5; James 2, 52, 80;
    Jobe 80; John 39, 66; Samuel 2,
    61, 62; Travour 80; Walter 5, 15;
    William 11, 80
TAYLOR Alce 37; Benjamin 70; Edward
    72; Elas 53; Elizabeth 25; Ester
    61; George 13, 23, 61; Hope 3;
    Humpphry 24; James 25, 71; John 5,
    12, 37, 38, 39, 42, 57, 58, 62,
    66, 67, 76; Jonathan 19; Joseph
    12; Peter 52, 72; Richard 70;
    Robert 52; Samuel 32, 42, 48, 80;
    Solomon 2; Thomas 5, 8, 25, 30,
    44, 45, 47, 72; Walter 13, 37, 42;
    William 5, 25, 34, 74
TEAT Gilbert 66
TEATE Thomas 73

TECKARE John 52
TEMPLE William 21
TEMPLEMAN John 82
TENLY James 2
TENNANT Thomas 27
TERENCE Adam 14
TERRIEHER Ann 41
TERRY George 8; Hugh 68; Thomas 85
THACKSTON Thomas 55, 56
THARP John 58; Peter 45
THARPE Abner 75; Isaac 76; John 76;
    Joseph 75; Ogle 76; Thomas 81
THOHON Andrew 74
THOLOW Edward 74; John 74; Samuel 74
THOMAS Allexander 38; Benjamin 75,
    77; David 4; Edmund 62, 66, 85;
    Elias 33; Ffrances 41; Ffrancis
    31, 39, 58; Grifen 2; Griffin 39;
    James 17, 28, 51, 55, 82; Jeremiah
    26, 31; John 72, 82; Lamber 39;
    Masune 34; Michael 21; Philemon
    75; Rebecca 39; Rich 43; Samuel 1,
    56; Thomas 66, 81; Trustram 23,
    62, 66, 73, 76, 83, 85; William
    20, 23, 42
THOMASINE Richard 72
THOMPSON Alce 60; Alexander 69;
    Augustine 62, 66, 67, 73; Clear 9;
    Daniel 29, 60; George 70; John 66;
    Joseph 69; Thomas 28; William 9;
    Willus 47
THOMSON Augustine 56; Daniel 20;
    William 4
THORLOW Samuel 49
THORNE William 34
THORNHILL Robert 72
THORNTON Mary 60; William 56
THOROWGOOD Ffrancis 39
THORP Isaac 28; John 28; Thomas 28;
    William 28
TIBBALLS John 46
TIBBATT James 55
TIBBELS John 28
TIL(LMAN) Widow 9
TILDEN John 1; Marmaduke 55
TILER Richard 61
TILGHMAMN Richard 56
TILGHMAN Richard 44, 48, 59, 63, 67
TILLARD John 1
TILLER John 31
TILLETTS ... 7
TILLIMAN Benjamin 78

TILLMAN Aaron 9; Gedieon 2; Gideon 37; John 79; Joseph 10; Moses 9
TILLMANS Gideon 35
TILLOTSON Beynard 77; Christopher 64; John 64, 66
TILMAN Giddion 62; Gideon 34; Ralph 61
TILMON Aron 80; Elijah 80; Elisha 80; Gedden 52; Isiah 80; Joseph 80; Nehemiah 53
TILOTSON John 77
TILTON John 70
TIMENS Thomas 5
TIMMONS ... 15; James 15; John 14; Joseph 15; Samuell 15; Thomas 15; William 15
TINDALL Charles 11; John 79; Ralph 11; Samuell 11
TINGELL Hugh 13; John 13
TINGLE Calab 83; Daniel 84; Hugh 37, 38, 79; Solomon 79
TINLEY JOhn 11
TIPLER William 22
TIPPEN William 31
TIPPINGS Henry 74; Thomas 74
TIPPINS Thomas 75
TIRPINS Nicholas Goldsborough 83
TISDALD William 39
TITBALD Richard 68
TITUM John 6
TOADVIN Nicolas 37
TOADVINE George 78; Henry 8; Isaac 8; Nicolas 8; Thomas 77
TOALSON Alexander 64, 66
TOBIN Edward 63
TODD Thomas 76
TODVINE Henry 53
TOLSON Andrew 58
TOMERLIN Samuell 3
TOMKINS William 37
TOMLIN Edward 45
TOMLINSON 29; John 29
TOMPSON John 8, 52
TOMSON James 15
TONGE William 48
TONNEY Thomas 68
TOOL Michall 76; Patrick 71
TOOMEY William 74
TOOMY John 26
TOPP Laynerd 76
TORNLEY James 1
TORRY Benjamin 50

TOULSON Allexander 74; Benjamin 74; John 74; Joseph 74
TOVY Samuel 31
TOWERS Thomas 66, 75
TOWLSON Alexander 49
TOWNSAND Brickhouse 15; Ezekiel 80; Jeremiah 15, 80; Joseph 80; Marshal 52, 80; Na'tt 80; Solomon 80
TOWNSEND Bowman 13; Charles 2, 61, 62; Daniell 2; Dantford 52; Elizabeth 2; James 2; Jeremiah 41; John 2, 62; Littleton 2; Saul 52; Wrixham 2
TOWNSLEY George 19; Thomas 75
TOWNSON Brickhous 83; James 66; John 34; Thomas 82
TOY Walter 66
TRAHERNE James 77
TRAILE William 38
TRAP William 54
TRASE John 71
TRAVERS Henry 72; Thomas 72
TRAYMAN Thomas 24
TREHAIRN James 52
TREHEARN James 6; John 6
TREHEARNE George 35
TRESZAR William 56
TREW John 56; William 55, 58
TREWS William 31
TRICE Abraham 6
TRIFORD John 35
TRIPP Henry 54
TRIPPE Henry 43, 72; William 83
TROTH William 46
TROTT Thomas 82
TRUEM... Robert 3
TRUET Thomas 2
TRUETT Job 42
TRUIT George 16, 79
TRUITT Benjamin 15; Eliner 16; George 14, 15, 16; James 16; Jobe 15; John 15; Joseph 15; Mordica 15; Philip 15; Samuell 16; William 15
TRULOCK Henry 57
TRUSHAW John 38
TRYALL Joseph 66
TUBMAN Rioch. 72
TUCKER John 37, 82; Nathaniell 76; Noble 82; Richard 72
TULL Benjamin 14; George 2, 37, 52, 61; James 53; John 13, 37, 39, 52,

62, 80; Jonathan 53; Joshua 53,
81; Noble 2; Nobold 52; Rachell
37; Richard 2, 34, 37, 52, 53, 78,
81; Samuel 6, 78; Sarah 6; Solomon
6, 52, 78; Stephen 53; Thomas 6,
41, 34, 37, 40, 53, 81; William 2
TULLE John 79; Richard 79; William 79
TULLINGTON Alexander 8
TULLY James 11; William 11
TUNEN Daniel 19
TUNSTALL John 9
TURBILLE William 13
TURBUT Richard 83
TURBUTT Anne 24; Michael 48; Rachel
25; William 62, 63, 67, 73, 85
TURITT ... 15
TURK Thomas 69
TURNER Absalom 83; David 28; Henly 2;
Henry 27, 72; James 2; Jane 28;
John 2, 56, 83; Joseph 29, 82;
Robart 75; Samuell 2; Thomas 17,
28, 29, 50, 82; William 11, 28;
Zadock 79
TURPIN Denwood 79; Elizabeth 38; John
78; Joshua 77; Mary 38; Nehemiah
81; Sarah 38; Solomon 11, 36;
Whittey 81; William 38, 52, 62, 81
TURVILE John 13
TURVILL John 83
TUTCHSTONE Christopher 68
TWIFOOT William 11
TWIGG John 57, 58
TWIGUE John 56
TWILLEY Robert 41
TWOLLY Robert 10
TYDER John 20
TYLER David 53; John 53; Jonathan 30;
Nicholas 38; Thomas 53
TYRAR Robert 41
TYRE Robert 13; Thomas 37

UMBERS John 85
UNDERHILL John 31
UNECK John 32
UNGLE Frances 27
URIN Jhn 69
USELTON Thomas 28
USHER Thomas 31, 59

VAINE John 24; William 24
VALENTINE Archibald 17
VALIANT Joseph 22

VALLENS Thomas 2
VALLENT Bennett 82; Thomas 82
VALLIANT John 27; Judith 59
VANABLES Pirkins 78
VANBEBBER Adam 70
VANCE Alexander 8; John 78
VANCOSLIN John 70
VANDERFORD Charles 62, 66, 74; George
66; John 76; Richard 74; William
66
VANDERGRIFT Nicholas 71
VANHORN Barnet 50, 71; Cornelius 71
VANNABLES Joseph 77
VANSANT Cornelius 71
VAUGHAM William 38
VAUGHAN William 31
VAUGHN Ephrim 80; Jethro 80; John 19;
Rowland 72
VEAZEY Edward 70, 85; George 50, 68;
James 69; John 49, 69, 71; Thomas
70; William 85
VEAZY William 78
VEITCH Thomas 72
VENABLES Dorathy 41; Joseph 62
VENNABLES Benjamin 7; John 8; Joseph
7; William 8
VENTON Daniel 22
VESEY Charles 12; William 12
VESTRY Mical 80
VHEYDEN Matt's 85
VICKERS Anthony 22; George 81; John
28; Joseph 81; Thomas 28; William
28, 66; William Brown 42, 81
VICTER Thomas 80
VICTOR John 14
VIGEROUS Ann 37, 39; Armewell Robert
39; Elizabeth 39; Ffrances 39;
John 37, 39; Mary 39
VINCENT Ffrancis 34; James 6;
Jeremiah 76; Thomas 6
VINEY Godfry 66
VINSON Mathias 80
VINTON Richard 81
VIRGIN James 17; Moses 2
VIRGON James 81
VITT... Joseph 52
VOCKARY William 75
VOSS James 27

W... William 1
WADE John 31
WADELL Robert 19

WAGGAMAN George 85; Jacob 11
WAGONER John 69
WAILES Benjamin 7, 41; John 77;
  Joseph 11, 62
WAINWRIGHT William 7, 40
WAIT Joseph 12
WAITE Jonathan 72
WAKEN John 34
WALDON Richard 22
WALE Edward 37; John 40
WALER John 5
WALERS Elizabeth 61
WALES Daniel 79; John 82
WALEY William 13
WALKER Charles 17; Charles 81; Daniel
  66, 75; Fflower 32; Henry 24;
  James 20, 68, 83; John 12, 24, 25,
  83; Robert 30; Thomas 7, 17, 54,
  62; William 25, 66, 72
WALL'R Thomas 49
WALLACE Hugh 54
WALLACE James 54; John 13, 50, 69,
  79; Mathew 5, 42, 69; Michael 69;
  Richard 5; Thomas 5, 13, 69
WALLER George 4; Hannah 41; Joane 41;
  John 4, 41; Laurawa 41; Major 4;
  Mary 41; Naomi 41; Nathanel 11,
  41, 80; Richard 80; Sarah 41;
  Thomas 11, 28, 36, 80; William 4,
  80
WALLICE John 21, 72
WALLIS David 41, 42; John 57; Matthew
  40; Richard 42; Samuel 55, 56;
  William 69
WALLS John 55
WALLTER Thomas 40
WALLTON John 31
WALMSLEY William 49
WALSON William 37
WALSSON William 81
WALSTON Benz 6; Charles 52; Joy 6;
  Thomas 36, 52, 53, 78; William 52,
  53
WALSTONNE William 36
WALTAN John 42
WALTER Daniel 41, 79; Henry 41; John
  41; Robert 79; Thomas 41; William
  79
WALTERS Benjamin 74; John 62; Robert
  62
WALTHAM William 33
WALTHOM John 56

WALTOM Job 79; Stephen 79; William 79
WALTON Benjamin 74; Fisher 12; John
  14, 64, 66, 84; Robert 62, 64, 66;
  Steven 12; William 14, 36, 62
WAMSLEY Robert 68
WANTLAND James 18; Thomas 18
WAPLES Paul 13
WARD (Also see Word) Bernard 40;
  Coll. 18; Cornelius 34, 40; Daniel
  29, 51; George 24; J. 49; James 6,
  52; John 26, 66, 85; Joseph 2;
  Lambert 83; Littleton 18; Mary 40;
  Matthew Tilghman 21; Richard 80;
  Samuel 53; Stephen 80; Thomas 18,
  32, 69; William 85
WARDE Peregrine 50
WARDELO Robert 24
WARFORD John 30; William 30
WARING Bazell 83; Henry 83
WARNER Charles 28; George 48, 53, 58;
  John 17; Joseph 58; Lamb: 81;
  Solomon 19; William 17, 43, 44, 45
WARREN John 58; Joseph 6; Richard 49;
  Robert 15; Sampson 76; Thomas 31,
  74
WARRIN Nicholas 15; Richard 37;
  Robert 16
WARRING Jacob 37; Sampson 29; William
  29
WARWICK Arthur 2; William 39
WASSEY Jane 67
WATERLY John 72
WATERS Edwart 5; Edward 80; Elizabeth
  5; Henry 5; John 40, 42, 52, 80;
  Richard 5, 10, 40; Thomas 40;
  William 5, 6, 35, 52
WATHERLEE James 53
WATKINS Peter 56
WATKINSON Cornelis 11
WATS John 13
WATSON Elizabeth 66; Ffrancis 62, 66;
  James 1, 55; John 12, 50; Luke 12;
  Peter 12; Robert 12; William 34,
  66, 72
WATT John 40
WATTLE Alexander 71
WATTS John 28, 47
WATTSON Charles 78; John 78; Peter 2;
  Robert 78
WAYAT Joshua 79
WAYMOUTH John 28
WEATHERBY George 52

WEATHERLE James 37
WEATHERLEE James 10; William 10
WEATHERLEY James 40
WEBB Carebra 61; Edgar 47; George 74;
  James 20; John 3, 14, 20, 36, 38,
  41, 56, 71, 78; Joseph 24; Park
  20; Peter 24; Richard 12, 20, 37;
  Sarah 24; Solomon 78; Timothy 66;
  William 45, 75
WEBBER Edward 38
WEBBS Edgar 44, 47
WEBSTER James 7, 21; Thomas 23
WEDG John 31
WEEB James 75
WEEDING Henry 74
WEEKS Joseph 31, 62, 64, 66
WELCH George 69; John 71, 85; Robert
  23
WELDING Charles 71; Robert 71
WELLBONE John 13
WELLING Joseph 23
WELLINGTON John 44
WELLS Brown 74; George 77; Humphry
  62, 66; John 64, 66, 67, 74;
  Richard 66; Thomas 33; Zerbuable
  48
WELSH John 76
WELTON John 17
WEPWORTH John 38
WERE Hugh 70; John 70
WERS Robart 5
WESCOTE John 70
WESSELS Gerrardin 48
WEST Anthoney 10; Elizabeth 39;
  Gabariel 13; George 13, 21, 50;
  Henry 21; James 5, 53; John 33,
  38, 39, 40, 41, 57, 58; Joseph 51;
  Lothan 21; Randall 41; Richard 32;
  Robert 13; Thomas 13, 39, 50, 79;
  William 27, 29, 41, 50
WESTLARKA John 34
WETHERBY Thomas 48
WETHERED John 50; Richard 50
WETHERLY George 56, 58
WETHERSLY George 58
WEYATT James 31; Thomas 32
WHAILIE William 50
WHALEY Daniel 56, 58; Edward 35;
  James 81; John 18, 78; Owen 56;
  Widow 18; William 18, 81
WHALING John 20
WHALLES Daniel 50

WHARTON Charles 42; Dan 50; Daniel
  13; George 79; Henry 27; John 13;
  Richard 35; Robert 64, 66
WHEATLER John 52
WHEATLEY Daniel 75; William 75
WHEATLY John 66; Sampson 51, 52;
  William 4, 38
WHEELER Edward 38, 41; Henry 43; John
  14, 39; Thomas 51
WHEELY Isaac 29
WHELER Samuell 5
WHEPLES Peter 36
WHETLY Edward 11
WHIDBE William 66
WHIDBY Richard 82
WHILEY Eliza. 67
WHITAKER Nathaniel 52
WHITE Ambrose 79; Andrew 38;
  Archabald 3, 38, 53; Davey 82;
  Dennis 22; Eben 54; Ffrancis 4;
  Henry 52; James 23, 40, 74; John
  2, 3, 5, 22, 27, 40, 41, 52, 54,
  62, 80; Joshua 80; Richard 23;
  Samuel 53; Sarah 55; Stevens 39;
  Thomas 26, 52; William 5, 17, 18,
  23, 39, 53, 59, 60, 80, 83
WHITEACRE Jonathan 22
WHITEHEAD John 70
WHITLY Ellin 34
WHITTE Richard 34
WHITTEY Richard 9
WHITTFIELD William 34, 38
WHITTINGTON Andrew 35, 38, 39;
  Benjamin 77; John 48; Southey 2,
  52, 62, 81; Thomas 25; William 2,
  16
WHITTINTON Thomas 83
WHITTOM William 69
WHITTON Samuel 70
WHORTON WilliamLee Thomas 77
WICKES George 20; Josh. 48; Matthew
  74; Samuel 56, 58; Stephen 74
WICKS John 66
WIGGINS John 66
WILCOCKS James 33
WILCOXS John 7
WILD Peter 62, 66
WILDING James 71
WILES John 23; Nathen 79; Robert 25;
  Thomas 6, 23, 25
WILIAMS Isaac 6
WILINS John 6

WILIT Ambrose 12
WILKENSON Thomas 75; William 75
WILKINS James 78; Thomas 58
WILKINSON Elizabeth 63; Henry 66, 74; James 74; Mrs. 19; Thomas 62, 66, 74
WILKISON James 4
WILKISSON Angelo 2; Isaac 2; Joshua 2; Patience 2
WILL..SON William 34
WILLCOX Henry 66
WILLES Burnaby 10; James 10
WILLET John 84; William 84
WILLIAM John 3
WILLIAMS Alixander 35; Anthony 17, 18, 74; Auldin 17; Charles 4, 11, 36, 41; Edward 64, 66; Eliza. 37; Ennion 29, 45; Henry 11, 76, 77; Hoplan 33; Hopton 55; Jacob 17, 50; James 24, 64; John 1, 15, 32, 50, 51, 52, 76, 78, 81, 82; John Guy 20, 28; Jonathan 6, 16; Joseph 26; Mark 26; Mathew 66; Mickell 35; Narthaniel 6; Oldern 81; Peter 21; Presgrave 16; Richard 29, 79; Robert 27, 69; Spencer 81; Thomas 1, 24, 31, 35, 38, 54, 55, 62, 74; Thomas Nathaniel 16; William 52, 81
WILLIAMSON John 29; William 15
WILLIARD Isac 38
WILLIN James 85; John 77; Levin 78; Robert 77; Thomas 7, 77
WILLING John 80
WILLIS Elizabeth 61; James 37; John 33; Richard 54; William 78, 80
WILLIT Jonas 74; Thomas 84
WILLMER Simon 1
WILLMORE Thoams 63
WILLOBY William 43
WILLOUGHBY William 72
WILLSCOTT James 21
WILLSON Alexander 17; Ephraim 60; George 8; James 29, 66, 74, 75; John 10, 18, 61, 66, 75, 82; Jonathan 81; Larkin 81; Mary 66; Michael 32; Phe. 4; Ralph 22; Robert 19, 36, 66, 83; Thomas 4, 29, 81; William 29, 71, 74
WILMER Lambert 33, 48, 55; Simon 32, 48, 55
WILMOT William 49

WILSON Abraham 4; Colebray 41; Denwood 85; Elexander 82; Epraem 49; George 58; Hugh 12; James 23, 31, 57, 85; Jane 41; John 6, 18, 33, 56, 58, 59, 85; Rachel 41; Robert 42; Samuel 85; Thomas 40, 41, 49; William 5, 12, 14, 39, 40
WILSONS Georgte 41
WILSTON Londan 41
WINCHESTER Isaac 74; John 31, 66, 74; Thomas 26, 83
WINDER John 34, 35; Thomas 34, 38, 41; William 77
WINDERS William 12
WINDSOR John 5; Lazarus 5
WINE John 39
WINFORD John 24; Richard 23
WING Robert 54; Thomas 73
WINGOD Thomas 35
WINIER Samuel 21
WINN Ephraim 66
WINRIGHT Cannon 62; James 77; Stephen 77; William 77
WINSER Henry 11
WINSLEY Benjamin 70; John 70
WINSOR John 11; 36
WINSTEDLEY Peter 21
WINSTER Mary 40
WINTERTON Ralph 9
WISE Anthony 45, 46; Christopher 29, 76; Ezekiel 79; John 27; Mathew 12; Mathias 50; Thomas 12
WITHERSPON David 50
WITHGOTT Joseph 23
WOLCOT James 83
WOLLAHAM Phillip 36
WOLLFORD Roger 34
WOLLOWHAND Frances 74
WOOD David 79; Edward 22; Hugh 71; John 69, 70, 71; Nicholas 70; Robert 71; Thomas 11; William 28, 52, 70
WOODALL John 33, 57, 66
WOODCRAFT John 13; Mary 13; Richard 13; William 79
WOODDALL John 74
WOODEN Edward 11; James 34; John 11
WOODLAND James 50; William 58
WOODLEY Edwart 5
WOODS Henry 20; James 14; John 76; William 79
WOODARD Benjamin 54; Mr. 43

WOOLFORD James 54; John 54; Roger 10;
  Thomas 54
WOOLISTON Cornelius 70
WOOLLAHAND Thomas 49
WOOLLFORD James 72
Woolmans 18
WOONETT Laurence 72
WOORELL Edward 1
WOORTH John 32
WOOTERS Jacob 28, 46, 47, 76; James
  76; John 75; Jonathan 75; Phillip
  66; Richard 66, 75
Wooters' Mill 44
WOOTTERS John 35
Wootters's Mill 45
WOOTTON Edward 36
WORBY John 45
WORD (Ward) Cornelos 5; Hopkin 5;
  James 5; Samuel 5; Stephen 5;
  Thomas 5
WORRICK William 80
WORTHINGTON Samuell 38
WORTON John 1
WOULD Joseph 42
WOUTH Hugh 32
WRAN William 55
WRATH Robert 41
WRENCH Henry 77; William 62, 66, 77
WRIGHT Abell 10; Alce 38; Ambrose 66;
  Bloice 38; Edward 38, 63, 64, 66,
  67, 73, 77; Fairclough 51; James
  54, 74; Jeremiah 9, 38, 61; John
  33, 36, 62, 64, 66, 67; Joseph 1;
  Judith 38; Katherine 63; Nathan
  76; Nathaniel 51, 66, 75, 77;
  Randal 10; Rebecca 38; Robert
  Norrest 62, 66; Samuell 76;
  Solomon 62, 64, 66; Thomas 4;
  Thomas Hynson 62, 66, 67, 76;
  William 7, 38
WRIGHTSON Francis 18; John 23, 45;
  Joshua 22; Mary 22
WRIN John 55
WROTH J. 48; Kinven 1; Robert 39;
  William 2
WYAT Ruth 66; William 79
WYATT James 58; William 74
WYNE John 38
WYNN Mathew 39

YATE John 72
YEAMAN Andrew 21

YEARLY Solomon 61
YEWELL Solomon 66; Thomas 44, 85
YOE Aaron 76; Stephen 75; Thomas 75
YONN John 48
YORKSON John 71; Yock 85; York 48
YOUNG Charles 11; Daniel 52; Edward
  66, 75; John 1, 9, 51, 55, 68, 75;
  Joseph 58, 68; Thomas 40; William
  11, 51, 69, 75, 79
YOUNGER Humphry 56; John 24
ZAVARY John 53
ZELISSOW Andrew 70
ZENGER John Peter 58

Other books by F. Edward Wright:

Abstracts of Bucks County, Pennsylvania Wills, 1685-1785

Abstracts of Cumberland County, Pennsylvania Wills, 1750-1785

Abstracts of Cumberland County, Pennsylvania Wills, 1785-1825

Abstracts of Philadelphia County Wills, 1726-1747

Abstracts of Philadelphia County Wills, 1748-1763

Abstracts of Philadelphia County Wills, 1763-1784

Abstracts of Philadelphia County Wills, 1777-1790

Abstracts of Philadelphia County Wills, 1790-1802

Abstracts of Philadelphia County Wills, 1802-1809

Abstracts of Philadelphia County Wills, 1810-1815

Abstracts of Philadelphia County Wills, 1815-1819

Abstracts of Philadelphia County Wills, 1820-1825

Abstracts of Philadelphia County, Pennsylvania Wills, 1682-1726

Abstracts of South Central Pennsylvania Newspapers, Volume 1, 1785-1790

Abstracts of South Central Pennsylvania Newspapers, Volume 3, 1796-1800

Abstracts of the Newspapers of Georgetown and the Federal City, 1789-99

Abstracts of York County, Pennsylvania Wills, 1749-1819

Bucks County, Pennsylvania Church Records of the 17th and 18th Centuries
Volume 2: Quaker Records: Falls and Middletown Monthly Meetings
Anna Miller Watring and F. Edward Wright

Caroline County, Maryland Marriages, Births and Deaths, 1850-1880

Citizens of the Eastern Shore of Maryland, 1659-1750

Cumberland County, Pennsylvania Church Records of the 18th Century

Delaware Newspaper Abstracts, Volume 1: 1786-1795

Early Charles County, Maryland Settlers, 1658-1745
Marlene Strawser Bates and F. Edward Wright

Early Church Records of Alexandria City and Fairfax County, Virginia
F. Edward Wright and Wesley E. Pippenger

Early Church Records of New Castle County, Delaware, Volume 1, 1701-1800

Frederick County Militia in the War of 1812
Sallie A. Mallick and F. Edward Wright

Inhabitants of Baltimore County, 1692-1763

Land Records of Sussex County, Delaware, 1769-1782

Land Records of Sussex County, Delaware, 1782-1789
Elaine Hastings Mason and F. Edward Wright

Marriage Licenses of Washington, District of Columbia, 1811-1830

Marriages and Deaths from the Newspapers of Allegany and
Washington Counties, Maryland, 1820-1830

Marriages and Deaths from The York Recorder, 1821-1830

Marriages and Deaths in the Newspapers of Frederick and
Montgomery Counties, Maryland, 1820-1830

Marriages and Deaths in the Newspapers of Lancaster County, Pennsylvania, 1821-1830

Marriages and Deaths in the Newspapers of Lancaster County, Pennsylvania, 1831-1840

Marriages and Deaths of Cumberland County, [Pennsylvania], 1821-1830

Maryland Calendar of Wills Volume 9: 1744-1749

Maryland Calendar of Wills Volume 10: 1748-1753

Maryland Calendar of Wills Volume 11: 1753-1760

Maryland Calendar of Wills Volume 12: 1759-1764

Maryland Calendar of Wills Volume 13: 1764-1767

Maryland Calendar of Wills Volume 14: 1767-1772

Maryland Calendar of Wills Volume 15: 1772-1774

Maryland Calendar of Wills Volume 16: 1774-1777

Maryland Eastern Shore Newspaper Abstracts, Volume 1: 1790-1805

Maryland Eastern Shore Newspaper Abstracts, Volume 2: 1806-1812

Maryland Eastern Shore Newspaper Abstracts, Volume 3: 1813-1818

Maryland Eastern Shore Newspaper Abstracts, Volume 4: 1819-1824

Maryland Eastern Shore Newspaper Abstracts, Volume 5: Northern Counties, 1825-1829
F. Edward Wright and Irma Harper

Maryland Eastern Shore Newspaper Abstracts, Volume 6: Southern Counties, 1825-1829

Maryland Eastern Shore Newspaper Abstracts, Volume 7: Northern Counties, 1830-1834
Irma Harper and F. Edward Wright

Maryland Eastern Shore Newspaper Abstracts, Volume 8: Southern Counties, 1830-1834

Maryland Militia in the Revolutionary War
S. Eugene Clements and F. Edward Wright

Newspaper Abstracts of Allegany and Washington Counties, 1811-1815

Newspaper Abstracts of Cecil and Harford Counties, [Maryland], 1822-1830

Newspaper Abstracts of Frederick County, [Maryland], 1816-1819

Newspaper Abstracts of Frederick County, 1811-1815

Sketches of Maryland Eastern Shoremen

Tax List of Chester County, Pennsylvania 1768

Tax List of York County, Pennsylvania 1779

Washington County Church Records of the 18th Century, 1768-1800

Western Maryland Newspaper Abstracts, Volume 1: 1786-1798

Western Maryland Newspaper Abstracts, Volume 2: 1799-1805

Western Maryland Newspaper Abstracts, Volume 3: 1806-1810

Wills of Chester County, Pennsylvania, 1766-1778

www.ingramcontent.com/pod-product-compliance
Lightning Source LLC
LaVergne TN
LVHW021502080426
835509LV00018B/2375